"Adios Nuevo Mexico"
The Santa Fe Journal
of John Watts in 1859

John Watts in his later years.
Courtesy Hallack Watts Hoag.

"Adios Nuevo Mexico"

The Santa Fe Journal of John Watts in 1859

Transcribed, Edited and Annotated

by

David Remley

Yucca Tree Press

First Printing   April 1999

Library of Congress Cataloging in Publication Data.

Remley, David

   "Adios Nuevo Mexico" The Santa Fe Journal of John Watts in 1859.

      1. Southwest United States - History.   2. New Mexico Territory,
         1846-1912 - History.   3. Personal diaries.   4. Watts, John.
      I. David Remley.   II. Title.

Library of Congress Catalog Card Number: 91-066179

ISBN: 1-881325-29-6

Cover design: Fine Line Design

For Grandpa, who,
in his quiet way,
would be pleased.

Fred Shelby Remley
January 10, 1871 — April 17, 1953

Table of Contents

List of Illustrations

Foreword

Historians know a good deal about the intriguing world of the Anglo-American merchants, lawyers, politicians, and soldiers who made Santa Fe their home after the US-Mexico War, but John Watts' recently discovered diary gives us an original view of that milieu through the eyes of a teenager.

The child of a locally prominent father, young Indiana-born and bred John Watts encountered a number of Santa Fe's leading citizens during his lengthy visit to New Mexico in 1859. In itself, Watts' bits of gossip about local personages makes his diary valuable and interesting.

Perhaps of greatest interest, however, is the diary's intimate view of daily life in Santa Fe. New Mexico's capital emerges from these pages as a place full of dogs where an Italian organ grinder made ear-splitting music, where the territorial governor had time to give daily French lessons in his office to John Watts and his brother, where the elite rode out to the countryside for a picnic, where men hunted birds a short distance from town, and where young men found it was difficult to bathe. Watts seems to have settled for washing his neck on Sunday mornings, before putting on a clean shirt.

John Watts' diary also gives us a rare glimpse into the daily life of an American teenager set loose in a frontier community that recently belonged to Mexico. He was apparently eager to understand his new surroundings. He read books like W.W.H. Davis's *El Gringo: or, New Mexico and Her People* and William Prescott's *Conquest of Mexico*. Mostly, however, he hung out at the pool hall at the Exchange Hotel (the site of today's La Fonda), devoted himself to billiards, thought about and occasionally visited girls, and lamented that he did not use his time more wisely.

Diaries kept by teenagers are scarce for this place and time. David Remley not only recognized the importance of John Watts' diary, but edited it scrupulously. His introduction puts the diary in context and his full annotations identify persons, places, and events that would otherwise mystify modern readers. Remley's clarifications also keep us from puzzling over the diary's eccentric spellings, as when Watts renders Fort Yuma as "Fort Uma" or corral as "carrol."

John Watts' diary opens up a new window on quotidian life in Santa Fe in the late 1850s, and David Remley's careful editing gives modern readers the optical assistance they need to appreciate the view.

David J. Weber, Director
Clements Center for Southwest Studies
Southern Methodist University
Dallas, Texas

Preface and Acknowledgements

Some years ago I was doing research on Judge John S. Watts, a land grant lawyer, justice of the territorial supreme court, and one-time New Mexico Delegate to Congress. Judge Watts had come out from Bloomington, Indiana, in 1851, having been appointed an associate justice of New Mexico's first territorial court. While I was searching the Monroe County court house records and the Indiana University Archives in Bloomington, I met a genealogist who told me he had seen a journal by a fellow named Watts in the Monroe County Historical Museum. I ought to go take a look at it. It might be my Watts.

Thus I came across *Adios Nuevo Mexico*, a boy's account of daily life in Santa Fe in 1859. The journal was that of teenage John Watts, the younger of the two sons of Judge John S. Watts. Having come to New Mexico in the fall of 1858 to recover from chills and fever, the boy began to keep a journal, much of which has survived in this single volume in the museum. The first one hundred sixty-seven pages of the original describe life in Santa Fe from March until October, 1859, when young Watts left New Mexico to return to Bloomington to complete college. Traveling by mail coach over the Southern Route through El Paso and Saint Louis, the boy carried the journal along. In that roundabout manner it reached Bloomington, where it turned up many years later on the top floor of a downtown building.

The curious story of the journal's discovery was told me by Pam Service, a curator, and Karla Nicholson, then director of the Monroe County Historical Museum. A well known Bloomington attorney died several years ago, leaving the Waldron Building on the downtown square to Indiana University. During the cleanup prior to renovation, someone discovered books and papers on the top floor, in Karla's words, "amidst the pieces of old furniture, broken chairs, and dead pigeons." Amongst this material lay the Watts journal. Dusted off, it was placed in a box with other stuff and given to the county museum. Much of the journal is reproduced here for the first time, with my sincerest thanks for the museum's permission.

Not only is the journal a record of events in Santa Fe from the point of view of a perceptive teenager, it is a compendium of little events in the lives of the town's citizens and sojourners for several months immediately before the Civil War. Since young Watts did not intend the journal for eyes other than his own, it is a personal record as much as an objective report. Written while he roomed with his brother, Joshua Howe Watts, it is a large volume measuring a little more than eight by twelve inches, bound in leather.

The ink is browned, the handwriting often written over when John wished to practice his hand. Some pages are missing. These include pages one and two, and those describing John's brothers' marriage. Pages 170 through 246 were written in Bloomington after John returned to college. Pages 247 through 297 describe a trip by rail to Washington, D.C., and events in Washington, Baltimore, and elsewhere (with large time gaps and blank pages) from July 1860, through March 1861. Only the New Mexico section is reproduced here.

My editorial methods are straightforward. I have transcribed the New Mexico pages of the Watts journal almost without changes or deletions, with variant spellings and punctuation preserved. Unclear words or phrases or probable words are bracketed with question marks. The footnotes offer biographical information on the persons Watts names, and background on events. The notes cite the sources in the order in which I used them or in what I consider the order of importance rather than alphabetical order. This order seems convenient for anyone interested in pursuing the sources. To save pages, I have not added a bibliographical essay. Some of the sources are archival, others are old standards known to any Southwestern scholar, and *all* sources are already cited in convenient order within the notes. For the sake of economy, I have not cited the names of persons I was unable to identify.

People who have helped with this project are, to use a trite phrase, too numerous to mention. Names of a few must do. Marc Simmons, for his encouragement and advice; Professor Howard R. Lamar of Yale University, for his past encouragement; Western historians Darlis Miller of New Mexico State University and Richard Etulain of the University of New Mexico, for their friendship and support; and Jane Elder and Professor David J. Weber of Southern Methodist University, for permission to use material from their manuscript edition of the very rich Webb-Kingsbury correspondence (since published in book form), I thank sincerely. I appreciate from Mary Jean Cook, of Santa Fe, the information on several of the women Watts mentions. My good friend Dr. Robert R. White gave unfailing encouragement and helped out in dozens of ways.

Fortunately the world still has generous archivists and librarians, who make the otherwise difficult life of the researcher possible. Such rare people are Pam Service and Karla Nicholson of Bloomington; recently retired J. Richard Salazar, of the New Mexico Records Center and Archives; Robert J. Torrez, the New Mexico State Historian; Arthur Olivas and Richard Rudisill of the Palace of the Governors Photo Archives; and José L. Villegas, Sr., NMSRCA Photo-Archivist. Among these rare citizens are Cheryl Pence, newspaper librarian, Illinois State Historical Library, Springfield, who cheerfully put all her other work aside to copy old newpaper accounts; Peggy Brooks, manager of an Indiana Department of Natural Resources Lincoln historic site at Gentryville, who provided information on Lincoln's stumping for Harrison for President in southern Indiana in 1844; Jane Jones and Marilyn Schmidt, of the Newton Public Library, Newton, Kansas, who brought out old obituaries and city directories and pointed my way to the Watts home; and Lecta Hortin, board member of the White County Historical Society, Carmi, Illinois, who opened the society's archives on a day when I was tracking Lincoln and Watts as Whig politicians.

Special thanks are due Gayle Cook and the Board of Governors of the Monroe County Historical Museum for permission to transcribe and edit the New Mexico pages of the Watts Journal. Robert Leffler is thanked for telling me about the Watts journal and for permission given 24 June 1993 to peruse copyrighted material from his typed commentary on it.

Hoosier friends Stephen and Candace Bailey of Bloomington gave me a place to stay while I did research in Monroe County; and Jerry Van Sickle, of Boulder, gave me a bunk while I worked at the University of Colorado library. Lillian Watford, of Silver City (presently of Denver), a Quaker lady of perpetual good sense, put me in touch with the William Penn House on Capitol Hill where I stayed while working at the National Archives and elsewhere in Washington. Craig Newbill, of the New Mexico Endowment for the Humanities, provided assistance.

A 1994 Senior Research Grant from the New Mexico Endowment for the Humanities provided for research trips to the New Mexico State Archives and Records Center; to Springfield, Illinois, and Indianapolis and Bloomington, Indiana; to Washington, D.C.; and to Irvine, California, as I traced the records of the Watts family across the country.

Mr. Hallack Watts Hoag, grandson of John Watts and great-grandson of Judge John S. Watts, welcomed me to his home near Los Angeles and made his large collection of family papers and photographs available. Mr. Hoag, like his male ancestors, is a graduate of Indiana University. With a law degree from Yale, he has practiced law in the Los Angeles area since 1932.

To these and to all the other helpful people, my grateful thanks!

INTRODUCTION

Judge John S. Watts—father of the boy who kept this journal—first stepped off the mail coach from Independence, Missouri, into the dusty streets of Santa Fe on June 26, 1851, after a twenty-three day trip across the plains. Newly appointed an associate justice of the New Mexico Supreme Court by President Fillmore, Watts was an experienced lawyer from Indiana. Born in 1816 in Kentucky, he had graduated with honors from Indiana University in 1835. After reading law with Judge Sullivan of Madison on the Ohio River, he had practiced in Versailles and Bloomington; had been prosecuting attorney for Monroe County from 1838-43; and had been elected to the Indiana house of representatives as a Whig in 1846-47. Somewhere during these years Watts had met Abraham Lincoln, lawyer and Whig politician from Illinois.

Judge Watts was a man's man. "He was a fine specimen of physical manhood," his son John wrote years later, "and could endure hardships with anyone I ever knew." Santa Fe trader Franz Huning recalled watching the Judge swim the Rio Grande in the summer of 1857, in very high water. Huning traveled the circuit with a party of lawyers going to Mesilla to hold court when Judge Kirby Benedict's ambulance became stranded across the river from Fort Craig. Watts volunteered to carry a message to the driver. "He was indeed a splendid swimmer," Huning wrote, "with his clothes tied on his head he swam the river, about one-half mile wide."

During the Civil War Judge Watts—by then New Mexico's Delegate to Congress —took his son to the White House to meet Lincoln. The President, harried but friendly, proposed a little ritual he often seemed to enjoy. He had the boy stand on a chair while he and the Judge stood back to back to see which was tallest. Placing a large book on their heads, John found that his father, at six feet two-and-a-half inches, was shorter than the President at six-four.

Thus the Judge was an imposing man, intimidating when necessary. An inveterate traveler, he crossed the Plains to Santa Fe more than fifty times. Once he stood off a band of Plains warriors who swooped down on horseback and commanded the stage to stop. Figuring to be robbed and even killed, Judge Watts leaned out the coach door with a rifle in his hand and ordered the driver to drive on. "The astonished Indians having no convenient trees or ravine to use for protection, rather than run the risk of being shot down, looked after the departing stage and especially the rifle in respectful silence," wrote Frances Watts Bancroft (the Judge's oldest daughter, wife of A.L. Bancroft, and sister-in-law of the historian of the West, Hubert Howe Bancroft).

On another trip from Washington during the War, Judge Watts carried secret orders to General E.R S. Canby, commanding in New Mexico. Arriving in Kansas City after the stage, supposed to wait for him, had already left for the West, Watts "immediately started after it on horseback, but failing to overtake it, traveled the entire distance, 850 miles, on horseback, reaching Santa Fe two hours later than the stage too exhausted either to speak or dismount," Mrs. Bancroft wrote.

"El Juez Guatches," as Spanish speaking New Mexicans knew him, brought his ailing son John to Santa Fe for his health in the fall of 1858. Born in Bloomington, Indiana, May 11, 1840, young John had been attending college at home. Having "studied too hard," as it was then believed, he was down with chills and fever when his father, by this time a well-known land grant lawyer in New Mexico and "claims agent" in Washington, D.C., stopped over in Bloomington on the way back from Washington.

"My father gave a glance at me and horrified my grandma by saying he was going to take me to New Mexico!" John wrote years later.

"'Why he will not live to travel over half the distance,' said Grandma.

"'Well, he will not get well here,' said Father, and finally he persuaded them all it was safe to take the risk.

"I was taken to the train in a buggy on pillows and a bed made on the seats and we started ... . At St. Louis he carried me up the steps of the Planter's Hotel."

From St. Louis, the two took a Missouri River steamboat to Wayne City Landing near Independence. The trip required a week, the river so low that boats had to pull one another off the bars. "I remember one bar that had eight on it and we helped them all off," John wrote. Father and son departed Independence in September 1858, on a coach heavy with passengers and mail. Fare was $175. The hardships of the crossing—of weather, of plain food, of regular exercise, of fresh air, and of sleeping on the ground— quickly improved John's health.

The stage passed through Black Jack, Burlingame, and Council Grove where the driver changed the mules. It was about a week beyond Council Grove to Bent's Old Fort on the Arkansas River. From there they took the "mountain route"—to Trinidad, Colorado, then over the Raton Mountains to "Maxwell's Rancho," Fort Union, and Santa Fe. Along the way the party saw "hundreds" of Indians and met the famed mountain man, Uncle Dick Wootton. "I saw thousands of buffaloes and killed one, the only one I ever shot," John recalled.

"The first night out we camped on Plum Creek, the drivers cooked. We had a wagon, and Concord mail coach, drawn by six mules, and a driver to each team and an 'outrider,' a man who rode along and whipped up the mules with a 'Blacksnake,' a long whip.

"Father spread down buffalo robes on the ground for our bed. I demurred at sleeping on the ground, would 'catch my death of cold,' but he insisted and I slept for the first time in my life with the 'Earth for a bed and the sky for a covering!'

"I had a great deal of medicine to take by the hour, pills, powders and much medicine. Father had me get it all out and show him! After it was all spread out and I explained when I was to take it, he gathered it all up, walked about a hundred yards away and threw it over the prairie as far as he could. I ... thought I was doomed sure.

"For several days I could not eat the coffee, crackers, and fat bacon they carried, but in a week or two I gained in every way ... . [We made] the trip in thirty days, and me strong and well, and I never have had any more chills and fever."

John spent a year in Santa Fe, rooming with his older brother Howe (Joshua Howe Watts, born March 28, 1838). The boys romanced the girls, played town ball (an early form of baseball), hunted, fished, played billiards at "the Fonda" daily, wrote letters, and kept journals. During that year Howe read law, passed the bar, and married Hattie Edgar, granddaughter of James L. Collins, the territorial Indian Superintendent and publisher of the *Santa Fe Gazette*.

Meantime John studied Spanish, took music lessons, learned French with Governor Rencher; and read, besides popular moral literature, the plays of Shakespeare, the current English novelists, George Bancroft's monumental *History of the United States* (1834-1876), William Hickling Prescott's, *History of the Conquest of Mexico* (1843), even *Pilgrim's Progress*, and the Bible in Spanish, as well as other books borrowed from O.P. Hovey's private library, "the best in town." Both boys combed the newspapers and journals which arrived fairly regularly on the mail coaches from Kansas City and El Paso.

They studied with tutors. Parson Samuel Gorman and Samuel Ellison, formerly private secretary to acting governor W.W.H. Davis, taught Spanish. Territorial Secretary Alexander M. Jackson taught the law. Governor

Abraham Rencher (perhaps the most civilized governor in New Mexico's history) taught French in his office at the Governor's Palace. Francis Bauer instructed in music. This system worked quite well, for the boys, in spite of the easygoing atmosphere of Santa Fe and the freedom from their parents, read widely and wrote almost daily. John used the current idiom: having "the blues" for example meant being melancholy, then as now; and "You bet!" meant "Yes." The boys also attended the Baptist Church, now Santa Fe's Presbyterian Church, on Grant Avenue at Griffin. Reverend Samuel Gorman preached each Sunday morning in English and in the afternoon in Spanish.

Friends, gathering daily to study Spanish, passed the language texts around. In one instance John and Willie Rencher "got our Spanish out of the same book" after Willie lost his. Sallie Rencher studied French with John and Willie and the other boys. And, when it came to learning, women could be *more than* servants to their families. Both Mrs. Pelham, the surveyor-general's wife, and Mrs. Gorman, the parson's wife, met with John and his friends at appointed hours to study Spanish with Rev. Gorman.

The power of the old-fashioned sense of reading and learning as truly important in themselves is striking in this journal. For Watts' community, reading was meaningful in profound ways that seem nearly to have disappeared with the coming of the computer and with "speed reading" for information. These were *remarkably literate* people. John and his friends *used* their books, then took them back and borrowed more. O.P. Hovey, without any doubt fully knowing their great value, loaned books freely from his large private library. John completed the fifth volume of George Bancroft's ten-volume *History of the United States* on April 2nd. He read the sixth volume by the 11th and returned it to Hovey that afternoon in order to borrow Prescott's three-volume *History of the Conquest of Mexico* "which," he noted, "were over at Mr. Jacksons." He read twenty pages of Prescott on April 12th, commenting "there are a great many notes in the first volume I see," eighty-four pages on the 13th, only three or four pages on the 15th, then lamented by the 16th that he was "not half through" Prescott yet. Having begun *The Conquest of Mexico*, he commented on April 21st: "I think quite a great deal of Prescott and I think I will be pleased with his Mexico." More than a way of sharing intellectual experience within the immediate community, reading a book for John and his friends was a means of becoming acquainted with the author himself. Through books, minds shared minds!

On Monday, October 17, 1859, John, packing his big journal along, left Santa Fe for Bloomington, Indiana, to finish college. With Judge Watts, he and Jimmie Edgar took the coach to El Paso. From there they rode the stage to St. Louis, a twelve-day journey, "without one night's sleep for eleven days." John added: "went to my first theater in St. Louis Murdock performed in one of the plays."

Arriving in Bloomington on November 15, John enrolled in college (where he soon became the university's "Deputy Librarian"). "I kept a Journal across in my note book with a pencil which I fear will be rubbed out before I have time to copy it off," he wrote. Unfortunately, that material was never copied into the main journal, which he continued keeping in Bloomington. He noted that his father had carried two bottles of wine all the way from the Rio Grande for Mr. Longworth of Cincinnati who had written "asking ... about the grapes and wine of El Paso."

While teenage John and his brother Howe lived in Santa Fe, they were intimate companions although marriage, professional choices, years, and distance may have separated them emotionally later in their lives. John eventually proved to be the settler, Howe the wanderer. John looked eastward, finally locating with a steady occupation in Newton, Kansas, while Howe looked westward, always moving from job to job and place to place. Notable in this journal is its detailed anatomy of the strong bond between young brothers as well as of John's sense of loss when Howe pulled away to marry. In an important way Howe seems to be a more modern type than John. Having the mobility of the modern man, he probably paid the price of being more rootless and perhaps ultimately less content.

In Santa Fe, in 1859, the brothers shared everything. They slept in the same bed. John was frightened and melancholy at the thought of sleeping alone when Howe decided to marry Hattie Edgar. In a good many of his journal entries written just before going to bed, John closed his day by noting what brother Howe was doing. Howe had been out to see the girls, had come in, or had not come in yet, or was sitting up reading, or writing, or smoking, or was suffering from a toothache, which was less painful today, or more painful today, than it was yesterday. There or not there, big brother Howe was a central figure in John's life.

Notable too is that John had no desire to stay in New Mexico. The time in Santa Fe was an interlude before he went back to Bloomington to complete college. Indiana, not New Mexico, was home. If many a nineteenth century western traveler's journal is a westering journal, this one—in terms of internal direction—is an eastering journal. Obviously that fact has much to do with John's age. The journal reveals the feelings of a homesick boy of genteel upbringing, not of an adventurous young man gone West to make his fortune. John's descriptions of New Mexico and of the people he met were always colored by his homebound boyish expectations. Thus, his woeful, but quite normal, teenage sexual inexperience made everything about women seem mysterious and exciting.

There was, for instance, the smoochy kissing that went on in the evenings after the Watts boys and their buddies Jimmie Edgar and Willie Rencher had gathered at the homes of Santa Fe's respectable families—Governor and Mrs. Rencher's home or the home of the Edgar girls. Everyone sang the popular sentimental songs, "Ellen Bane," "Gentle Annie," "The Long, Long Weary Day," "We have Lived and Loved Together," "Thou Hast Learned to Love Another," and "Don't Be Angry Mother," while Howe strummed the guitar, or the marriageable daughters tinkled away on the piano. Afterward their mothers served freshly baked cake. When time came for the boys to go home, the girls followed them out onto the portal to bestow big smackers on their cheeks—so loud they could be heard all over the house.

Or there were the days when the boys and girls went hiking together, and the other days when the men and boys hiked alone, while, for reasons seemingly obscure to John, the girls remained home, sometimes with a headache, sometimes sick in bed, sometimes because the weather was too warm. John dreamed of Bettie, a girl in Indiana, but in Santa Fe he wore Sallie Rencher's ring, yet stoutly denied to his journal that he had any interest in her.

By contrast was the overtly strong sexual appeal of Santa Fe's local women—ladies such as the beautiful Lola Numen, "Lolita" as she was called, and Miss Campbell—in the warm hours of sleepy late afternoons. John noted that the boys and men, particularly the womanizer "Col. Means," learned Spanish from these ladies during their afternoon visits although such language practice as went on was undoubtedly largely an excuse for the visit itself. Learning Spanish in Santa Fe was one of the benefits of having an adventure with a local woman. The *bailes* which Howe and John and their buddies attended at night at Tom Valencia's were another exciting foray away from the "respectable" families and their daughters.

The journal also details the usual teenage symbols of growing up, as well as the characteristics of small town life everywhere, for Santa Fe in 1859 was very much a small town. Everyone knew the business and the whereabouts of everyone else, and rumor traveled fast. Spanish-speaking and English-speaking citizens lived side by side in a cooperative arrangement, then as now. Elections might pit the one against the other briefly as Whig or Democrat, nativist or nationalist, member of this tribal clan or of that. Local Catholic *fiestas* seemed alien and mysterious to John and his friends of the Midwestern Protestant world, who sat on a rooftop and watched the show, much as tourists do today. But the daily billiards matches at "the Fonda" went on between men of English speech and men of Spanish speech as if billiards were all that mattered and there were no ethnic or cultural differences anyone cared anything about. Thus, Santa Fe's democratic experiment went forward.

Meantime John did the kind of things American boys have always done although—unlike them—he read a very great deal, often borrowing books from the pretentious O.P. "Don" Hovey. He grew a mustache, bought a razor and strop, went fishing and bird hunting, rowed a boat, rode a horse, played alley ball, foot ball, bull pen, and townball with a "solid cake" (a ball of India rubber), took a bath once a week, put on a clean shirt on Sunday mornings, threw snowballs at the girls, went on picnics superintended by an adult, got his lessons, berated himself for being lazy, counted the number of pages he read in his book each day, thought French hard to pronounce, wore Sallie Rencher's ring, and attended church regularly, where, quite clearly, the good sermons, for him, were the short ones. So far as we can tell from reading the journal, the only thing memorable about the Reverend Gorman's Sunday sermons was that nearly all of them were too long.

From a boy's point of view, the journal describes the daily round in the territorial capital, occasionally exciting, more often humdrum. Here are glimpses of the Utes come to town to parley, dancing round the plaza and shooting off their guns. The Governor teaches French in his office at the Palace. An Italian organ grinder's organ is badly out of tune. Miguel Antonio Otero and Jose Manuel Gallegos battle for the position of Congressional Delegate on election day, while the liquor flows freely, and wagons carrying banners parade the candidates' names. Governor and Mrs. Rencher and Territorial Secretary and Mrs. Jackson own black slaves and keep them in Santa Fe.

A pistol scrape at Dr. Kavanaugh's office in which men fire several shots, but no one gets hurt. A grand welcoming party for a visiting Congressman, who disappoints the whole town with his personal appearance. A posse chases a horsethief all the way to Algodones, to find the thief asleep under a tree. Army officers, saloon keepers, and stage drivers. A famous gambler from "Washington City" spends a few nights at "the Fonda." Someone names Judge Watts' "$150 horse" after the Taos scout who had already become renowned— "Kit Karson." Governor Rencher's wife doctors John's sty with calomel, and packs basket lunches for fishing trips.

Dogs run out to bite passersby. Men, when drunk, attack one another with knives. A group in the Governor's carriage takes a joy ride out to the race track. Boys row girls around the town pond. A picnic gets rained out. A boy, bored, spends too many hours at the billiards table, as boys waste precious time today playing videogames. A free black man called "Uncle Tom" makes his way by carrying out fireplace ashes, shining boots, and cleaning messes off the carpet (considering free blacks a nuisance, the legislature had passed an act in 1856 restricting free negroes to a maximum of thirty days residence in the Territory).

"*Adios Nuevo Mexico*" provides a visual cross section of daily life in territorial Santa Fe, not the kind of stylish town it is today, where the cultured attend the opera and live in fashionable adobe homes, and the visiting rich spend fortunes having fun. In 1859, New Mexico was a "howling wilderness" and Santa Fe only a dreary little place where, to pass the time, both men and boys hunted and fished, drank too much, fought with knives and guns, partied the women, and— trying to escape the mindless boredom of an isolated frontier village—spent hours each day playing billiards. John Watts' journal is an inventory of Santa Fe's citizens and sojourners *as they were*, with their least admirable characteristics, including their violence and boredom, and as a teenage boy, who never intended his entries for any eyes but his own, experienced them.

Curiously, in all the later pages of his journal describing exciting events and people in Washington, Baltimore, Bloomington, and elsewhere, John mentions playing billiards only one time. Relieved of the boredom of daily life in Santa Fe, he no longer feels the need to escape to the billiards parlor which takes up so many of his hours at "the Fonda." Some sense of the intellectual drowsiness of life in territorial New Mexico was suggested by Leonidas Smith, when, in a speech to the Literary Club of Santa Fe on February 10, 1857, he spoke of the "inertia" and the "sleeping lethargy" of "the spirit of literature" in New Mexico Territory of the day.

In *The Killer Angels*, a prize-winning novel of the Civil War, Michael Shaara noted of the period: "It was a naive and sentimental time, and men spoke in windy phrases." Shaara added that "the religiosity and naiveté" of the day "were genuine" nonetheless. In "*Adios Nuevo Mexico*" Watts' candor reveals a genuine innocence, an artless viewpoint, and a dual morality on his own part and that of the adults in Santa Fe in 1859, simple attitudes that are alarming when one recalls that the great Civil War loomed only months away. While John was in New Mexico, both houses of the territorial legislature passed and Governor Rencher on February 3, 1859, signed a law for the protection of slaves as property. The law would be known as New

Mexico's "slave code." Both Governor Rencher and Territorial Secretary Alexander M. Jackson kept black slaves in Santa Fe; and John, as well as everyone else he moved with, seems to have accepted the "peculiar institution." At least he notes nothing unjust about the condition in his journal.

The simple level of intellectuality of the men and women who appear here, including the brightest and best educated, matches this artlessness and doubleness. Looking backward from late in the twentieth century with all its industrial and technological development and its massive violence, one would think that Santa Fe's adults of 1859 were little more than intellectual (as well as moral) children. "The finest and most useful thing" Watts could imagine was an evening spent with Governor Rencher's wife going out to look at the stars through Captain John Macomb's telescope. Then Chief of the Corps of Topographical Engineers in New Mexico, Macomb was without doubt the most capable, best educated man ever to hold that position. This was "the first [telescope] I ever looked through," Watts wrote. "It was an exceedingly fine treat to me and Mrs. Rencher." Young John and the governor's wife were also thrilled at seeing Captain Macomb's sextant.

More than naive, the people of Watts' journal were sentimental too, to an extent that seems quaint and even embarrassing today. Over the years after 1859, John and Howe carried on a voluminous correspondence, and, though they saw one another less frequently, their letters flow with a brotherly sentiment which was a mark of their time and their culture. One instance: After John returned to school in Indiana, Howe stopped to visit him in Bloomington. It was March 1861. Howe had gone from Santa Fe to Washington "without stopping having some official papers from [Surveyor General] Wilbar and others for Congress or the President."

On his return journey to Santa Fe, Howe spent a day in Bloomington with John, who described their parting in the journal thus: "Howe (God take care, guide and preserve him!) ... came home and staid one day—yesterday March 22nd," John wrote on the 23rd. "How long will it be before I forget that day ... . O what will result from the talk of last night before we closed our eyes!—may God direct. Poor Boy—he embraced me as he left just before entering the cars and I slowly walked home with a heavy sad heart ... ."

Such sentiment must have seemed simple and good, but its ironies were costly, for while it may have bonded genteel families and marked an American age, there is little doubt that it was an element in the unquestioning patriotism that vastly multiplied the violence of the Civil War. These were times, after all, when men fought duels with pistols over largely imagined personal insults as did Judge Watts and Miguel Antonio Otero while John was in Santa Fe. These were days when people took sides quickly without critical thought as did the West Point graduates who deserted the officer corps of the United States Army and left New Mexico for the Confederacy as the War began.

Through the pages of John Watts' journal march the territorial and family characters, Spanish-speaking and Anglo, military and civilian, male and female, cordial yet bored, generous yet violent, bright yet simple of thought, moral yet unjust, naive and sentimental. Picnics. Hunting. Hours of playing billiards. Dancing. Little piano and violin concerts. Playing the guitar. Eating cake at parties. Looking at the stars through Captain Macomb's telescope, and wondering at his sextant. Hours upon hours spent reading, with little critical thought. These were the social and intellectual activities and attainments of Santa Fe's citizens, and these suggest the fabric of their feelings and their loyalties, about to be tested and redefined in the fire of America's great Civil War.

"*Adios Nuevo Mexico*" offers tiny vignettes of life in Santa Fe in another time: Howe "hawks" when he walks in the front gate just like Pa. Governor Rencher looks "very sour" at Willie's coming in late to French class. With Secretary Jackson out of town, the boys get by with playing in his office. John rolls a six-pound cannon ball around the plaza "for exercise." Men, women, and children all turn out for horse races, a form of entertainment well established in New Mexico by 1859. A mother and children sit under the portal of the Palace of the Governors to listen to a band concert on the plaza. John finds Mrs. Edgar in a bad mood, "from some reason—was crying," and wonders why.

Then as now, the plaza was *the* center of the community's activities, as well as the physical center of the town. Here were located "the Fonda" (then the Exchange Hotel), and the main drygoods stores. Here on sunny afternoons the band played, the old men gathered to talk, and the boys played ball. Here arrived the wagon trains from Missouri, and the stages from El Paso and Kansas City, packing the newspapers, the letters from friends back home, and the travelers who came to settle or to exploit the territory.

Late one August afternoon in 1994, I sat on the plaza enjoying my coffee. I watched two Mexican-American boys, four or five years old, play stickball. They used an old sock rolled up and tied with a string. Their sticks were crooked limbs broken from trees. One boy speared the sock and threw it at the other, who took his turn doing the same. There was a good deal of yelling and squealing.

Across the plaza a circle of older boys played a game a Santa Fe friend of mine called hacky-sacky. They stood barefoot or in socks. One boy kicked a cloth ball into the air. A second caught it with his toe and kicked it high toward the next boy. And so on. The object seemed to be to keep the ball in the air without quite breaking the circle, but to do it with great style, and much hopping about, using the heel, the toe, or either side of either foot. Touching the ball with your hands was *the thing* you must not do!

Down San Francisco Street from where I sipped my coffee, in plain sight from the plaza, modern-day mountain men, bearded, hard-eyed bikers in black leather trousers and caps, lazied in and out of Evangelo's bar. Their shiny Harleys, parked slantwise into the curb, wore California plates. From time to time the bikers left the bar, mounted the Harleys, and roared away in smoke as if they had to get someplace now! Circling a block or two, they coasted quietly in, backed their Harleys gently into the curb, and lazied once more into Evangelo's.

This, I thought, was about the way life looked from the plaza on any sunny afternoon in John Watts' day, except that in those times the mountaineers would have worn beaver skins and point-blanket coats, and the Harleys would have been horses.

BOOK I

Spring 1859

"I did not put on a clean shirt this morning. I thought the one I had on was clean enough." — *Sunday, 6 March 1859*

"I went to church this morning and heard a sermon by Mr. Gorman and one thing good about it was it was short." — *Sunday, 3 April 1859*

"This month will soon be out and then perhaps father will come with ma and then we will get our socks and shirts mended." — *Thursday, 21 April 1859*

"There are more dogs in Santa Fe than any place I ever was in before— there are two dead over on the side of the road as we go up in Town." — *Thursday, 5 May 1859*

"This ... is fathers eighteenth trip across the plains—he looks quite ruff when he first arrived but got shaved and put on a clean shirt and now looks considerably better." — *Friday, 27 May 1859*

March 1859.

Friday; 4

Here I am again another day having simply flown. I [rose] about my usual time and went up with Howe to breakfast. I have not played any pool to day. I and Howe went up at 11. O clock [and recited] our lesson [to] the Governor [with the rest of] the class. I played one game of billiards [tonight after the] Sunday with Willie Rencher and he beat me of which he made a great fuss — it was [on] the upper table. I have not [paid] my billiard [bill] for this month yet. Howe and Willie and myself all went out by the capitol where there were a lot of boys (grown) playing town ball and they asked us to play which of course we were glad to do. We had a pleasant time — they played a little different from what I have been used to playing — they catch one fellow out three times hand running it puts all out. It was fine exercise and I enjoyed. I have read some little to day in "Ralph Railton" but I am not getting along as fast as I would like. I practiced on the guitar some to day. Howe went and said his law lesson as usual. To day has been a very pretty day — the sun shone out warm all day. I helped snowball some boys or more girls there was three boys with Jesus — him and I against three or four. It was back in the corral and we could n't see each other. I hit one of the women in the belly and knocked her down so they tell me

Saturday; 5.

To day has been a very blustery cold day. It has snowed hard all afternoon or rather drifted about. It has been quite a snow storm. I rose about my usual time and Howe and I went up to breakfast. I and Willie said our Spanish to day to Mr Eliason at our usual time. I have played no pool nor

Three pages of the original diary are included in this book. The diary was legal size and the diagonal squiggles were John's attempts to improve his penmanship.

Chapter I

March 1859

Friday; 5

Here I am again another day having swiftly flown. I rose about my usual time and went up with Howe to breakfast. I have not played any pool to day. I and Howe went up at 11, O'clock and recited our lesson to the Governor with the rest of the class. I played one game of billiards to night at the Fonda with Willie Rencher[1] and he beat me of which he made a great fuss—it was on the upper table. I have not paid my billiard [bill?] for this month yet. Howe and Willie and myself all went out by the capitol where there were a lot of boys (grown) playing town ball[2] and the[y] asked us to play—which of course we were glad to do. We had a pleasant time—they catch one fellow out three times [hard?] running it puts all out. It was fine exercise and I enjoyed [it]. I have read some little today in "Ralph Rattlin" but I am not getting along as fast as I would like. I practiced on the guitar some to day. Howe went and said his law lesson as usual. To day has been a very pretty day—the sun shone out warm all day. I helped snow ball some boys or more girls there was than boys with Jesus—him and I against three or four. It was back in the carrol and we couldn't see each other. I hit one of the women in the belly and knocked her down so they tell me.

Saturday; 5

To day has been a very blustery cold day. It has snowed hard all afternoon or rather drifted about. It has been quite a snow storm. I rose about my usual time and Howe and I went up to breakfast. I and Willie said our Spanish to day to Mr. Elison[3] at our, usual time. I have played no pool nor billiards to day. Vigil was over here this afternoon and after he had gone Willie came over. I have spent the day mostly in reading in "Ralph Rattlin." I had such a nice dream last night—I dreamed that I was at home up stairs in Bettie's[4] room sitting in the old rocking chair and that Bettie was sitting by me—I dreamed that we had a [...?] and she having "snugged down" in my arms I gave her three sweet kisses which has made me feel better all day to day when I thought about it—[...?] got up and went to breakfast. The mail did not get in to day and therefore I have neither letters nor papers. Howe is reading "Vanity Fair" by W.M.Thackery—I think he borrowed the book of Hovey.[5] There is a bitter cold wind blowing to night and drifting the snow about. I am getting along in the French very slowly—it is so hard to pronounce. I have on a ring of Sallie Rencher's[6] that she gave me to look at and I put it on and wore it off. We got the Gazette this afternoon. Howe said his Law as usual—I staid at the Fonda[7] until he got through. I went "back" a little while and saw Pageans[8] going it and also George Waldo playing at "Twenty-One." I have not touched the Guitar to day neither has Howe that I know of. I think I have written all I can think of and I will cease.

Sunday; 6

Well we have been treated very well to day and could not complain of there being [...?] in our church. I did not put on a clean shirt this morning. I thought the one I had on was clean enough. I wrote an answer [to Martha's?] letter this morning and then went to church and listened to a sermon preached by Mr Gorman.[9] We had a most [...?] at the Fonda today. This afternoon I wrote a long letter to Bettie although I have not received a line from her for two months and I think it is time she was answering some of my letters. Howe wrote four or five letters to day I only two. I went to church this afternoon and listened to a sermon in Spanish by the same man that preached this morning. I have another sty coming on my eye so I went up and let Mrs Rencher[10] try her hand at curing it—she put some calomel on it and gave me some to put on before I went to bed at night. I have read some in my Bible to day. It has been cold and disagreeable. I saw the notice of Prescott death in Boston on the 30 of Jan. Mr. Elison went to San Miguel to day.

Monday; 7   <u>9 O'clock and 11 minutes.</u>

I rose about my usual time this morning and after dressing went up to breakfast. I got a lesson in French and with the class recited to the Governor at 11 O'clock our regular hour. I played two games of billiards to day on the big table with Davison[11] and beat both. Howe played pool on the big table some to day. I played on the little table with Willie and Vigil and came out as usual—behind. I have run up an account with Vigil and Willie both—the former I owe two dollars and the later six bits. Howe has gone to Jackson's[12] to say his law lesson. There is a baile at Tom Valentia's[13] to night. I read one hundred and forty pages to day and to night together in "Rattlin" which I finished. I have not paid my board bill or billiard bill I mean, for this month yet. To day has been a very pretty day. Jesusito was in a few minutes ago in his bare feet and with his coat off. I have not practiced any on the guitar for a long time.

Tuesday; 8   **8 O'clock.**

This is rather early to write in my Journal but as I may go to a baile at Tom Valentia's to night I thought I would post up quick and on time. Howe and I went to a baile at Tom's last night and to night is the last one there will be for a long time because "Lent" commences soon and there are no bailes I believe until it is over which is forty day[s] I think. I recited French to day. Samuel [Ellison] being away we cannot recite in Spanish. There was a horse race this morning but I had no way to go down to the track so I staid at home. Kavanaugh's horse and Jones pony I believe were the ones that run— Pointer and Jones bet—$300 I believe. Pointer gave Jones twenty feet I believe and beat him twenty. Howe bought some marbles and a ball this afternoon and he Willie R. and I all played marbles. I beat Colorado this evening two games of billiards. I got another book of Hovey—"Percival Keene"—which I have commenced—I am wearing a ring of Sallie Rencher's. I played town ball this morning.

Wednesday; 9   **10, O'clock less 11 minutes.**

Another day's rotine has been gone through and the last act before I go to bed is to work in my Journal. Rose about our usual hour and went to breakfast. We also recited our French lesson which was the second congugation [...?] and the seventh lesson in Oldendorff. I did not play any billiards on the large table to day. I read some this afternoon in "Percival Keene" and played pool with Willie and Vigil this afternoon—I came out as usual behind but not much. Howe has gone over and not yet returned from saying his law lesson. To day has been a very fine day but there is quite a strong wind blowing to night. I got my French lesson for tomorrow this afternoon and read a little in French. Howe read some in French to the Governor this morning. I owe Howe $5 dollar[s] of money I have borrowed of him. At home I was always lamenting for time to read and now I have plenty I do not improve as I ought, however I am reading some and learning otherwise very important information. I did not go to the baile last night. We burn two candles constantly.

Thursday; 10.   **9 O'clock and 11 minutes.**

Well to day has been exciting and full of adventure. I rose about my usual hour and went to breakfast. I with Howe and the rest of the class recited at the usual hour. Willie and Vigil played pool a good [while] this morning. There was a fight this morning up at the Fonda between Col M enes[14] and Leo Smith. The Col sneaked up on Leo with a cane and lit into him and whipped him before he had any chance to retaliate. And again this afternoon there was a big fight down at Kavanaugh's Office between Drue and Menes chiefly but Leo Smith helped Drue. There was considerable shooting of pistols and some how or other Rogers was in the scrape—all four were shooting. Dr. Kavanaugh[15] said he never saw so many deliberate shots without any lasting effect—he said there were ten or twelve shots. Col I believe run them through. We moved our little table up to the shop of a workman that fixed the Fonda billiard tables who is going to fix our little table up nicely. We have obtained the small [rondo?] balls—eight in number and a new cloth for our table of Green and we will have things fixed up right. I read a piece of or rather the whole story in a little book for children in French to the Governor this morning. I got my Oldendorff this afternoon and also looked over the verb. I have read almost a hundred pages to day in "Percival Keene." I have enough now to keep me employed. I have not done much in the music line. I have not practiced those pieces Bauer[16] gave [me]— two of my teachers are away now Bauer and Mr. Elison.

Friday. 11.   <u>10 0' clock</u>

Another day has passed and I am now performing the last thing more before I go to bed. Tomorrow is the day for the mail which I am glad of and hope will get in in time with some letter[s] for me and one from Bettie especially. We recited in French this morning at our usual hour. I played four games of billiards to night with Colorado—the first he beat me the rest I beat him and beat him playing off. I have played eleven games this month and they have cost me nothing. We have a neighbor in the room ajoining our[s] where we had our billiard table—his name is Crump[17] he has just taken up his quarters here to day—I do not know what kind of a man he is— I am not acquainted with him. Howe and I had a game of "back out" this afternoon out by the new capitol with a solid cake that Howe bought. I have read over a hundred pages to day and finished "Percival Keene." I went up to night to get another book but Hovey was sick. I am going to read Bancroft if I can get it and finish it and be like it was at home. I studied French a little this afternoon. Pointer won some thirty odd dollars to day off of Nicholas Pino[18] playing billiards—Pointer gave him ten points—the first game Nicholas beat which was fifteen dollars, the second Pointer with thirty odd dollars bet. Howe has posted for to night.

Saturday; 12.

To day has passed away. We did not recite any in French to day. I took back "Percival Keene" which I had finished and and have got into my old stand by Bancroft's United States. I have the third Volume which I had read about half through. The mail came in this afternoon and I recieved two letters—one from Fannie[19] in Washington City and the other from Bettie in Evansville which I have been looking for and expecting. Howe recieved some papers and one letter from ma. Howe and I and our neighbor Mr Crump went over to the baile to night at [...?] which I thought was contrary to the Catholics it being Lent. I played two games of billiards to day with Don José—he giving me ten points—he beat me—two dollars were bet one dollar on each game. José was in extra good luck. I, Howe and Mr Whiting[20] took a walk this morning but it was to windy—I was in Mr. Crump's room to day—he has a large dog. Willie was over here this morning. I have played on the guitar some today. The Gazette came round as usual. Ma[21] said she was getting ready to come to Santa Fe.

Sunday; 13.

Well another week has commenced. I rose this morning and washed myself and put on clean clothes. I answered Fannie's letter this morning and then went to church. Mr. Gorman preached—they are baptists—I thought it was the episcopal church but I found it is not. I wrote or answered Bettie's letter this afternoon—that was all—I only wrote two letters this mail. The bugle has sounded once and there it goes again. Howe has been reading "Pendennis" by Thackery. I read a little in my Bible to night. We had quite a nice dinner to day—Mr. Elison is back—came last night. To day has been a tolerable good day. Miller[22] was in our room this afternoon—he and another man has a rancho below Hatches. Jim Sabine[23] was in this afternoon and we all three sung sacred music—I also—Jim bass Howe air. Hovey also was in here this afternoon—staid a short time.

Monday; 14.

Well to day I believe has been like the most of them—about the same old thing. I went up and recited with the class but it was the poorest I have ever done yet. We (Willie and I) get a Spanish lesson tomorrow. I read ninty pages in the third volume of Bancroft to day—that is making more progress than I did at home—I expect I will make it a hundred before I go to bed to night. I played three games of billiards to night with Colorado and beat him the three. Cotton who was drunk to night played Quintana[24] at the discount—Barry Simpson bet $10 with Cotton and won it—Barry went away and I too. Howe and Col Menes have gone out sparking. Howe took Lola over to her Aunts where they were to rendezvous. I have a bad cold which I do not know where I caught but which gives me a headache. Nothing of vast importance has happend to day that I know of now.

Tuesday; 15.

Here I am another day having swiftly glided away. I rose about my usual hour and went up and got my breakfast. I got my lesson in Spanish this morning and about 7. O'clock having gone in for Willie who was just getting out of bed—after he dressed we went in and recited to Don Samuel [Ellison] who hears us in the morning early because he has to go to court. I read in Bancroft this afternoon and to night—I have read just a hundred pages to day. I got the French this afternoon too—Adire or Adyre[25] was in here this afternoon loafing and bothered Howe considerably who was getting his law lesson.Whiting was in this afternoon and went out riding in Self-defense—Howe went with = in a carriage. Percy Eyre[26] was in this morning and wrote the assignment and land warrant. I played one game of billiards to day—before supper with Davison and beat him. Tom Valentia won $33 dollars off of George Waldo[27] to day—beat him five straight games. Cotton played George at fifteen and the discount. Howe is saying his Law lesson.

Wednesday; 16.

Another day has passed and I have to fulfill the last act before I go to bed. I rose about my usual hour and went to breakfast and as I went got some eggs at George Estes'[28] and had them for breakfast. I got a French lesson this morning and when the time came went up and recited. Willie came in a little late for which his pa looked very sour at him. I got the fourth volume of Bancroft this afternoon and have read twenty-five pages in it. I played one game of billiards to night with Chastine[29] giving him forty and then I beat him. I spent the evening with Willie Rencher. I went into the parlor where I was introduced to Dr Connelly[30]—Lieut. Craig[31] was also there with whom I had a little talk and who is more sociable than I expected as he and father are not on good terms. Howe went over and said his law lesson. I spun a top of Jesusito's this afternoon some—I am trying to learn to spin it and catch it in my hand the same as these Mexicans. I have had a bad cold for two or three days. It hailed a little to day. Percy and Hovey have bought out "Mac's" daguerrotype establishment.[32] [Dunn?][33] is here and I had a talk with him this afternoon.

Thursday; 17.

Here I am again I will do my writing up in a hurry to night. I rose and went to breakfast about our usual hour. I forgot all about the French for tomorrow and read in Bancroft all morning—I read eighty pages to day. This afternoon I lounged around the Fonda all the afternoon watching them play pool. Colorado and I got in a way of playing and played six games in all—I got cleaned two of them. At night Cotton and Tom Valencia played for money Cotton giving him twenty-five and the discount. Tom won some off of him I think in the long run. Pigeans was winning like everything when I came away. I studied my French some to night. Howe has gone to bed and I am going to follow suit.

Friday; 18.

The week is closing up fast and I am glad of it for I wish the mail to come in for I want some letters from home. I rose about as late as usual—went to breakfast and when I came back got the French lesson. I am learning to throw a top and spin it in the air and catch it in my hand—I am doing very well. This afternoon Willie and I played with dollars throwing them against a post and letting them bounce off. I and he and a lot of other fellows had a game [...?] against the side of the church—ball ally and before long we knocked one of the balls on top and then I came and got my solid cake and before we quit we had it knocked on top too so we after much debate went in and got a ladder at Hovey's and then climed up on top—a Mexican—and got one of the balls but could not find the others so I went up myself and after a little hunting found it in the middle of the church[34] —I then came down and went to supper. I played three games of billiards to day with Don José and beat all. I read a little in Bancroft to night—I may read more. Howe went to bed to night with the tooth-ache.

Saturday; 19.

I rose about my usual hour this morning and went up and got my breakfast. We did not recite as we ought to have done to Mr Elison in Spanish this morning. The court is going on. The Navajos and Utahs met here in Santa Fe and made a peace—they (the Pueblo some said) marched round the plaza singing stopping at intervals and singing firing their guns and dancing—this I saw and it reminded me of descriptions of the Indians in the time of "The Old Thirteen Collonies" in Bancroft. We knocked both balls on top again on the church and when we got them down went and played knock and catch[35] and bull pen—Dick Simpson[36] was with us to day. I was at the Governor's to night—staid until 9 O'clock. Howe still has the tooth ache. The mail came in this afternoon. I received two letters one from ma and one from Mary Miner[37] —both of which of course were acceptable. When we were playing ball—there were but few of us, there came up a wind so strong and full of dust—sand that we had to quit. I played marbles with Hary Whiting this afternoon. Howe is having a bad time with his tooth—I went up to night and got him two cigars and a plug of tobacco. He received some letters I think. I spun Jesusito's top this afternoon. I read a little in Bancroft to day. Mrs Rencher brought me in some of the soup she had for dinner to day it was very nice. Sallie is not nor has not been well—has a severe cold. Our friend Crump took a ride this afternoon—I saw Tom Smith[38] to day—he has come back I suppose. Piggians breaks the bank every night most. Howe got Waverly Magazine in the mail—Did not hear from father.

Sunday; 20.

Another week commenced with today. I rose and put on clean clothes having washed my neck and ears. I went to church this morning and heard Mr Gorman preach. We had a very good congregation to day better than usual. The Governor and lady, Miss Knellie[39] and Mr Kavanaugh with Mrs Wilkins[40] and others were there. I answered ma's and Mary Miner's letters this afternoon. Mr Crump was in here this morning writing letters—he writes left handed—the first I ever saw and very fast. We had quite a fine dinner to day. It has been a very blustery day. Howe has had the tooth ache all day and went to bed with [it]. He has been smoking and chewing tobacco for it all day but I guess he found very little relief. I have been reading the Waverly Magazine all day most and to night to Howe in bed. It is a very good periodical I think—it is excellent. I have [not] read a word in my Bible to day. Pointer has gone home to Taos and Tom Smith is here. Percy was in a short time this afternoon.

Monday; 21.

Well to day passed away with its pleasures and duties. This morning at 11. O'clock we went up and recited in French [after] which we went over to the Fonda and Crump and I played a game of billiards with José and Watkins—they beat us—a bottle of champagne was bet which we had for dinner. This afternoon I and Willie with some more had a game of ball out in the commons by the Capitol. To night Adair came over a little after dark and asked me to take a walk with him down to see Lola[41] which we did and met Howe and Col Menes coming from there. We had quite a nice time. I played on the guitar some for them while Adair talked to them in Spanish. I read thirty pages in Bancroft to day—but must do better tomorrow.

Tuesday; 22.

To day has been a beautiful day—the sun shone and very warm. I rose about as late as usual. Read in [...?] Latin Grammar all morning but did not recite our lesson to Mr Elison[.] we have not recited for a long time. I spun Jesusito's top some this morning. This afternoon I read in Bancroft and to night also and will read more before I go to bed. I have read so far to day just fifty-two pages or seventy-two I mean. I have played three games of billiards to day—one with Davison—one with Louie Felsenthorf [42] which we did not finish for the sheriff arrested him for playing cards and gambling I believe it has just been cleaning all the gamblers out. I played one game with Col Menes giving him twenty-five and he cleaned me. To night I read in Bancroft —I am in a hurry to get through all the volumes. My watch has got so I cannot wind it[.] the key slips. Howe still has the tooth-ache occasionally.

Wednesday; 23.

Well to day passed off as usual I believe. I got and recited with the class a lesson in French. I played a good many games of billiards to day three games with Louie Staub[43]—he giving me fifteen the first two games and the last we played even—I played one with Mr Erwin—and Bob and I played against Editor and Davison—the[y] beat us and then Bob and I drew to see who should play for it and I beat him—all of the former I beat. But to night we had the fun. Howe and Col Menes had a private party over at Lola's aunt's I believe—I dressed up while Howe was down at Mr Jackson['s] and went up to the Fonda and when Howe came he was with Mrs Bowler.[44] I stopped for Frank [O'B?] —Col Menes sent us back for Bary Simpson but that only provoked him who with Cader[45] swore they would give one and kick out any of our crew out that came. We had an excellent time and I danced every thing I knew how and ever thing else[.] I learned the round and Viana waltz and the [...?] which I never tried before in my life. I had laid by my watch because I had no key that would fit—the one I have has got so it will not wind the watch—it slips.

Thursday; 24.

I rose rather later than usual this morning on account of being out so late last night. To day was the day for Spanish but Mr Elison is to busy at court. I studied some though in [Cooke's?] grammar—Howe is translating sentences from Ollendorff—Spanish and French. Howe has been writing letters through the week. George Waldo beat Howe playing off today twice— so there is $3. for to day. I played two games and half to day and lost one. I played one [and] a half with Willie and one with Boone[46]—Willie beat me one game. I read seventy-two pages in Bancroft—took a ride West with

Adair. I was over to see Bauer who with his wife are very sick[.] he has the fever. I and Adair went down to see Lola to night found Col Menes there but [scared?] him off. I played some on the guitar. Mr Watkins was in to see us a little while—his dog brought Howe's Magazine in his mouth. Mr Watkins thinks a good deal of his dog—I think he is a pointer[.] he looks like one. We had a nice time to night—at Lola's. I am learning the Spanish as fast as I can.

Friday; 25.

The end of the week is drawing near. Tomorrow I will look for some letters if the mail arrives. I rose about as late as usual and Howe and I went up to breakfast. After breakfast I came down and got the lesson in French in the grammar—having got Oldendorff and also read two stories in a French book Howe borrowed of Mrs Rencher—the pronuntiation is what I am trying chiefly to learn. I am getting so I like the French. This afternoon I played three games of billiards with Louie Stabb—the first he beat—almost strung me I the second and beat him the third playing off—the second and last games he gave me fifteen points. I read in Bancroft some this morning—twenty or thirty pages. Mr Crump and Bauer and wife are all sick yet. We had a game of "cat"[47] in the plaza this afternoon and also a game of bull pen. While we were playing the band came out in the plaza and played several tunes—Howe and I came home. After supper I played two games of billiards with Colorado and beat him both so I have played five games which cost me nothing. I read in Bancroft to night and finished the fourth volume—in all I have read ninty pages to day. When I came down home I came in company with Mr Yost[48]—I could not get in my room the door was locked—Howe had gone away some where so I had to roust Jesusito out of bed and get his key. Our table I suppose is coming on fine. It has been a pleasant day but rather warm in the afternoon. The time will come when I'll read this with pleasure and perhaps with Bettie by my side.

Saturday; 26.

This is the last day of the week—Willie and I did not recite our Spanish to Mr Elison to day—he is too busy now in court. I rose about as late as usual. I have played seven games of billiards to day two with Juan [somebody?] a Mexican—one with Joe that used to stay at the Fonda giving him twenty—two with a man with black whiskers from Alburqueque and two with a tall fellow with sid[e] whiskers. I beat all except one with Juan. I studied the Spanish grammar some to day—I exchange[d] the fourth volume of Bancroft—which I finished last night for the fifth volume. The mail arrived this afternoon—I got one letter from mother—Mackinstery[49] brought it [and?] the man that brought pa and I to Council Grove and gave me a can of currant jelly which [Hall?] grumbled at so. We received Harper's Weekly and Magazine in the mail—no news from pa. There is going to be a ball on Monday night. Adair was over to see us to night. Willie was down here to see us to day.

Sunday; 27.

The first day of another week has passed and I am now going to write the events of it. I rose about my usual hour—washed my neck, ears, hand[s] and face, put on clean shirt[,] undershirt and clean clothes all around. I wrote two letters this morning one to Seth P. Tuley and one to Samuel W. Dodds.[50] I did not answer ma's as she would not get the answer before starting for here[,] Santa Fe. I went to church this morning and heard a sermon by Mr Gorman which was pretty good. There were not many out but a fair congregation considering the disagreeable day which has been blasting the dust about in whirlwinds. I also went this afternoon when he preached in Spanish—very few there. I and Howe and Mr Crump went up to see Whiting—we saw his lady—I had a little chat with the boys and Cora.[51] I have read some in my Bible to day. To night it still storms. Howe went to church both times. I read over the French to night.

Monday; 27.[sic]

Well the chief event of to day was at night. I with the class recited in French. I bought me a pair of pantaloons to day at Kingsbury's[52] at $4.50 which I wore to the ball to night. Well to night I went up to Beck and Johnson's[53] with Mr Crump who got a pair of kid gloves and then we went up to the Fonda—from there I and Willie went down to the baile of the batchelors at Col Collin's[.][54] We had a fine time. Howe went after Lola who had gone up to Mr Bowler's but Howe had a row with the old lady and she would not let Lola come. I took a fancy to Charley Conclin's sister who is a very fine girl I think—I danced with her and she danced very easy. The wife of Jesus Cena[55] was also there and very good looking. We had an excellent time. John Ward,[56] Lieut. Craig and Mr Wilkins all got "tight" as "bricks"— the dance broke up about 2 O'clock.

Tuesday; 29.

Well I felt tired this morning when I rose which was not very early. We went to breakfast after which I came home and went to studying Spanish.

Howe had a little fuss with Jesus whom he made pay three bits that Jesusito stole—Jesus was very mad but the little buggar of a son of his has stolen powder, candy and other things from us—I expect Howe will send Jesus off and get some other man. We did not recite in Spanish to day at all—I went up at 11 O'clock and found Mr Elison there but Willie never came at all. Bob is writing for Mr Elison—he is employed there I expect. I have read very little in Spanish but have studied the grammar hard. I have read none in Bancroft of any account to day. I have played no billiards. Howe bought a can of pine apple to day which we opened and got into. I took a nap this afternoon and so did Howe—Willie came over while I was asleep. I copied a couple of [songs?] out of Howe's book into mine.

Wednesday; 30.

Well this month will soon be out and I have not a cent to pay my billiard bill with—I do not know what I will do for Some. I rose this morning a little later than usual I believe. I got the french this morning and recited with the class as usual. I have idled away to day—I went up with Willie to see how our table was getting along which as usual was very slow. We played ball against the church and accidently knocked it on top and so away went Willie's ball. I played ball a good deal and billiards too—I played three games with Mr Crump and beat him all of them—then a four handed game—Willie and I discounted Jones and [McEvan?][57]—we beat them too. I have read very little in Bancroft to day and if I do not read more I will be as bad as at home —three months on a volume. I have been studying Spanish this afternoon. I went down to see Lola this evening with Adair and we had a nice time—I am getting so I understand the Spanish pretty well. Howe went up to the Fonda while we were at Lola's and played billiards. I studied the French a little to day also.

Thursday; 31.

I rose this morning about our usual time. Howe has sent Jesus off and we employ an old negro they call Uncle Tom.[58] This morning was the first time he has come—he built a fire and blacked our boots for us nicely. I and Willie as usual did not recite to day in Spanish—Mr Elison was too tired and busy. I played two games of billiards to day—a four handed game I and Jones against Willie and Louie Dickens[59]—we beat one game and them the other and then we banked to see who should pay for the game I or Jones and he went in the pocket and he beat me he said but by the request of the fellow that keeps the table I read the rules and when one goes in the pocket he loses. So I pay nothing for to day for billiards. We had a game of bull pen in the plaza this afternoon and I gave Willie a good one. I have read a hundred pages in Bancroft to day. I looked over the French to night. There were two men in here to night and Howe gave one a good coat and pair of pants. This is the last of the month.

NOTES: March 1859

1. 1 have not identified "Willie" Rencher. The 1860 U.S. Census, as well as biographical sources on the Governor and Mrs. Rencher, state that they had three daughters. No son is mentioned. In writing of the Rencher family, April 12, however, Watts says "Willie caused his ma some anxiety," suggesting that Willie was the Governor and Mrs. Rencher's son. The point is further confused by an entry in which Watts notes that Willie "showed us his name in one of the N. E. papers where he lives." Since the Renchers were from North Carolina, it seems strange that if Willie were their son he would have been mentioned in such a way. Perhaps he was a visiting nephew. See entries for April 12 and May 22.

Born in North Carolina in 1798, Governor Abraham Rencher graduated from the University of North Carolina Law School in 1822 and was elected to Congress, where he served ten years. He lived in Switzerland and was U.S. Minister to Portugal. He was a poet and essayist as well as a lawyer and politician. Curiously, he tutored students in French in the governor's office in 1859. Without any doubt that office has never again been used for so civilized a purpose.

Having actively sought the territorial governorship, Rencher was appointed by President Buchanan, August 17, 1857, and he and his family arrived in Santa Fe November 11. The editor of *The Santa Fe Weekly Gazette* wrote of the incoming governor and the territorial secretary, Alexander M. Jackson, that "we feel justified in predicting an enlightened and liberal administration ... guided by an elevated regard for the interests and rights of the people and a scrupulous reference to the aims and wishes of the Federal Government towards this people."

Although his four-year term was stormy, Rencher had two important accomplishments: promotion of public school education for all New Mexicans and reduction of the debt.

Unlike other civilian and military officials of southern background, Rencher chose to stay with the Union as the War approached. Although he wished to be reappointed governor, Lincoln appointed Henry Connelly to the office in 1861.

See "Southern Patriot: Abraham Rencher, 1857-61," in Calvin Horn, *New Mexico's Troubled Years: the Story of the Early Territorial Governors* (Albuquerque, 1963), pp. 73-91; Thomas A. McMullin, and David Walker, *Biographical Directory of American Territorial Governors* (Westport, CT, n.d.), pp. 239-40; Ralph Emerson Twitchell, *The Leading Facts of New Mexican History,* Vol. II (Cedar Rapids, Iowa, 1912), p. 314 ff; and *The Santa Fe Weekly Gazette,* 5 Dec 57.

2. An American form of the English game rounders, "town ball" (also called "old-cat," "one old-cat," "round ball," "barn ball," "burn ball," and so on) was one of several early versions of baseball.

Ball games were probably common among children along the Santa Fe Trail and in New Mexico in this period. Marian Russell also mentions them. Traveling the Santa Fe Trail in 1852 with her widowed mother and her brother Will, she played with the other children around the campfires at night. "Between the two night circles formed by the wagons was a bit of no-man's land which the children used as a playground," Marian wrote. "The ball games that went on there! The games of leap-frog and dare base."

From 1852 until 1856, the Russells lived in Santa Fe and Albuquerque. Little Marian and Will played games with the New Mexican children in the dusty streets. They made up a game called "Steal the Dead Man's Bones" which they played with human bones amongst the eroded graves of the Fort Marcy cemetery, and the New Mexican children taught Marian and Will a game called "kanute" in which betting for beads and piñon nuts went on.

See Harold Seymour, *Baseball: the Early Years* (New York, 1960), pp. 5-8; Geoffrey O. Ward, and Ken Burns, *Baseball* (New York, 1994), p. 3; and Marian Russell, *Land of Enchantment: Memoirs of Marian Russell Along the Santa Fe Trail as Dictated to Mrs. Hal Russell* (Albuquerque, 1981), pp. 20, 36, 47, and 48.

3. Born in Kentucky, Samuel Ellison was private secretary to acting governor W.W.H. Davis after Governor David Meriwether departed Santa Fe in May 1857. When Davis left for the States on October 15, Ellison remained in charge until Governor Rencher's arrival on November 11, 1857.

A political jack of all trades, Ellison survived by working at any job that provided a little income. Besides tutoring local students in Spanish in 1859, he was a United States Court clerk, a member of the territorial house of representatives, and by 1882-83 the territorial librarian.

See Horn, *Troubled Years,* p. 75; "Executive Record Book 1," p. 182,

New Mexico Records Center and Archives, Santa Fe (hereafter cited NMRA); 1860 U.S. Census; and Twitchell, *Leading Facts*, II, p. 492.

4. "Bettie" was Miss Bettie Ruter of Patriot, Indiana, with whom young Watts corresponded. See "Letters Written," Watts Journal, p. 407.

5. A Vermont native, Oliver P. Hovey was a long-time resident of Santa Fe. A private with Cerán St. Vrain and Colonel Sterling Price, he had helped put down the Taos Rebellion in January 1847. In February and March 1849, with a party of seven men and a wagon, Hovey traveled from Santa Fe to Independence in forty-three days. Attacked by Indians, the men walked more than 350 miles.

In the fall of 1847, Hovey and Edward T. Davies began New Mexico's first newspaper, the *Santa Fe Republican*. Using a press purchased from the U.S. Government, Hovey purportedly had 700 subscribers at $5.00 a year. He had earlier printed 500 copies of the "Kearney Code," the laws proclaimed for New Mexico in late 1846.

A member of the legislative assembly in 1858-59 and 1861-62, Hovey had an extensive private library. In 1860, at thirty-three years of age, he was listed as a "commission agent" who owned real property in Santa Fe valued at $18,000 and personal property at $35,000. His wife, Ysabel, twenty-seven years old, was Charles M. Conklin's sister. The Hoveys had four children.

The self-important Hovey was called "General" Hovey by Kearney's men, "Don" Hovey by young Watts, and "the great Lord Hovey" by W.W.H. Davis. He owned a share of the Mora Grant, lived in a grand house across the street from the Baptist Church, and was a poor business risk. At least Santa Fe merchant Kingsbury thought so, for he wrote of Hovey: "I have no confidence in him ... . There is little hope of recovering anything of him. He continues to spend money fast & foolishly if anything more extravagantly than when you was here." He was generous, loaning books, mules, and even a bathtub.

See Jane Lenz Elder, and David J. Weber, eds., "Trading in Santa Fe: John M. Kingsbury's Correspondence with James Josiah Webb, 1853-1861," unpbl. ms. (1994), Ch. 7, p. 13 (hereafter cited Elder and Weber, "Trading in Santa Fe"). The latter was published as a book by the Southern Methodist University Press (Dallas, 1996) since the writing of these notes. George P. Hammond, *The Adventures of Alexander Barclay, Mountain Man* (Denver, 1976), pp. 214-15; Ralph Emerson Twitchell, *Old Santa Fe: The Story of New Mexico's Ancient Capital (Santa Fe, 1925)*, p. 282; 1860 U.S.

Census; and William A. Keleher, T*urmoil in New Mexico*, repr. (Albuquerque, 1982), pp. 118, n. 25, and 503, n. 108.

6. "Sallie" was Sarah Rencher, the governor's fifteen-year-old daughter. See 1860 U.S. Census.

7. "The Fonda" is a Santa Fe landmark. It seems to have been an inn at least by the time Americans arrived in 1846. Soon afterward it operated as the "U.S. Hotel" and somewhat later as the "Exchange Hotel." In the 1850's it served as a gathering place for local people as well as a stopover for travelers on the Santa Fe Trail. It had a large, attached corral which reached down to the Rio Chiquito (today's Water Street), and its main doorway was on the corner diagonally across San Francisco Street from the southeast corner of the plaza. The Exchange Hotel burned early in the 20th century. Afterward the present-day "La Fonda" was built on the site.

Twitchell called the hotel "the most notable landmark of the Santa Fe Trail." It was, he wrote, "the rendezvous of the scouts, pioneers, and plainsmen from the earliest days of the trail" and "its gaming tables were the attraction that lured the prospectors, soldiers, traders, trappers, and mountaineers for miles around ... . " The editor of the *Gazette* called the "Exchange Hotel" under proprietors B. Frank Green and Thomas Bowler in 1858 "one of the best kept houses we have ever seen—certainly superior to any hotel west of St. Louis." Green and Bowler managed the inn while John Watts kept his journal in 1859.

As early as 1848, the *Santa Fe Republican* contained a description of the Fonda, at the time operating as the U.S. Hotel, managed by Humphrey and Coulter. The writer described the place as "well supplied with beds, and large and ventilated rooms;" its "table has everything that the market will afford." Its "bar has the best of liquors of every kind, and also an ice house, the only one in the city. Attached to the house is a splendid pasture and a large correll for animals, and the only one in the vicinity of Santa Fe."

In December 1856, James Ross Larkin took his horse out of the Fonda's stable to board it with Dr. Kavanaugh because of the expense. "I took my horse from the Fonda stable yesterday, & keep him in company with Dr Kavanaugh we sharing the expense," Larkin wrote on December 12th. On January 10th, he noted: "Paid Dr Kavanagh [sic] $16.62 being for food &c. for my horse kept in his stable to date—for one month, being much cheaper than keeping him at the Fonda." This rate does seem high although it undoubtedly included grass hay, some grain, and minimal care.

The billiard tables which daily lured young Watts from his studies, and the gamblers who loitered about the Fonda must have tempted the straight citizens of Santa Fe. J.J. Webb warned his business partner Kingsbury of this temptation: "New Mexico is now the place of resort of the worst characters," Webb wrote on October 6, 1859. "My advice is to have nothing to do with them. Don't cultivate their acquaintance, even for purposes of trade .... Play no billiards, keep away from the fonda as much as possible and pursue such a reserved course as will be rather a barrier to the cultivating of your acquaintance."

Nonetheless, the Fonda has remained a plaza landmark. Trees were planted along one side of the plaza as early as February 1858, when the *Gazette* noted: "The example of our public spirited citizen, Mr. Preston Beck, Jr., in planting shade trees in front of his store, has been speedily followed by Mr. John Kingsbury and Levi Spiegelberg, who have extended them along two-thirds of the length of the east side of the plaza. Our friend and neighbor O.P. Hovey, has also planted four trees in front of his private residence. If they all grow, they will go far to beautify our city."

See Twitchell, *Leading Facts*, II, p. 138; *Gazette*, 27 Feb, and 17 Apr 58; Twitchell, *Old Santa Fe*, p. 237, n. 481; *Santa Fe Republican*, 17 June 48; *Reluctant Frontiersman: James Ross Larkin on the Santa Fe Trail, 1856-57*, ed. and ann. by Barton H. Barbour (Albuquerque, 1990), pp. 109, 115; and Elder and Weber, "Trading in Santa Fe," Ch. 12, p. 26, n. 40.

    8. Watts here spells this name "Pageans," elsewhere "Piggians," "Pigeans," and even "Piggeans." He was probably Alexander Valle, or "Pigeon" as everyone called him, the French-American proprietor of "Pigeon's Ranche," an inn on the Santa Fe Trail near the top of Glorieta Pass.

Valle got his nickname by "cutting a pigeon's wing," that is strutting like a pigeon at fandangos. He seems to have been an inveterate gambler, for Kingsbury remarked of him in a gossipy letter to Webb: "Pigeon's luck has come back to him again, in the last two or 3 weeks he has wone [sic] between $12,000.+ & $14,000. The most of it from Old Falez [sic] Garcia. The probability is he will not keep it long."

"Pigeon's Ranch" became famous as the site of the Battle of Glorieta, for up and down the boulder-choked canyon near the inn Confederate and Union forces fought the decisive battle between March 26 and 28, 1862. The Rebels finally broke off and retreated into Santa Fe after Chivington's troops, guided in the field by Lt. Col. Manuel Chaves, destroyed the supplies, wagons, horses, and mules which had been left under light guard in the Confederate rear near the mouth of Apache Canyon.

See Elder and Weber, "Trading in Santa Fe," Ch. 10, p. 42; Francis L. Fugate, and Roberta B. Fugate, *Roadside History of New Mexico* (Missoula, 1989), p. 137; Alvin M. Josephy, Jr., *The Civil War in the American West*

(New York, 1991), pp. 78-85; Ray C. Colton, *The Civil War in the Western Territories* (Norman, 1959), p. 50; Hubert Howe Bancroft, *History of Arizona and New Mexico, 1530-1888,* (San Francisco, 1889), pp. 694-97; Twitchell, *Leading Facts,* II, pp. 380-85; and Howard Roberts Lamar, *The Far Southwest, 1846-1912: A Territorial History (New Haven, 1966),* pp. 118-20. A dramatic first hand account is Ovando J. Hollister, *Colorado Volunteers in New Mexico, 1862* , ed. by Richard Harwell (Chicago, 1962), pp. 97-124.

9. Samuel Gorman, a Baptist clergyman, would be forty-four years old in 1860. Born in Ohio, he came to the territory in 1852 as a Pueblo missionary and established a school at Laguna. In 1859, he and his Massachusetts-born wife Catherine served Santa Fe's Protestant community from the Baptist Church, located across the street from Fort Marcy on the one side and Oliver P. Hovey's great house on the other. Fluent in Spanish, Gorman preached in English on Sunday mornings and in Spanish in the afternoon.

The Gormans had three children living in Santa Fe by 1860: James, 13, Milton, 5, and Eugena, 2, the youngest two born in New Mexico. Apparently they also had an older daughter who was in school in the East in 1859.

The Baptist Church, the first Protestant church built in Santa Fe, was dedicated on January 15, 1854. The Presbyterians purchased this property during the Civil War. It remains today the site of the Presbyterian Church.

See 1860 U.S. Census; Twitchell, *Leading Facts*, II, p. 350; *Gazette,* 17 June 54, 7 Aug, and 2 Oct 58; Lewis A. Myers, *A History of New Mexico Baptists*, Vol. 1 (n.p., 1965), pp. 42-43, 49-50; and Frank D. Reeve, *History of New Mexico*, Vol. II (New York, 1961), p. 85.

10. Formerly Louisa Mary Jones of Chatham County, North Carolina, Mrs. Rencher married Abraham in 1836. The Renchers had three daughters living with them in Santa Fe in 1860: Sarah, 15, Charlotte, 11, and a one-year-old baby, Susan. The two oldest had been born overseas—Sarah or "Sallie" in Portugal while her father was U.S. minister, and Charlotte in Switzerland.

The Renchers kept black servants, no doubt slaves. The oldest, Margaret, 20, born in Maryland, could neither read nor write. Samuel, 18, and Mary Ann, 7, were both born in North Carolina.

According to the 1860 U. S. Census, the Renchers owned real estate in Santa Fe valued at $15,000, and personal property—probably including the slaves—valued at another $15,000. They also gave splashy parties. The *Gazette* described one given for the legislature in January 1858, as a "handsome entertainment." The editor wrote that "the beauty and *elite* of Santa Fe were there," and that "the guests were all making the most of the pleasant occasion." The party was, he concluded, "an incident in the monotony of our city that will be an occasion of pleasant recollection by our citizens."

See McMullin and Walker, *Territorial Governors*, p. 239; 1860 U.S. Census; Twitchell, *Leading Facts*, II, p. 314; and *Gazette*, 23 Jan 58.

11. Possibly William A. Davidson, in 1860 a twenty-four-year-old supreme court justice. Born in Louisiana, he had arrived in New Mexico in October 1858, the first person to be appointed Register of Public Lands for this land district. Davidson was licensed to practice law in 1859.

See 1860 U.S. Census; *Gazette*, 30 Oct 58, and 30 July 59; and "Land Offices, Registers and Receivers," *New Mexico Blue Book*, p. 122, xeroxed pp. in file entitled "Indian Agents, #114," NMRA.

12. Born in Ireland in 1823, Alexander Melvorne Jackson came to Alabama with his parents in 1829. After clerking briefly in Memphis, he moved in 1840 to Marietta, Ohio, where he was educated by private tutors and where he began to study law. Moving to Holly Springs, Mississippi, in 1842, he passed the bar and began practicing law with Judge Nathaniel S. Price of Ripley. Jackson also helped Price edit the Ripley *Advertiser.*

During the Mexican War, he was Captain of Company E, 2nd Mississippi Volunteers. At the war's end he went back to Ripley to practice law. In 1849 he married Cordelia C. Kavanaugh.

Shortly afterwards, Jackson entered politics. In 1852 he was appointed special district attorney in Oxford, Mississippi, was an elector for the district Democratic Convention, and then a member of the Democratic State Central Committee. In 1857, he nearly won his party's nomination to the U.S. House of Representatives when he was deadlocked at the convention with two other men through fifty-nine ballots.

In September 1857, President Buchanan appointed Jackson Secretary of New Mexico Territory, a position he held for nearly four years. According to John M. Kingsbury, Jackson was "a very good man ... becoming popular and will get along well." His salary was $500 per quarter, that is $2,000 a year.

Resigning his office in order to serve the Confederacy, Jackson left Santa Fe for El Paso on June 11, 1861, accompanying the secessionist Col. William W. Loring, former commander of the Military Department of New Mexico, and his chief of staff, Lt. Col. George B. Crittenden, former commander at Fort Stanton.

As assistant adjutant-general to Sibley in the New Mexico campaign, Jackson carried a request for a truce to Col. Slough's Colorado Volunteers after the fierce fighting of March 28, 1862, at Glorieta. This request was merely a cover for Sibley to begin retreating after Chivington's men had destroyed his wagons and mules near the mouth of Apache Canyon. Due to poor health, Jackson left the Rebel army and was appointed Chief Justice of Arizona by President Davis, a position he never assumed because the Confederates lost New Mexico.

After the War, Jackson moved to Austin to practice law. In 1876, he was appointed court reporter of the Texas Court of Appeals, a position he held until his death in 1889.

While serving as secretary of New Mexico, Jackson tutored young J. Howe Watts—and perhaps others—in the law. In 1858 and 1859 he also practiced law with John S. Watts. The two advertised in the *Gazette* as "Watts and Jackson, Attornies at Law."

By 1860 Jackson and his wife Cordelia Kavanaugh Jackson had four children with them in Santa Fe: Nat, 9; Alexander, Jr., 7; Mary, 4; and a one-year-old daughter, Florence. Nat and Alexander attended school in Santa Fe in 1860. The Jacksons kept a fifty-year-old black servant—probably a slave—who had been born in Missouri and who could neither read nor write.

See Josephy, Jr., *Civil War in the American West*, pp. 37, 84; "Biographical-Historical Sketch," Alexander Melvorne Jackson Papers, McCain Library and Archives, University of Southern Mississippi, Hattiesburg; Twitchell, *Leading Facts*, II, p. 372; 1860 U.S. Census; *Gazette*, 24 Apr 58, and 19 Nov 59; and Elder and Weber, eds., "Trading in Santa Fe," Ch. 9, p. 17, and Ch. 11, p. 33.

13. "Tom Valentia" may have been one Tomás Valencia, a fifty-two-year-old farmer, whose thirty-eight-year-old wife, Guadalupe, owned real property in Santa Fe valued at $2000 in 1860. Namecio, a laborer, Josepha, and Refugio, were probably their children. See 1860 U.S. Census.

14. "Col Menes" (spelled "Means" elsewhere in the journal) seems to have lived to pursue the ladies, although occasionally he played billiards. Called a *"flojo"* by Mrs. Campbell, he was probably Thomas Means, 44, the Irish born "computer" in the surveyor general's office in 1859 and 1860. He did not keep his job under Surveyor-General Wilbar in 1861. No "Col Menes" (or "Means") is listed in the Fort Marcy Post Rosters. See *Register of Officers and Agents ... of the United States* (1859), p. 84, and (1861), p. 77, National Archives; Elder and Weber, "Trading in Santa Fe," Ch. 12, p. 37, and Ch. 13, p. 4; and 1860 U.S. Census.

15. Dr. Finis E. Kavanaugh advertised regularly in the *Gazette* in 1857

and 1858 as a physician and surgeon. He also drank heavily, owned a race horse, formed a company with 0. P. Hovey and Nicolás Pino in 1858 for a trading expedition to Utah, attended Santa Fe's social events, and served in the territorial house of representatives, for which the pay was low. He received $30.00 from Secretary Jackson "for mileage and attendance at the session of the Legislative Assembly of the Territory" in Santa Fe on December 5, 1859.

In the winter of 1859 Dr. Kavanaugh and Dr. Beck performed major surgery on victims of severe frostbite. They "amputated the leg of Mr. 0.C. Perkins below the knee, and have yet to amputate the other one lower down. They also cut off the foot of ... Juan Sandoval." Both patients were put under chloroform and both, wrote the editor of the *Gazette,* "are now doing well." In May and June 1859, the Army employed Dr. Kavanaugh, a "citizen physician," as post surgeon in the absence of the Fort Marcy Army surgeon. The *Gazette* said that he had "a very f ine reputation in New Mexico as a surgeon and physician." F.E. Kavanaugh may have been related to Cordelia Kavanaugh Jackson, wife of the territorial secretary.

See "Tenth Legislative Assembly, December 5, 1859 - February 2, 1860, Miscellaneous Papers, Legislative Expenses," NMRA; *Gazette,* 12 Dec 57, 3 Apr, 30 Oct, and 13 Nov 58, and 8 Jan 59; Fort Marcy Post Rosters, NMRA; and "Biographical-Historical Sketch," Jackson Papers, University of Southern Mississippi, for a photograph of Kavanaugh.

Of the men involved in the pistol scrape at Dr. Kavanaugh's office on March 10, 1859, "Drue" may have been William Drew, a surveyor who assisted A.P. Wilbar, the deputy surveyor, in February 1858. See *Gazette,* 27 Feb 58. He may have been William Drew, early publisher and part owner of the *Gazette*. See *Gazette,* 6 Aug 53. Most likely the latter is the same as the "Mr. Drew" whom an 1859 issue of the *Gazette* said would "deliver the anniversary address" to the "Santa Fe Literary Club," then in its third year of existence. See *Gazette,* 29 Jan 59. Drew was president of the Santa Fe Literary Club, organized in 1856 to debate important issues. See *Barbour, ed., Reluctant Frontiersman*, pp. 176-77, n. 109.

According to John M. Kingsbury writing in September 1859, one William Drew drowned in the Rio Grande near Santo Domingo while trying to cross the river in high water. See Elder and Weber, "Trading in Santa Fe," Ch. 12, pp. 6, 18.

"Rogers" was possibly T.M. Rogers, twenty-six years old in 1860, a Georgia born machinist. T.M. Rogers would be convicted of murder in 1860. See 1860 U.S. Census.

"Leo" Smith may have been Leonidas Smith, in 1856 the secretary of the Santa Fe Literary Club. See Barbour, ed., *Reluctant Frontiersman*, p. 177, n. 109.

16. Francis Bauer, besides tutoring music students, directed the Third Infantry Regimental band in Santa Fe in 1858-59. The band gave Tuesday and Friday evening concerts at the court house during November and December. The musicians played "the choicest pieces of Il Trovatore and La Traviata and all other kind[s] of good music." The local editor wrote that "the leader of the band, Mr. Francis Bauer, is a very talented young musician and shows great taste in arranging the pieces. The whole band indeed, deserve the highest credit for their zeal, great attention and perfect execution." Large crowds reportedly attended. See *Gazette*, 18 Dec 58.

17. Often mentioned in the journal, "Mr Crump" may have been J.R. Crump, the civil engineer and astronomer with Edward F. Beale's government party that improved a road from Fort Smith to Hatch's Ranch via the Canadian River in October to December 1858. Beale's road party wintered at Hatch's in January and February 1859, and broke camp for Albuquerque, February 26. Apparently Beale had gone on to Albuquerque and Santa Fe where he paused to write letters. He also went to Taos to visit Kit Carson before returning to Hatch's. This schedule may have put Beale, and perhaps also Crump, in Santa Fe while John Watts was writing the journal. "Mr. Crump is married," Watts wrote, "his wife is in Philadelphia." See Gerald Thompson, *Edward F. Beale and the American West* (Albuquerque, 1983), pp. 112-14; and Watts Journal, May 15, 1859.

18. Nicolás Pino was apparently one of several New Mexicans involved in a conspiracy to overthrow U.S. forces under Col. Sterling Price in Santa Fe in December 1846. After the conspirators were punished, however, the Pinos became loyal citizens. Nicolás Pino was one of Cerán St. Vrain's volunteers who defeated the Taos insurgents. He was a colonel of New Mexico Volunteers during the Civil War, a member of the legislative council in 1873 and 1878, and president of the council in 1869. He died in 1896.

"All of the Pinos were of noble mold," Twitchell wrote. "They were of a brave and chivalrous class ... . Don Nicolás was a man of large means. He was charitable and kind, as was he gallant and brave." See Twitchell, *Old Santa Fe*, pp. 276, 280-81; and Stella M. Drumm, ed., *Down the Santa Fe Trail and Into Mexico: the Diary of Susan Shelby Magoffin, 1846-1847*, repr. (Lincoln, 1982), pp. 183-84, n. 77.

19. Frances Watts ("Fannie")—Watts' sister—married A.L. Bancroft, whom she had met while she and her mother were visiting Greenport, Long

Island. Fannie raised her family in San Francisco, where her husband was the business associate of his famous brother, Hubert Howe Bancroft. See David Remley, *Bell Ranch: Cattle Ranching in the Southwest, 1824-1947* (Albuquerque, 1993), pp. 39, 313, n. 15.

20. David V. Whiting belonged to a frontier type—a jack of all trades who could perform any paying job. In the absence of territorial secretary Allen, Governor James S. Calhoun appointed Whiting (illegally) "Acting Secretary" from April 5 to June 20, 1851, at a salary of $425. Governor Calhoun's certification that Whiting's appointment had been "absolutely necessary" and that his work had been "satisfactorily performed" was required, however, along with correspondence between the U. S. Secretary of the Treasury and the Speaker of the House of Representatives before Whiting could receive his pay.

He also served as "Translator of the Territory" from March 8 to June 20, 1851, although not until February 5, 1857, did he receive his salary of $567.05 (at the rate of $2,000 per annum) for his approximately 3 1/2 months' service. He was "Acting Surveyor General" early in 1859. At one time he was also the postmaster.

In 1863, Whiting was Miguel Antonio Otero's partner in a Kansas City forwarding and commission agency called "Whiting and Otero." By 1879 he was living in Austin, Texas, where he was a "resident agent of the Texas State Agricultural Fair." In addition, he was a charter member of the Historical Society of New Mexico, organized in 1859.

By 1860, Whiting had several children, born all over the country— Harry, 12, in Pennsylvania; Joe, 10, in New Jersey; and Cora Luz, 6, in New Mexico. He seems to have been a thoughtful father. Sending an order East for Christmas presents in October 1858, the merchant John M. Kingsbury wrote James J. Webb: "Mr. Whiting requests that you will purchase for him and forward by express ... about $20.+ in toys and little tricks suitable for his children. He wants them to get here before Christmas. For the little girl send a large Wax doll with eyes to open and shut. Select what you please for the boys."

See Elder and Weber, "Trading in Santa Fe," Ch. 9, pp. 37-38; Twitchell, *Old Santa Fe*, p. 415, n. 755; Horn, *Troubled Years*, p. 26; 1860 U.S. Census; *Gazette*, 8 Jan 59, and 30 May 63; "Seventh Legislative Assembly, December 1, 1856 - January 29, 1857, Miscellaneous papers, Legislative Expenses," NMRA; "D.V. Whiting, Esq., Letter from the Secretary of the Treasury," 6 Mar 52, 32d Congress, 1st session, HR Ex Doc. 81; and *Weekly New Mexican,* 1 Mar 79.

21. John Watts' mother, Elizabeth Anne Howe, was the daughter of Joshua 0. Howe, Sr. (1784-1868), who had come from Maryland via Kentucky. A prominent Bloomington merchant, he was appointed to the board of trustees of Indiana Seminary in 1821 and later served as a trustee of Indiana College and of Indiana University. His photograph reveals that he was a big jawed, Lincolnesque figure. Born May 11, 1817, Elizabeth Anne Howe married John S. Watts in May 1837.

Her sister, Louisa Jane Howe, married Dr. James D. Maxwell, for many years a trustee of Indiana University. Their son, Allison Maxwell (Elizabeth Anne's nephew and the cousin of John Watts), would later become Dean of the Indiana University School of Medicine. Young John Watts, his brother Joshua Howe Watts, and their father John S. Watts were all Indiana University graduates, as is Hallack Watts Hoag, John's grandson.

See Theophilus A. Wylie, *Indiana University, Its History from 1820, When Founded, to 1890* (Indianapolis, 1890), p. 175; Burton D. Myers, *Trustees and Officers of Indiana University, 1820 to 1950* (Indiana University, 1951), p. 24; Remley, *Bell Ranch*, p. 43; obit., "Joshua 0. Howe, Sr.," n.p., n.d., Indiana University Archives; and typescript giving names and dates of family of Joshua Owen Howe, Indiana University Archives, Bloomington, Indiana.

22. "Miller" may have been David J. Miller, in 1860 a twenty-nine-year-old clerk in the surveyor general's office. Born in Alabama, Miller was also briefly co-editor of the *Santa Fe Gazette* in 1857. From 1850 to 1854 he had lived in Austin, Texas, where he was a translator in the General Land Office. He left Austin to take the job of chief clerk and translator in the surveyor general's office in Santa Fe. David J. Miller was treasurer of the Santa Fe Literary Club in 1856.

See 1860 U.S. Census; copies of *Gazette* for August and September, 1857; Elder and Weber, "Trading in Santa Fe," Ch. 12, p. 37; *Santa Fe New Mexican,* 7 Nov 80; and Barbour, ed., *Reluctant Frontiersman,* p. 177, n. 109.

"Miller" may also have been one William A. Miller, who in 1853 had been in charge of "the publishing department" of the *Gazette.* See *Gazette,* 6 Aug 53.

23. James E. Sabine was a jeweler, clockmaker, and daguerreotypist who also sold guns, magazines, and stationery. Active in Democratic politics, Sabine came and went from Santa Fe. In the fall of 1858 his shop was located on the east side of the plaza. The Gazette called him "one of the

cleverest fellows above the ground" and "an old citizen among us." See *Gazette,* 20 Oct 55, and 20 Nov 58; and Richard Rudisill, compiler, *Photographers of the New Mexico Territory, 1854-1912,* (Santa Fe, 1973), pp. 51, 22.

24. "Cotton" may have been M.L. Cotton, a thirty-two-year-old Mississippi-born trader; or Thomas L. Cotton, a twenty-year-old Mississippi-born clerk. Both men owned real property in Santa Fe valued at $10,000 in 1860.

Although there were many Quintanas in Santa Fe, this may have been Nicolás Quintana, whom Governor Rencher appointed a justice of the peace for the 4th Precinct of Santa Fe County on Nov 21, 1857.

Barry Simpson may have been W.T.B. Simpson, a twenty-three-year-old Kentucky-born clerk who owned real property valued at $3000 in Santa Fe in 1860. See 1860 U.S. Census; and "Executive Record Book 1," p. 184, NMRA.

25. His name spelled "Adire," "Adyre," and "Adair" in the journal, this man may have been one Abner E. Adair, "foreman" of the "printing office" of the *Gazette,* in 1858. See *Gazette,* 2 Oct 58.

26. Percy Eyre (also spelled "Eyers" in the journal) was a twenty-nine-year-old Pennsylvania-born clerk. See 1860 U.S. Census.

27. Although his is the name of an important family in New Mexico, George Waldo has not been identified. Dr. David Waldo, who was born in Clarksburg, Virginia, in 1802, went to Lexington, Kentucky, where he earned a medical degree from Transylvania College. After practicing medicine briefly in Missouri, Dr. Waldo formed a partnership with David Jackson for trading on the Santa Fe Trail. Twitchell wrote that by 1831 Dr. Waldo was active as a merchant in Chihuahua and Taos and that when war began with Mexico he "had already amassed a large fortune in business."

In 1846, Dr. Waldo became captain of Company A, First Missouri Mounted Volunteers, mustered into service at Fort Leavenworth on June 6. He and his men rode in Doniphan's regiment throughout the Santa Fe and Chihuahua campaigns and were mustered out at New Orleans, June 22, 1847. Fluent in Spanish, Dr. Waldo gave invaluable service, largely as a translator of official documents and of the so-called "Kearney Code." After the war, he returned to trading.

Dr. Waldo received the contract for "the first vehicular transportation of United States mail across the Great Plains under a Congressionally authorized, four-year contract." Under the name Waldo, Hall and Company the first mail coach left Independence on July 1, 1850, for Santa Fe. The company later operated on a semimonthly and then a weekly schedule by 1858 (when John Watts arrived in Santa Fe). Dr. Waldo died in 1878 in Independence, where he had lived almost fifty years.

Lawrence L. Waldo, the doctor's younger brother, was also a prominent trader on the Santa Fe and Chihuahua Trails. He and several other men were ambushed and killed near Mora on January 19, 1847, while eastbound with a caravan.

Henry L. Waldo of Las Vegas was the son of Lawrence L. Waldo. Howard R. Lamar calls him "the most respected lawyer in the territory." A partner of Thomas B. Catron and Stephen B. Elkins, a territorial chief justice and attorney general, a solicitor for the Santa Fe Railroad, and a member of the so-called "Santa Fe Ring," Henry L. Waldo was a Democrat, who, according to Lamar, "was as open, trustworthy, and frank as anyone in the territory" and "respected by friend and foe alike."

See Ralph Emerson Twitchell, *The History of the Military Occupation of the Territory of New Mexico from 1846 to 1851 ...*, repr. (Chicago, 1963), pp. 323-35; Twitchell, *Leading Facts*, II, pp. 118, 133, 244, 245, 419, 421, 484-85, n. 395; Drumm, ed., *Susan Shelby Maqoffin*, pp. 64-65, n. 25; Lamar, *Far Southwest*, pp. 63, 146, 160, 174, 175; and Morris F. Taylor, *First Mail West: Stagecoach Lines on the Santa Fe Trail* (Albuquerque, 1971), pp.1, 13, and 16.

28. Born in Virginia, George H. Estes was one of the grantees of the "Scolly Grant" along the Mora River in 1843 with John Scolly, William T. Smith, James M. Giddings, and others. By 1860 he was a forty-one-year-old merchant, who owned real property valued at $250 and personal property valued at $5000 in Santa Fe. In early 1860 he sold out his mercantile stock at an estimated value of $3500 or $4000 to Vicente Garcia.

John M. Kingsbury wrote on Christmas Eve, 1859, that Estes, Dr. Kavanaugh and others were drinking heavily. "Kavanaugh is drinking very hard, if he does not hold up he will go off as poor Hugh [N. Smith] did," wrote Kingsbury. "Geo Estes takes all that he can chaimber, there are lots more in the same fix. When shall I get out of this hole of disipation."

See 1860 U.S. Census; Elder and Weber, "Trading in Santa Fe," Ch. 12, p. 39, and Ch. 13, p. 17; and James Josiah Webb, *Adventures in the Santa Fe Trade, 1844-1847* (Glendale, 1931), p. 74, n. 104.

29. One Chastine was stabbed and killed by a man named Houston in a fight. "I do not remember any one being killed except Chastine he was stabbed

by Houston, & Houston is still in jail waiting trial. We have had any number of fights but nothing fatal," Kingsbury newsily wrote his partner Webb on November 6, 1859. See Elder and Weber, "Trading in Santa Fe," Ch. 12, pp. 17-18.

30. Lincoln would appoint Dr. Henry Connelly Governor to replace Rencher. Inaugurated September 4, 1861, he was already a well-known citizen of the territory.

Born in Fairfax County, Virginia, Dr. Connelly received a medical degree from Transylvania College in 1828. After practicing briefly in Liberty, Missouri, he went to Chihuahua as a trader. There he owned his own store by 1830. He married a Catholic woman in 1838.

After trying to pioneer a new trade route directly across Texas to Missouri in 1839, Connelly formed a partnership with trader Edward J. Glasgow in 1842 or 1843. By then, according to Glasgow, he was "moderately well off and in good standing and credit as a merchant of ability, integrity, and fair dealing, besides enjoying the personal friendship of many of the influential Mexicans and all of his own countrymen." While visiting Chihuahua in April, 1847, Josiah Gregg spent an evening shut away from a noisy street crowd in Dr. Connelly's store. "I retreated with my old friend Dr. Connelly to his store," Gregg wrote, "where we shut ourselves up snugly in his backroom, remote from the scene of confusion, and thus secured a quiet evening." Connelly also visited Susan Shelby Magoffin and her husband, the trader Samuel Magoffin, in Santa Fe during August and September 1846. What Susan wrote of Connelly's friend, Kentuckian Lucius F. Thruston, she might well have said of Connelly himself. Thruston, she wrote, had "become so well iniciated [sic] in the manners of living and ways of Mexico, he will not be in much of a hurry to visit his native land."

A friend of Manuel Armijo, Connelly was in Santa Fe in 1846 while Kearney's army advanced westward. According to Calvin Horn, Dr. Connelly at that time acted as "the principal intermediary between his friend Armijo and General Kearney." Later, however, when Dr. Connelly rode to El Paso to ascertain the conditions under which trade might be resumed, he was arrested, taken to Chihuahua and jailed.

After his release, he returned to New Mexico in 1848. His first wife having died, he married Dolores Perea Chaves, widow of Don Mariano Chaves. For many years Connelly and Dolores maintained a showplace of a home at Los Pinos near Peralta where they entertained well-known guests from far and wide.

Shortly after New Mexico became a territory in 1851, Dr. Connelly was elected to the territorial council and served from 1853 to 1859. He also kept up his mercantile trade, operating business houses in several of New Mexico's villages. "He established," wrote Stella M. Drumm, "the largest mercantile business in New Mexico, having houses at Peralta, Albuquerque, Santa Fe, and Las Vegas."

As governor, Connelly termed the Union war effort "the holy cause" in his first legislative message in 1861. He then demanded and achieved the repeal of New Mexico's slave act of 1859. He also influenced many powerful citizens not to become allies of Sibley's Confederate invaders in 1862. He was visiting Fort Craig in February 1862 when the Texans defeated the Union soldiers at the Battle of Valverde. As the Texans rode into Santa Fe in March, Connelly moved the territorial capital to Las Vegas.

While remaining generally popular with both Spanish-speaking and English-speaking citizens, Governor Connelly was not a friend to Indian people. He joined General Carleton in crafting the disastrous civilize-or-die policy which placed so many natives on the Fort Sumner reservation. There they died of disease and starved by droves. Those who survived learned to hate.

Governor Connelly also had other enemies. Legislator Theodore S. Greiner in a letter to Secretary of State William H. Seward called him "the amiable incumbent" who "has been a passive tool of the powerful and unscrupulous enemy of all Mr. Lincoln's friends in General James H. Carleton." Nor did the merchants Kingsbury and Webb speak well of Connelly. In private correspondence, Webb wrote Kingsbury from Kansas City in 1858, "You had better be a little careful of Connelly & Co. Connelly is [a] hard man. I am told there are several thousand dollars indebtedness about here two years old. He owes a good deal in St. Louis and I presume in the East also." Kingsbury replied: "Have kept clear of him, have refused to sell him except for cash, offered him good bargains for cash but could not trade."

Twitchell remarked of Connelly, however: "Socially he was a man of great refinement and intelligence. His services to the territory deserve a monument." Often ill throughout his later years, Connelly died in Santa Fe on August 12, 1866, less than a month after his term as governor had ended. The requiem mass was celebrated by Bishop Lamy, and Dr. Connelly was buried in Rosario Cemetery.

See Maurice Garland Fulton, ed., *Diary and Letters of Josiah Gregg: Excursions in Mexico and California, 1847-1850* (Norman, 1944), pp. 100-101; Drumm, ed., *Susan Shelby Magoffin*, pp. 104, 126-27, and 105, n. 37; Twitchell, *Leading Facts*, II, pp. 391-92, n. 316; Horn, *Troubled Years*, pp. 93-111; McMullin and Walker, *Biographical Directory*, pp.

240-41; Elder and Weber, "Trading in Santa Fe," Ch. 9, p. 33; and Keleher, *Turmoil*, pp. 122-23, n. 38.

31. Bringing his wife with him, Lt. William Craig arrived in July 1858, as aide-de-camp to General Garland. He was post commander at Fort Marcy in October and December 1858, and for some months in 1859.

Appointed to West Point from Indiana in 1849, Craig graduated in 1853, 52nd in his class. He served in the 3rd and 8th Infantry and was promoted to captain in May 1861. Captain Craig was later the depot quartermaster at Fort Union. He resigned from service in April, 1864, and died in May 1886.

See Fort Marcy Post Returns, NMRA; Francis B. Heitman, *Historical Register and Dictionary of the United States Army*, Vol. 1 (Washington, 1903), p. 334; Leo E. Oliva, *Fort Union and the Frontier Army in the Southwest* (Santa Fe, 1993), pp. 298-99; Chris Emmett, *Fort Union and the Winning of the Southwest* (Norman, 1965), p. 287; and *Gazette,* 24 July 58.

32. "'Mac's' daguerrotype establishment" was probably a studio of one "Professor MacEwen," a photographer in New Mexico in 1858 and 1859. The *Gazette* called Mac Ewen "the distinguished Daguerrean Artist." See *Gazette,* 2 Oct 58; and Rudisill, *Photographers of the New Mexico Territory*, p. 41.

33. "Dunn" may have been J.W. Dunn, an Ohio-born clerk in the surveyor-general's office in 1860. An 1858 issue of the *Gazette* noted that James L. Collins, the Indian Agent, had recently "purchased the premises immediately north of and adjoining his residence from Mr. J.W Dunn." Collins intended to use the Dunn building as the Indian Office since the previous office "in the old Palace building" was "neither sufficient or convenient." J.W. Dunn had also advertised his services as a teacher of English and Spanish in the *Gazette* as early as November 1856.

See 1860 U.S. Census; *Gazette,* 15 May 58; and Barbour, ed., *Reluctant Frontiersman*, pp. 178-79, n. 120.

34. Since the boys got the ladder at Hovey's house located across the street from the Baptist Church, the building where they played ball was undoubtedly that church.

"Ball ally" may be a transposition of "ally ball," or it may be the name the boys gave the street from which they threw or batted balls against the church. This church, now the First Presbyterian Church, is bounded by Grant Avenue on the east and Griffin Street on the west.

The game was probably a variant of one in which a ball is thrown or hit against a wall and caught or hit again by one of the players. Some such games are "wall spud," "wall stunt-catch:" "wall scramble ball," "one wall handball," "one wall squash," "wall tennis," and "ledge ball." Had the object been to throw the ball over the church to a team on the other side, the game would have been a form of "Anthony over" (also "handy over," "andy I over," "ante over," etc.). See Darwin A. Hindman, *Handbook of Active Games* (New York, 1951), pp. 128, 158, 245, 286-87, and 294-95; and Paul G. Brewster, *American Nonsinging Games* (Norman, 1953), pp. 84, and 89.

35. "Knock and catch" was probably a game similar to "one old cat" (or "two old cat," "three old cat," etc.) in which a pitcher serves the ball to the hitter. It may also have been a form of "fungo," in which the batter throws the ball into the air for himself, then hits it toward the fielders. "Bull pen," is an old game in which a baseman throws the ball at a player among those grouped on a playing field, or inside the "pen." See Hindman, *Handbook*, pp. 314-16, and 323-24; and Brewster, *Games,* pp. 82-83.

36. Dick Simpson has not been identified; perhaps he was a brother of Barry Simpson.

37. Mary E. Miner was a friend in Bloomington, Indiana. See "Letters Written," Watts Journal, p. 407.

38. Tom Smith was a gambler who, according to Kingsbury writing on September 24, 1859, had been tried and acquitted in El Paso for the murder of the mail contractor George Giddings. James Ross Larkin mentioned in December 1856, that he found his room at the Fonda "too noisy from neighboring gambling room, & proximity to Mr Tom Smith & Lady" and so had moved "to a room opening on the carrelle—a much more pleasant one." Larkin added: "Gambling tables are doing a grand business now at the Hotel —faro, Monte, etc. A Lieut in the army won $460.00 tonight." This may not have been the Tom Smith Watts mentions. See Elder and Weber, "Trading in Santa Fe," Ch. 12, pp. 5-6; and Barbour, ed., *Reluctant Frontiersman,* p. 108.

39. "Miss Knellie" was probably Nelly Shoemaker, a daughter of Captain William R. Shoemaker, who had been in charge of the military department's ordnance depot since 1848. He was transferred to Fort Union as ordnance officer in 1851 when the fort was established. Remaining there

throughout most of his military career and most of the life of Fort Union itself, Captain Shoemaker retired in 1882 and died at his home at Fort Union in 1886. Marian Russell wrote that he "was esteemed and respected by both the civilian and military population" and that "Shoemaker Canyon" on the Mora River was named for him.

Nelly Shoemaker was later engaged to Dr. J.J. Beck. Beck was killed in a fight with Henry O'Neil in 1860 before he and Miss Shoemaker could be married.

See Russell, *Land of Enchantment,* p. 83; Elder and Weber, "Trading in Santa Fe," Ch. 13, pp. 26-27, 31; and Oliva, *Fort Union,* pp. 59, 600-602.

40. "Mr. Wilkins" may have been Lt. John Darragh Wilkins, stationed in Santa Fe at least as early as 1856. Lt. Wilkins and his wife were sociable people who often attended parties and entertained visitors.

Lt. Wilkins was named, along with Felipe Delgado, Dr. Kavanaugh, C.P. Clever, Caspar Ortiz y Alarid, Clemente Ortiz, O.P. Hovey, Manuel Spiegelberg, David J. Miller, and R. Frank Green, to the "Committee of Finance" for a celebration at the Exchange Hotel during Missouri Congressman John S. Phelps' visit in 1859.

A native of Pennsylvania and an infantryman all his life, Wilkins graduated from West Point forty-sixth in his class. He had served as 2nd Lt. in the 3rd Infantry from 1846 to 1851 and as 1st Lt. since November 1851. He retired as a colonel in 1886 and died in 1900. He was breveted "for gallant and meritorious service" in the Mexican War (the battles of Contreras and Churubusco) and the Civil War (the battles of Malvern Hill, Fredericksburg, and Chancellorsville).

James Ross Larkin noted social visits to the Wilkins home on more than one occasion, and on November 21, 1856, he wrote: "Attended a party at Lieut. Wilkins, a very delightful affair. Col Bonneville, Maj Thornton, Capt Easton, Lieuts Clitz, O'Bannon & Howland, & Maj Nichols were present; as also Gov Merriweather[,] Squire Collins &c. Quite a handsome supper was spread." On December 3, 1856, Larkin accompanied Mrs. Wilkins to "a very pleasant party given by Mrs Dr Sloan USA" and, on the same day, "a fine Concert given by the 3d Infty Band."

On still another occasion, after attending a meeting "of the Debating Society of Santa Fe," Larkin went to "a danse [sic] at Mrs. Wilkins."

See *Gazette,* 21 May 59; Heitman, *Historical Registry,* p. 1036; Elder and Weber, "Trading in Santa Fe," Ch. 13, p. 55; and Barbour, ed., *Reluctant Frontiersman,* pp. 104, 105, 107, 108, and 109.

41. "Lola" was probably Dolores Newman, or "Numen" as Watts spells her name. In 1860, Dolores was a seventeen-year-old woman who lived— along with José, 14; and Jesus, 10—with one Allagracia [sic] Newman, a forty-three-year-old woman, probably their mother. Also living with the Newmans was a fourteen-year-old servant, Petra, from Paguate.

Born in New Mexico and listed as a "seamstress," Allagracia had real estate in Santa Fe valued at $1000 in 1860. Lola was clearly an attractive young woman and the Newman house a pleasant place to visit, for the boys and young men regularly went there to enjoy the female company. See 1860 U.S. Census.

42. Louie Felsenthorf was a Prussian-born twenty-eight-year-old clerk in Santa Fe in 1860. It is also possible that Watts is thinking of Louis Felsenthal, another Santa Fe resident of the day. See 1860 U.S. Census.

43. Louie "Staub" (probably "Staab") was no doubt a member of a well-known family of Jewish merchants in Santa Fe. Following the lead of Elsberg and Amberg, the Spiegelbergs, and the Seligmans, who had arrived in Santa Fe in the 1840s and 1850s, Zoldac and Abraham Staab of Westphalia opened a general store in Santa Fe in 1858.

Begun as the retail business "Zoldac Staab and Brother," the firm moved toward wholesaling until in the sixties they were, Twitchell writes, "the largest wholesale trading and merchandising establishment in the entire Southwest .... The firm filled many immense contracts for supplies to the government .... These contracts covered all sorts of native products, hay, grain, chile, beans, flour, and buffalo meat, giving employment to many of the native citizens of New Mexico, who gained their livelihood as sub-contractors for this firm."

See Twitchell, *Old Santa Fe*, p. 479; William J. Parish, *The Charles Ilfeld Company: a Study of the Rise and Decline of Mercantile Capitalism in New Mexico* (Cambridge, Mass., 1961), pp. 7, 8, 358,.n. 28; and appropriate pages in Henry J. Tobias, *A History of the Jews in New Mexico* (Albuquerque, 1990).

44. Mrs. Bowler would have been the wife of Thomas Bowler, a familiar resident of Santa Fe. Tom was proprietor—with R. Frank Green—of the Exchange Hotel as well as a mail contractor. Born in Virginia, thirty-five years old in 1860, he listed real estate in Santa Fe valued at $17,000 and personal property valued at $30,000.

About the time young John Watts arrived in Santa Fe, Bowler contracted with the U. S. Post Office Department to carry the mail from Neosho, Missouri, to Albuquerque over route 10615 starting October 15, 1858. After windy speeches over a celebratory dinner, the mail coaches rattled out of Neosho, in the southwest corner of Missouri, on the morning of October 16. Frank Green, Bowler's old friend and business associate, was in charge.

Today, the party's troubles would seem insurmountable. Their guide John Britton was, according to historian Morris F. Taylor, confused about the route (historian W. Turrentine Jackson says that Jesse Chisholm was the guide "all the way"). Eventually the coaches joined Edward F. Beale's government survey party, who were assigned to improve a wagon road from Fort Smith to California via Albuquerque along the Canadian River. Green's coaches and a cluster of immigrant wagons needed Beale's party, which was supposed to have a military escort, to offer protection across the no man's land of the Comanche and the Kiowa. By the time they reached New Mexico, winter weather had become a deep freeze.

When Beale's party went into winter quarters at Hatch's Ranch in December and January, the mail coaches pushed ahead alone. Reaching Anton Chico, an old outpost on the eastern New Mexico frontier, by January 1, 1859, they took the left-hand fork of the road toward Albuquerque. From Albuquerque the party of four gold-lettered passenger coaches with baggage wagons rattled on into Santa Fe.

The citizens of Neosho believed this departure "an epoch in the history of Neosho." The editor of the Neosho *Herald* wrote the editor of the *Gazette* that "although the amount of matter sent is small, it is accompanied by the warmest wishes of hundreds of our citzens for the success of this great enterprise." And "The Press of Neosho" addressed New Mexicans: we "trust that it is only the forerunner of a more speedy line from here to the rich plains of New Mexico."

Following one or two more attempts to cross the plains along this route, the post office discontinued the contract. Joseph Holt, the new Postmaster General, wished to retrench. The dangers of the route and the small volume of mail carried were factors. "Apparently that was the end of service on the Neosho-Albuquerque mail route," Taylor wrote. "The way was difficult and the patronage was slight."

Tom Bowler and Frank Green were involved in various other enterprises. They bought and sold draft animals and equipment, purchasing James Ross Larkin's mules, harness, and ambulance in January 1857. The mules brought Larkin $250, the harness $15, and the ambulance "$280.00 Cash." Larkin noted that he lost on the mules, but made about $80 over the cost of the carriage in St. Louis.

See *Gazette,* 17 Apr 58, and 8 Jan 59; 1860 U.S. Census; Taylor, *First Mail West,* pp. 56-57; appropriate pages in W. Turrentine Jackson, *Wagon Roads West: a Study of Federal Road Surveys and Construction in the Trans Mississippi West* (New Haven, 1965); Thompson, *Edward F. Beale,* pp. 111-13; and Barbour, ed., *Reluctant Frontiersman,* pp. 118,120.

45. "Cader" was probably Tom Cater, in 1860 a twenty-five-year-old farmer born in Alabama. See 1860 U S. Census.

46. "Boone" was probably Judge Boone's son. A Catholic from Phila-delphia, Judge William T. Boone was sworn in as associate justice of the territorial supreme court on September 28, 1858. Assigned to the Second Judicial District (Taos), he had arrived by stage on Sunday, September 26, bringing a son with him. Sickly, Judge Boone left New Mexico in December 1859, and soon died in the East. See *Gazette,* 2 Oct 58, and 20 Nov 58; and Aurora Hunt, *Kirby Benedict: Frontier Federal Judge* (Glendale, 1961), pp. 136, 143.

47. "Cat" had many variations—"catball," "one old cat," "two old cat," etc. In general, a pitcher served the ball to a batter, who, if he got a hit, ran to first base, then home again. The fielders tried to throw the runner out either by hitting him with the ball or by throwing it to the catcher at home. If the runner got home safe, he batted again. Otherwise, he gave up the posi-tion to the next fielder in line or to the man who put him out. See Hindman, *Handbook,* pp. 314-16, 337.

48. Samuel M. Yost, from Missouri, was the Navajo Indian agent sta-tioned at Fort Defiance in 1858 and 1859. Governor Rencher, critical of Yost's part in the so-called "Navajo War" of 1858, wrote Lewis Cass, Secretary of State, November 29, 1858, "The war, in my opinion, was unwisely precipitated upon the Indians, and might have been avoided by prudence and fairness on the part of the Indian agent." Yost edited the *Santa Fe Gazette* for several months in 1858 and in January 1859.

See Keleher, *Turmoil,* p. 100; editorial pages, *Gazette,* 18 Dec 58, and Jan 59; "Indian Service," *New Mexico Blue Book,* pp. 122-23, NMRA; and *Register of Officers and Agents ... of the United States* (1857), p. 93, and (1859), p. 94, National Archives.

49. "Mackinstery" was without doubt D. Mc Kinstrey, the conductor of the eastern mail coach. See *Gazette,* 7 Aug 58.

50. Seth P. Tuley, of New Albany, and Samuel W. Dodds, of Bloomington, were Indiana friends of John Watts. Tuley was enrolled in Indiana University in 1859 when Watts was a student there. See Wylie, *Indiana University,* p. 456.

51. "Cora" was probably Whiting's daughter, Cora Luz, who was six
years old in 1860. See 1860 U.S. Census.

52. Located on the plaza, "Kingsbury's" mercantile store belonged to
John M. Kingsbury and James Josiah Webb. Born in Connecticut, Webb
clerked in dry goods stores in New Jersey and New Haven, then opened a
clothing store in Savannah, Georgia, in 1841. Moving to St. Louis in 1843,
he and a partner opened a dry goods store near the levee at Third and Pine.
In July 1844, Webb stocked up on trade goods and left for Independence,
intending to enter the Santa Fe trade.

He soon became a prominent Santa Fe-Chihuahua merchant, forming
successful partnerships, first with George P. Doan ("Webb and Doan"), then
with William S. Messervy ("Messervy and Webb"), and finally with John
M. Kingsbury ("Webb and Kingsbury"). Webb and Kingsbury formed in
1854, after Messervy decided to retire.

Born in Boston in 1829, Kingsbury came to Santa Fe probably in 1851
while clerking for Messervy and Webb. When Messervy retired Webb
offered the young clerk a junior partnership. From February 1854, until
May 1861, Webb and Kingsbury continued in business. After August 1857,
Webb generally remained in the East for purchasing while Kingsbury
remained in Santa Fe for trading. By 1857 the partners were shipping goods
over the trail twice a year, spring and fall, and were doing business all over
New Mexico, western Texas, and northern Mexico. By 1859, they had
decided to close, but it took over a year to sell off their stock. Not until May
4, 1861, did Kingsbury close the doors and leave Santa Fe for good. Webb
retired to his farm home, Spring Glen, near New Haven, while Kingsbury,
having lost both his wife and young son, returned to Boston where he worked
as an accountant and treasurer, at least during the 1890's. See "Introduction," and "Afterward," Elder and Weber, "Trading in Santa Fe;" and Webb,
Adventures in the Santa Fe Trade, pp. 21-37.

53. "Beck and Johnson's" was a mercantile store in Santa Fe.

54. James L. Collins was born in Crab Orchard, Kentucky, February 1,
1800. He moved to Franklin, Missouri, where he was a justice of the peace,

then to Boonville. In 1826 or 1827 he made his first expedition to Santa Fe, then engaged actively in the Chihuahua trade. He left Chihuahua to settle in Santa Fe when the Mexican War began. During the war he was an interpreter and despatch bearer for Colonel Doniphan. He had a large home not far from the plaza.

"I well remember the squire and his appearance," wrote J.J. Webb of Collins as he looked in 1844 when Webb met him at San Miguel. "He was then advanced in years (but brisk and quick in all his motions as a young man of twenty-five), dressed in [a] well-worn broadcloth suit (but neat and clean without a particle of stain or dirt) and an old-fashioned plaid camlet cloak. I think his was the last one I ever saw of the genuine oldstyle."

Trader, politician, newspaperman, Collins had a long-time connection with the *Santa Fe Weekly Gazette* as owner or as editor, at least as early as 1853. W.W.H. Davis, retiring as editor, wrote, February 16, 1856: "With the present number of the *Santa-Fe Gazette,* we cease our editorial connection with the paper ... . The office and all the fixtures pass into the hands of James L. Collins ... to whom the establishment belongs." In the next issue, February 23, 1856, Collins, now editor, announced that the *Gazette* would be: "Independent in all things—Neutral in nothing." He also mentioned his "conducting the paper in 1853, when it was under our charge."

President Buchanan appointed Collins the first Superintendent of Indian Affairs when the office was separated from the governor's office in 1857. Although he was "an intelligent, well informed Indian expert," Howard R. Lamar wrote, he was also, as editor of the *Gazette,* a blunt critic of Colonel Fauntleroy, commander of the military department, with whom he carried on a "press war." Meantime, Apache and Navajo increased their hostilities during Collins' administration.

After Governor Rencher also criticized Colonel Fauntleroy's policies and Delegate Miguel Antonio Otero jumped on Rencher, it became obvious that the military and civilian leadership of New Mexico was confused and divided. In 1863 Collins was removed from the Indian office and replaced by Dr. Michael Steck.

A loyal Union man during the War, Collins later served as Receiver of the Land Office and as United States Depository and Disbursing Officer, that is as custodian of federal funds in Santa Fe. In 1869 he was robbed and murdered. During the search, much of the missing $100,000 in federal funds was discovered in a building near the depository. An investigation by the House Committee on the Judiciary later concluded that Collins, a man "of high character for integrity, patriotism, and courage," had been "wickedly and cruelly murdered while bravely attempting to defend the property of the United States against unknown thieves and robbers."

In remarking on his life, the *Gazette* said of Collins that he had "served his country's cause faithfully, patriotically, and bravely."

See Lamar, *Far Southwest*, pp. 98-99; Bancroft, *Arizona and New Mexico*, p. 662; Keleher, *Turmoil*, p. 484, n. 10; *Gazette*, 16 and 23 Feb 56, and 12 June 69; Emmett, *Fort Union*, pp. 347-48; Webb, *Adventures in the Santa Fe Trade*, p. 77, n. 108; and "Indian Service," *New Mexico Blue Book*, pp. 122, 124, NMRA.

55. Jesus Cena (Sena) may have been Jesus Sena y Baca, a member of the Santa Fe Literary Club in 1856. See *Gazette*, 20 Dec 56.

56. John Ward, in 1860, a thirty-eight-year-old clerk in the Indian Department, was born in Spain. His twenty-six-year-old wife, Maria, was from Mexico. They had four children, all born in New Mexico. Of these, Refugio, 11, and Trinidad, 8, attended school in Santa Fe in 1860. In 1861, Ward's title was "Pueblo Indian Agent."

An article in the *Daily New Mexican*, reprinted from the *Denver News*, noted that Ward had died of pneumonia in 1875 in Cañon City, Colorado, while returning to Denver from a conference with Chief Ouray at Saguache. He had served as the interpreter for J.B. Thompson, the Ute Agent, and had been "for ten years preceeding 1867" the Pueblo Indian Agent in New Mexico. The *News* said that Ward "conversed in the Ute tongue very fluently."

See 1860 U.S. Census; "Pueblo Indian Agents, Santa Fe," *New Mexico Blue Book*, p. 122; and *Daily New Mexican*, 12 Oct 75.

57. The identity of "Jones," who appears elsewhere in the journal, is guesswork. "McEvan" may have been "Profesor MacEwan," that is "Mac," the daguerreotypist.

58. "Uncle Tom" appears to have been a free black man.

59. Louie Dickens was probably Louis Dickens, born in Illinois. In 1860, Dickens was a twenty-seven-year-old surveyor. See 1860 U.S. Census.

J. H. Watts (*l.*) and John Watts, May 11, 1895.
Courtesy: California Historical Society, FN-29908.

Chapter 2

April 1859

Friday; 1.

On to day commences a new month and the day father said he would leave home with ma and the rest of the family for Santa Fe. I have no money to pay my billiards with so they will have to credit me or I play no billiards. I recited with the rest of the class to the Governor in his Office. I never have seen such a day like the one to day, before in my life—it blew terribly all day with such an amount of sand that some times you could not see six feet before you[.] I staid in the house most of the time and read in Bancroft—I have read ninety-four pages during the day and I do not know how many I will read to night. Miller was over here two or three times this afternoon and so was Col Menes here—Willie was also here and went up to see about our table which is getting along finely. We got Colorado to make little iron "fixings" for the pockets. I missed my supper to night by playing billiards—one game with Charley Conclin[1] which I beat and one with a fellow from Alburqueque who beat me—we played two half games. I have rather a large [...?] for the beginning of this month which I did yesterday or day before I have forgotten which. To night the wind has abated. Mr Crump was in here this morning also. I have almost got "<u>blues</u>" reconciled to me now since I go out in the Corral so much. They were playing pool at the Fonda when I came away.

Friday [sic]; 2.

I rose this morning about as usual and and found Uncle Tom had blacked my boots nicely as usual—I read in Bancroft this morning steady and fast—one hundred and forty-two pages and finished the fifth Volume this afternoon—in all one hundred and fifty during the day. The mail came in to day—I received four papers—three "Advocates" & the Republican but no letters. Howe received quite a number of magazines and papers one new one—which I have been reading to night called "Ballon's Dollar Monthly

Magazine." I have been reading miscellaneously all night, one piece entitled, "American Artist" was good, also another, Isaac Newton. Willie and I played ball with Sandy against the church and then went up to see our table which is getting along as slow as expected. I played two games and a half to night of billiards and lost one game—one and [a] half with a fellow from Alburquerque and one with a fellow they call Gardenhire[2]—I beat the first and got beat the second. Howe received some letters which he has been answering but I got none—we did not get any word from father in [the] form of a letter. Howe went to sleep to night sitting in his chair. Charley Thayer[3] came up in the this afternoon—I saw him and shook hands with him. Whiting was down to day to see us—we did not recite any to day.

Sunday; 3.   **8. O'clock and 10 minutes.**

And the first day of another week has passed. I rose about our usual hour washed myself and put on clean clothes and then went to breakfast—Howe bought some eggs for breakfast which we had fried. I wrote one letter to day which was to Bettie. I went to church this morning and heard a sermon by Mr Gorman and one thing good about it was it was short—there were few out—fewer out than common. We had an excellent dinner which I like the most of the boarders did justice to. Charly Thayer has got fat while he was gone. They played billiards all day to day as usual. This afternoon I read in the Western Christian Advocates mother sent me. I went over and heard Mr Gorman preach in Spanish this afternoon—I as a matter of course could not understand it but some sentences I could make out. There were exceedingly few there only four besides his wife and child. The exercises were very short—about twenty minutes the whole services were which is not too long. To night while setting by the fire Hovey knocked and said that Jesus had shot himself—I went out and found them all the boys and women looking for him and found against the door that leads to the corral being tight "no mas." I came back and went to reading. I have read one chapter in the Bible in Spanish. Howe had his likeness taken to day by Mc Ewin. "Buenos Noches."

Monday; 4.   **11. O'clock less 7 minutes.**

I finished reading the fifth volume of bancroft Saturday and got the sixth volume this morning. I went to breckfast about my usual time—Studied and recited the lesson in French to the Governor at 11. O'clock as usual. We had intended to go fishing but Whiting could not go—and it was rather cold any how. We had a game of ball this afternoon up by the Capitol—there was only five of us. I played eight games of billiards or nine to day and all with Colorado—we played eight—or seven to night—We played until after 11. O'clock—I put four or five on him and he two on me. I came home and found Howe writing who thought it was about 10.0'clock. Piggeans broke the bank to night—of one thousand dollars—there is a terrible hard wind blowing to night and cold at that. I have read eighty pages in Bancroft to day. The Band played in the plaza this afternoon—I see Bauer is up again which I am very glad to see. Howe bought some nuts to day at Kingsbury's.

Tuesday; 5.   **10 O'clock & 25 minutes.**
    To day like yesterday has been rather windy. I went to breakfast about my usual time with Howe. I did not go up at 11 O'clock to day for I expected that Willie would not be there but I found he was and recited also. This afternoon I played two games of billiards with a fellow by the name of Gardenhire—he beat the first—and I the second. I have read over a hundred pages in Bancroft to day. I made a calculation and I find I will have to read eighty-eight pages a day to get through this volume this week. I have also read some in Ballon's Dollar Monthly Magazine. Howe has gone to bed. Willie came by this afternoon and we went out and had a game of ball— there was four but we lost one fellow so we had but three. Our table is doing tolerable well—Piggeans lost a thousand dollars at Monte. To day the quarter master in the army was dealing. He lost very quick too. I looked over Ollendorff to night. The wind is blowing some to night.

Wednesday; 6.   **10. O'clock less 19 minutes.**
    I rose this morning about my usual hour and went to breakfast. Howe have our boots blacked every morning by Uncle Tom. I recited with the rest in French this morning to the Governor. This afternoon I played two games with Jim Houston[4] and he one I the other [sic], the same was the case with Colorado and I—he beat the first and I the second. The blacksmith where Colorado works caught fire to day and burned down—it was the only fire I have ever seen in Santa Fe—they soon pulled it down and kept it from burning the rest of the houses close or joined to it rather. These are terrible houses to put out when they get afire and burn for a long time. I did not learn whether it caught from carelessness or by accident but the house was full of fodder which helped it along—it was about 2 1/2 O'clock when I found it out—I was playing billiards. There was quite a number there. I played ball a little in the plaza this afternoon. I have read over a hundred pages in Bancroft to day and have only two hundred more when I will have finished the sixth and last volume that Hovey has. Hovey and Joe Whiting were with me playing this afternoon.

Thursday; 7.

Well to day shall be employed in describing our fishing expedition. We started about 9. O'clock and rode about eight or nine miles up the cañon directly East. We got up there about 11. O'clock. The party consisted of Howe, Battail,[5] Crump, Captain Chapman[6] and myself. We had a lunch given us by Mrs Rencher which we eat as soon as we got up there and then all scattered along the creek which contained nothing but trout. We only caught three—I, Howe and Battail caught one a piece. Howe fell down and caught his hook in his finger which spoiled all his fun. They had a bottle of brandy but I took none nor Howe. We came home pretty fast[.] I had the Governor's pony. Crump, Battail and I came before Howe and the Captain. I caught the head ache—went to bed early very tired and sleepy.

Friday; 8.

Well I rose this morning considerably relieved and free of my headache. I eat a hearty breakfast as common. I have recited with the class in French. I have read a hundred pages in Bancroft to day. We had a lesson in French to day. I staid at home most of the day. This afternoon Howe and I went over to see Mrs Jackson who has four children and we had quite a pleasant time. Howe played on the guitar and we both sung. I sung bass he air. We then came to supper at the Fonda. After supper I and a fellow from Alburqueque had a game of billiards and I cleaned him. While we were at Mrs Jacksons the mail came. I received two letters—one from ma and one from Sam Dodds, which I answered to night. Whiting was here a short time.

Saturday; 9.

I rose early this morning and after breakfast I went over to see Willie for we intended to go fishing. I tried to get Dunn's pony but it was not at home so Willie borrowed Lieut Craigs and I took his pony. We started about half past eight O'clock and got up there at about 10. O'clock and went up the creek and fished until we got tired and then came down the creek where our horses were and eat our dinner after which we took another fish and then got on our horses and came home and got here about 5 O'clock when Mrs Rencher gave us some lunch after which I went out into the plaza and rolled a cannon ball—six pounder I believe for exercise and then went in and played two games of billiards with a man from Alburqueque who works for Hovey—he beat me both. The General (Pelham)[7] and Mr Howard[8] came back to day— the General's wife has not arrived yet. Mr Howard and Whiting were both down here to night and Mr Howard gave us a sketch of his travels in Zuni. But I am tired, and sleepy from my trip to day and want to go to bed.

Sunday; 10.

To day is the first day of another week and I was awakened this morning by the firing of cannon which I have learned was in honor of the death of the Post-master General Brown[9] who died lately in Washington—they have continued to fire all day about a half an hour intervening between the shots. I also noticed when I went to breakfast that the flag was only half way up. I have written two letters to day one to ma and one to Bettie. I went to church this morning and so did Howe[.] there was a pretty fair congregation. I also went this afternoon and listened to the Spanish sermon only a little of which I could understand. I read a little in my Spanish testament with the aid of the English. Col Menes was over to night and sat and chatted a while with us. We had an excellent dinner to day as usual. I also looked over the French to night. It rained a little or drizzled rather this morning. General Cowart[10] is back arrived to day. Piper[11] is also here. As usual they have been playing billiards all day at the Fonda.

Monday; 11.

Today has been rather cold—the wind has been blowing pretty briskly all day. I finish the sixth volume of Bancroft this afternoon and the last that Don Hovey has. I studied the French this morning and recited at 11. O'clock with the rest of the class. Howe, Willie, Sallie and I all went out and threw and caught a covered ball of Sandays which we got off of the church with Willie's ball—he went up this morning—Howe, Vigil, Juan Tapia,[12] and myself holding the ladder for him. It has been blowing the sand about considerably. I took Bancroft back and got Prescott, "Conquest of Mexico" which were over at Mr Jacksons. I went up in town to night and played four games and won all—one with Hoveys clerk from Alburqueque and three with Colorado—we played until almost 11. O'clock. We got the top part of our desk from Hovey to day. I have not begun Prescott yet[.] I may though to night.

Tuesday; 12.

Well I have gone through another day and played one game of billiards with Mr Crump and he beat me. I got the Spanish lesson but did not recite until this afternoon at 4. O'clock—he was not at home this morning. I played two games of billiards with Eva Rencher[13] but I think I came[?] if I said backgammon—I do not know whats got into me to night. I read twenty pages in Prescott to day—there are a great many notes in the first volume I see. I and Willie took a game of ball alley against the church this afternoon and then went up to see how our table was getting along and we found they have done nothing to it. I wrote two letters to night to go in Frank Green's[14] mail—one to Mary Miner and one to Mc Neil. Howe wrote two or three also. Willie and I watched the soldiers exercising this afternoon. I think Prescott and I will get along very well as soon as I get [fairly?] started.

Wednesday; 13.

I went through my regular rotine to day as usual. I got and recited a lesson to the Governor in French as usual. The clerks [have?] to be a little more dutiful and industrious now the General[15] is here. I played a four handed game of billiards this afternoon. Willie and I against Louie Dickens and Gardenhire and we beat them although they run away ahead of us in the beginning. I have read eighty-four pages in Bancroft or Prescott I mean to day. The house was full of company this morning and I did not get half a chance to read or study any. Willie and I played ball up against the church this afternoon and as usual soon had it up on the church but we got Howe and he and I held the ladder and Willie went up and got the ball but we soon knocked it up again and then we could get no one to help us any more. I have got considerable of a billiard bill [al]ready and if I keep on I will have a big one at the end of the month, Howe and I spent a pleasant evening at the Governor's to night with Sallie, Eva[,] Willie and the rest of them. Mrs Rencher played the piano.

Thursday; 14.

Again another day has closed and when I look at what I have done to day I ought to be ashamed. I have not read a single line in Prescott the whole day but then I have a painful sty which might palliate the negligence a little. I and Willie recited our lessons to Mr Elison who got a little vexed at Willie's conduct—one thing was he took Mr Elison's shucks and smoked them—Mr Elison put us through[.] we recited longer than we have any time yet. I played one game of billiards with Mr Mandel[16] and one with or rather three with Davison and he beat me playing off—I gave him twenty. [My] billiards for to day are therefore $2.00 and my billiards bill for this month already is $6.50. 1 noticed the other day a Mexican plow which I presume is like the ancients—it is a rough looking tool made entirely of wood. I have a pain in my bowels to night from some cause.

Friday; 15.

Well I am again brought to the close of another day which like all others has passed away very quickly. I rose this morning about my usual hour and went up to breakfast after which I came down home and got the French

Grammar lesson for we did not have Oldendorff for we have to take it up the night before we recite to Willie and Sallie. We went up at 11. O'clock and the Governor heard us and just as we were getting through the first time going over Squire Collins Came in and then we quit. I gave Sam a picaune which I owed him for finding Sandy's ball. I have spent a great part of the afternoon with Mr Elison who has the rheumatism unfortunately. The Band played in the plaza this afternoon—Bauer is not completely well yet[.] I have not seen him for some time. Howe and I spent the evening with the Governor's family—we had a big game of blind fold—Miss Knellie Shoemaker was there. We had some fine fun[.] we played Jack Partner also. We came home at 10. O'clock. I beat Mr Mantel a game this afternoon. Willie and I had a game of foot ball this afternoon. I intend riding this afternoon with Willie, Sallie and Knellie but could get no horse. Mr Gorman was here this afternoon to get Howe and to go to Santo Domingo with him tomorrow[.] the Indians are going to have a treaty or consultation or some thing of the kind but after trying every body in town I could get none so I cannot go so far. I could not get a horse even to take a ride this afternoon with Miss Knellie. I have read three or four pages in Prescott to day. I have my sty yet which gets worse and worse. Harry Whiting has the mumps.

Saturday; 16.   **10. O'clock.**

And now I come to the close of another week and instead of getting through with the first volume of Prescott I am not half through. Willie and I got our Spanish out of the same book—he says, he has lost his. We with Vigil and Juan Clamaca[17] played against the church until time to go up and then we went up and promptly recited. The mail came in this afternoon in good time and I had the pleasure of hearing from three of my warmest friends—from Grandpa[,] McNeil[18] and from Bettie who has got safely home from her late visit to Evansville where she spent Chrismas—she is in a bad state of health as she has been all winter which I am very sorry to hear. She says she would like to take a trip to New Mexico but says she never expects to but if she lives and I live she may some day in the future, "Quien Sabe"! Howe got some papers and so did I get one, which was from home. I am writing with a steel pen which is some thing uncommon for me but the world is full of wonders. Howe told me that the Chinese trick of a man sitting in the air has been discovered at last and by a Yankie who is in Europe I believe who saw the man do it I believe. I beat Mr Mantel to night one game of billiards which is all I have played. I have read thirty-four pages in Prescott to day and to night. Howe has gone to bed to read. I have been up to see Mr Howard[19] since he moved into Jim Sabines shop who has left. He finished moving in day before yesterday. We did not get a single word from pa or Fannie.

Sunday; 17.   **8. O'clock & 20 mins.**

To day was Sunday and is yet until midnight. Our parson has gone down to Saint Domingo and if I could have obtained a horse I would have also went down—and therefore we had no church no services of any kind. I staid at home and wrote letters three in number—one to McNeil—one to grand pa and one to "H.B." I read some in my Bible to day in Psalms. I went up to see Howard this afternoon and he came down home with me and I gave him two quires of foolscap paper—he is writing quite a lengthy piece for the Tribune New York entitled, "A Trip from Santa Fe to Tiwia." I intended to take a walk this afternoon with Mr. Elison but he was not at home. Willie was here this afternoon about four O'clock but soon went away with Howe. Howe has been reading the, "Newcombs" by Thackery nearly all day. We had a nice dinner to day at the Fonda to which I did ample justice. To day has been a most magnificent day—the sun has been shining out very nice and warm. Mr Boone the son of Judge Boone was in to see us this morning with Col Menes. I witnessed quite a pretty sight to night[.] I waited and watched until the moon rose over the mountains which was quite a treat a most beautiful sight. I read the French lesson over to night, the book we take in the morning as we go to breakfast.

Monday; 18.   **10 O'clock and 7 mins.**

I am trying a new pen Howe got to day—all the clercks[20] in the office got one. Howe is very much pleased with it and I think myself it is a good one. I rose about or a little earlier than common and went to breakfast. I got my French but as Mr Craig[21] is going away there was to much bustle to hear us so the Governor said we could come tomorrow at 11. O'clock—Mr Elison is not in Santa Fe[.] he has gone to Peña Blanca to court. Mr and Mrs Craig left just after dinner this morning for the States—they [have] quite a nice outfit. Miss. Knellie Shoemaker is with them as far as Fort Union. The[y] had one avalanche[22] to ride in of four mules and one with bedding and eatables. The Lieut rode on his pony. I have done very little to day compared with what I might and ought to have done. I have read fifty-four pages in Prescott so far. This afternoon I took a walk with Col Menes and we went up to see Miss Campbell[23] at whose house I never was before. The Col went up to say a Spanish lesson which he did and I listened and amused myself. We had quite a nice time and I got a scolding because I had not been there before but I promised to come often. We went down to see Miller whom we found at home. We came to the Fonda from there and eat our supper. After supper I took two games of billiards with Mr Mantel and beat both of them[.] the first game I strung him and beat him thirty or forty points the second. I met and spoke to Lola Numen this afternoon.

Tuesday; 19.   **11. O'clock & 9 mins.**

I have just been six months in New Mexico or Santa Fe to day[.] I got here the 19th of Oct. I rose about my usual hour this morning and went to breakfast—we had eggs for breakfast to day. I and Willie were in the parlor at the hour to recite but the Governor is unwell and and he says he does not like to proceed without Howe who was not there to day. I bought a razor, Strop, mug and brush to day at Beck and Johnson's, all of which cost $3.10 which I think will pay for themselves in Six months. I shaved this afternoon with my new razor but I made a poor [cut?] as I had no warm water. I have played two games of billiards and a half to day—I lost the half from Willie Rencher and beat the [two] with Mr Mantel. Howe played two games to night with Quintana—the first game he got beat forty points and beat the second thirty-five. There came very near being a big bet to day on Bob beating Howe even game—General Pelham offered to bet $250 on Howe and the others backed out and after he left Bob came in with a $50 to bet and gassed considerable about it. Willie was over here this morning and carried off Sandy's ball which I have had for a week. He and I were over to see Bauer this afternoon. I have read ninty pages in Bancroft to day. Howe went to bed with the tooth ache. Our washstand is gone—it was the General's. To day has been a fine day. I am sorry for Howe.

Wednesday; 20.

Well to day has passed away and I find I have done little to what I ought to have done. The Governor being sick with the rheumatism we did not recite in French. Howe was [up] all night with the toothache and this morning it hurt him badly so he just went over to Doctor Kavanaugh's and had it pulled and it bled more he said than any tooth he ever had pulled—it has been bleeding all day and he was so weak that he could scarcely go to dinner. I have read twenty-six pages in Prescott to day. I have been idling around all the afternoon. Nothing new except Willie's breeches which he displayed to great advantage. The band played in the plaza this afternoon—I was in Howard's room at the time. Willie has all the balls in the crowd now he took the one we had. I went to see Bauer at 10. O'clock this morning but his wife was not well and he could not hear me neither Willie. After supper Louie Dickens being drunk got up a game of billiards and every body most bet high on the game. Louie bet $5. with Chastine and so did George Waldo that Howe could beat Bob. Howe had come home and I came down for him and he went up and they Set in and drew for the lay out and Howe beat him. Howe got the start of him and kept it and beat him <u>sixty points!</u> Mantel and Percy Eyers were betting—the former on Bob. George Waldo, Estis and Henry Mercure[24] I think also—of course they all won that bet on Howe but they were not satisfied with one game and took another. Howe beat for the lay off again. Bob got the bulge on Howe the second—he struck of[f] and kept ahead a good piece but Howe [caught?] him and beat him <u>seventy points</u>!! They quit then. Editor, Cotton, Cater and others—the braggers out of pocket! Estis won $40. I think. Waldo $50, Barry $25, Eyers $40, Louie Dickin $150. this I cannot tell whether it is exactly true or not. I will find out tomorrow perhaps. Barrey[25] did not get there in time to bet which he regred for he would have won sure—he always bets on Howe. I guess it will stop their bragging now. Bob said he would stake his existence that he would beat him but he slipped up badly. But I have said enough now.

Thursday; 21.

Another day has passed with its rotine of duties. Again we did not recite French to day by some bad arrangement. I have read thirty-four pages in Prescott to day and I ought to have read a hundred. Here I am with nothing in the world to do and access to Hoveys library—the best in town and what am I doing? Why nothing but playing billiards and—loafing about——tis a shame—I will see the time when I will surely regret this lost time. To day has been a pretty day with the exception of this afternoon when it was windy and the dust made it disagreeable to go out. Mr Bowler's dog Charger has taken quite a fancy to Howe and I and has been in our room nearly all day— he follows us around—Howe says he was a circus or show dog in the States. I find I am about twice to much in my statements of the winnings of last night. Tomorrow is the great day of the Mexicans—they have been preparing for the last week for it. I think quite a great deal of Prescott and I think I will be pleased with his Mexico. I and Willie went down to see Sam Elison in his new quarters—he has left the Palace—he was in the house of Repsentatives—perhaps we can get that room for our billiard table—which Christian[26] has not finished but gone to Moro and left it with [...?] so. I think I shall write at least a page in my journal after to day and not merely give the simple events of the day but observations and comments of all kinds—I have been practicing in penmanship for the last week but do not improve much as far as I can see. Howe and I went up to the Fonda to night—I listened to a tale of Charly Thayer's about two little half men and animals which he saw in the States that could lift seven hundred pounds without much trouble—tweny-six and eight feet [high?] and that the keeper said he would bet a $1000 that the largest could lift fifteen hundred pounds. There are men here also who say there is a pond about 15 miles from here with fish in it with four legs—this gets Howard down, he says he is going up there and get some of them. Mr Howard says he has a fish at home (New York I suppose) that is part fish and and part eel and that you can feel the place in its back where the two different kinds of animals meet. Col Street keeps a Mexican lady called "Blanca" who they say negras used to keep and who a good many fellows have caught the clap and pock from. Tom Cater and George Waldo played billiards all night last night and were still at it when I came from breakfast. They had drunk an even dozen bottles of porter. I have played six games of billiards to day and lost one game—five I played with Colorado and he beat me one and then we had a four handed game. Louie Staab and I against Willie and Vigil—we beat them twenty-two points I believe. I saw Bob up there to day and neither nor any other of his bragging backers except Chastine and he has had very little to say. Howe won a dollar and a quarter at pool this morning I think. This month will soon be out and then perhaps father will come with ma and then we will get our socks and shirts mended. I went over at 10. O'clock and recited my lesson to Bauer. I played ball with Willie and talked with Sallie this afternoon—I also took a little walk with Mr Elison. I am making quite a long day out of to day. I read a little in Howe's Spanish reader this afternoon. Willie was here this morning and afternoon both I think. I have lately got in a great way of flourishing and twice out of three times I make an ugly one. Sallie played and sung on the piano for me this afternoon. I expected the Mexicans were going to march in a procession this afternoon but they did not—will I not have a long letter to write to Bettie about it and to Grand Pa. All the Señoritas as Col Menes says are busy now and we cannot go to see them which is a hard old outfit. Howe has been to bed an hour I suppose—it is twenty-five minutes of 12. O'clock. I saw the old Indian doctor to day who said with his hands that he was forty-one years old and which Doctor Kavanaugh burlesqued very good to the amusement of by standers. I think I have written quite enough now so I'll read some in Prescott—until I get tired—and then go to bed.

Friday 22

Of all the strange and unheard of religious ceremonies—to day beats all. To day is one of the Mexican Catholic's great days and I am glad I had a chance to see everything. This morning I was on hand when the ceremonies came off and at which I am somewhat surprised. I and Willie went up through Mr. Johnson's and got on the last house closest to the church where we had quite a fine view of every thing that was going on. The ceremonies began about 11. O'clock—there was and immense crowd there of between two and four thousand. Howe with others records that there were twenty-five hundred and the least said fifteen hundred. The church was cramed full and the outside was full to you might say—at least the placita. There was one man with a comic looking cap on on a horse that looked as if it had paint on it and then another who was supposed by some to represent Pilate who as the former was dressed in a mask of fancy clothes. There were some fifteen or twenty with long sharp poles who went on each side of the procession and kept the watchers back. First three little boys marched out abrest the middle one carrying an image of the Savior, then came the effigy of Jesus who was to be crucified borne by four strong men, with the crown of thorns on his head and bearing the heavy cross—then three or four priests one of which with two or three little boys were singing—then came the effigy of the Virgin Mary who was born by four <u>virgins</u> (?) with lamps among whom was Lolita—there followed masked Mexicans—but before the front of the procession the thirty [guards?] or soldiers who guarded <u>Him</u> and cast lots for his garments would run before and as Windham said, "scratch in the dust"—make out as though they were dividing his garments. The priest made them a sermon on a raised pulpit—of about 10 minutes long and then they very deliberately marched back into the church. They had a small drum which the[y] gave three expressive taps continually with short intermissions also a whistle—such is a short sketch of the first procession.

This afternoon another procession came off similar almost to this morning's except that they brought Jesus out in a coffin ready for burial. They had an effigy of some one else dressed in white with a book in his hand —they only marched a short way to the corner where the North Street turns to the West, and then back again. Sallie, Jennie Green[,] Mrs Rose[27] and here mother in law I suppose was on a house across the street from us. Barry Simpson, Howard and Windham curse the whole proceeding as a humbug and a sacrilege—they are disgusted with it. I played ball with Willie this afternoon and to night I went up and say the same things by torch light which varied very little from the preceding. I have played a sight of billiards to day—three games with Colorado one of which I lost, one with Gardenhire, and a half—one with Vigil—gave me fifteen on which Don José bet and won a dollar—one with Mantel and a four handed game—Editor and I against Bob and Mantel and one with Col Menes giving him twenty-five and he came near stringing me. I beat all I played with but lost two games in all. I have played entirely too much and need not play any more for a long time.

I have read just thirty pages in Prescott to day—very little[.] I ought to have finished the book to day. After the excitement of the day I feel tired and sleepy. I bought five cents worth of apples to day which was <u>two</u>! I am tired and sleepy and fear that reason will not extend any observations but rest the body weary from the excitement of the day. I almost forgot to say that Charley Thayer had a fuss with a Mexican to day. And Leo Smith got drunk and got to brandishing his knife and the sheriff took him in charge.

Saturday; 23
Another week has closed over my head and I find to my regret that I have done not only little to day but Comparatively nothing to what I ought to have done. I have read forty-two pages in Prescott to day which finishes the first volume which I ought to have finished last week—I have just been two weeks on it. I found an effigy hung by the neck this morning before the church when I went up to breakfast—I went up and saw it and then to breakfast. I got and went over at 10. O'clock and recited my music to Bauer and then came home and studied a little and then went up to say my Spanish lesson to Mr Elison which we did—Willie made rather a poor out at the beginning but after a good long hour we got through and Mr Elison let us off and we went up to dinner. We had the conjugation of the irregular verbs of the first or rather the second conjugation. Willie and I took a play in the plaza this afternoon, we rolled Mr Mercure's six pound cannon ball and while we were thus playing the Southern mail came in bringing two men and three ladies—all relations of Col Collins'—Willie and I tried to catch a peep at them but could not make the trip—they drove down to Col Collins and dismounted from the coach. There was a horse race this afternoon between George Bell[28] and Cater I believe of $50. 1 do not know which won as I did not go and have not heard. The Eastern mail came in and I recieved two letters—one from ma and the other from Seth Tuley who has left college and is in N. Albany. There was a fellow who came in the Eastern mail to day who was down to see us—knows Howe by the name of Hager[.][29] there was also another passenger with him. Howe sends a ring to "M.E.H." with his first name engraved on the inside. Howe recieved an abundance of news papers which I have been reading. Whiting was here to night but no news of father for him.

Sunday; 24
Well another Sunday has passed and a new week begun and I hope to improve it better than the last. I stopped as I came from breakfast and had some calomel put on it for a sty that is coming on my left eye. I have been

taking salts all week by Whiting's advice but as I have been advised by Mrs Rencher and as the sty is going away I intend to cease. I am well pleased that it is going away for the last one was a very bad one and I am getting tired of them anyhow, I think I have had enough for one person. I washed this morning as usual my neck and put on clean clothes. I wrote two answers this morning one to Seth P. Tuley and one to Grand pa answer of ma's letter. I went to church to day and we had quite a fine sermon by Parson Gorman. General Pelham and the Governor and family were among the congregation—they wanted and expected to see the Misses Collin[s] whom they expected would certainly be out but as they say out here they "slipped up." I and Mr Howard took a walk far beyond Fort Marcy and when I came back I was very lazy. I read some in Psalms to day and also in the Repository ma sent me. Howe to night while reading in a catalogue in the back of "Mens Wives" stumbled over a book that ma read when young and has been trying to get for many years[.] it is called, "James Monjoy" or "I have been Thinking" and he immediately sat down and wrote a letter to the publishers for it. Howe is smoking a cigar to night[.] he only smokes a little and then quits. I have been thinking what fine subjects for compositions was, "Vera Cruz" and "Buena Vista" for I have been reading about the former in Prescott's Mexico for it was founded by Cortes. I will begin the second volume Monday—if I live. Howe I think wrote eight letters to day and yesterday for the mail. To day has not been very pretty[.] it has been rather windy and dusty— Uncle Tom still does all our work and it well. I think I will write as Howe says, "a [...?] and that is little enough. There are some two or three strangers boarding at the Fonda. There is a distinguished gambler from Washington City here—arrived a day or so since in the mail.

Monday; 25

I have done some thing to day anyhow or as the common expression here is, "that I know of." I went through the same mill to day as usual—eat my breakfast as usual—which is a thing not at all uncommon. Well we are at French again which I am glad of. After French Willie and I were playing ball and I knocked it through the window above the door—I immediately gave Willie a hit and cut a streak for the Fonda. I played two games of billiards to day with Don José—I beat the first he the second—he wanted to play off but I was to sharp for him. I began the second volume of Prescott to day and read thirty-two pages. Willie has not been over all day—"Mirable Dictu". I went over and said my lesson to Bauer this morning and now he has given me a song, "Mary of Argyle" which I do not know. To night there was a baile at Tom Valencia's—I and Howe went down with a crowd—

I danced once and lost all the money I had—my woman called for [dances?] and away went the fifty cents Howe loaned me—it was quite a good baile and full. I got a glimpse of one of the ladies that came with the last mail to Col. Collins. It has been quite a bad day[.] the wind blew much and full of dust at that. I went down to see Lolita Numen this afternoon about 3 O'clock—she was hard at work and so was her mother with another Mexican woman there, "yo no sea quien." As usual she wanted to know why Howe did not come to see her and I did not tell her for I want Howe to settle that himself. She told me that I had been over to see Miss Campbell once with Col Menes which is the truth—women hear things quick and know all about things that we would not think they knew any thing about. Howe cuts and flourishes about considerable with his new gold pen with which he is much taken up. I am going to make a hearty blow—fill at least a page to day if not more. I have read, a little miscellaneous literature to day from Harper's Magazine. I am going to finish the sec-volume this week, "si possible"— and learn all the Spanish I can which I am doing pretty fast.

Tuesday; 26   **10. O'clock & 20 minutes.**

Aqui estoy un otra vez! Well I must post up and go to bed as Howe has just done. I rose about my usual time and went to breakfast—after breakfast I came down home and got the Spanish Grammar lesson for Mr Elison which was the irregular verbs of the third conjugation as laid down in Coke's Grammar. I got my music lesson and went over and recited it and then went up and recited the Spanish which Willie and I both recited very well if I do say it myself. I saw one of those ladies at Mr Collins' this afternoon—Willie and I both—she had bought some thing at Johnson's—a man was a long with her—she is not tall but low and fleshy and very good looking. Willie and I had a game of ball this afternoon in the plaza but was ended by Dick Simpson knocking the ball, a solid cake of Indian ruber on the palace. I played two games of billiards to day—one I lost the other won—both were with Don José on the lower table. Col Menes and I went walking this afternoon and we went to see Miss Campbell who was not at home but who came before long. we found Lolita and her mother in with Mrs Campbell talking. I had quite a fine chat with Lola and the Col kept pretty silent—but learned one word which Mrs Campbell applied to him—"flojo"—and which he repeatedly mispronounced. We met Juan Tapia up there and he found out where the Col was going who had often refused to tell him—Col called the word, "flajo"—"floco"! We or at least I had fun. We stopped a short time to see General Garland's[30] woman whom I saw at the baile last night. There is a terrible wind to night. I read thirty-six pages in Prescott to day, and to night. I and Howe both smoked a cigar to night—and he has gone to bed to read. Willie was here this afternoon—he has seen Christian who has not got our table finished yet. Miller was in here to night and took a cigar. I am making poor progress in Prescott to what I ought to do[.] I idle and fiddle away entirely too much time—I must try and do better.

Wednesday; 27.   **25 min. of 5 O'clock.**

By way of variety I have taken my seat by the window to see and write down what is passing with whatever reflections I may wish to make. I[t] snowed this morning and the clouds are now gathered round the sumits of the famous Rockey Mountains which over look Santa Fe. Old Bauly is in the distance with his snowed crowned cap. I have just been reading in Prescott of the Spaniards ascending a volcanoe in Old Mexico—I have just come to where they have entered Mexico and seen the Great Montezuma. This is such a large book that I cannot get myself seated rightly in order to write well—for I write poorly anyhow. All the Clerks have left the Office and Howe among the rest. I have recited my french and music to day as usual at the proper hour. It is now snowing in the mountains but none here in Santa Fe. I[t] looks still except that I hear the "pajaritos" which have nest under the portal. Ah! there is some thing now—yonder goes a man galloping a mule with a half a dozen dogs after him which is quite a common thing—a person cannot ride around Santa Fe without a lot of dogs following him. There the bugle has just sounded[.] the soldiers I suppose must run. It is a fact that there is none of the soldiers here that are Americans but they are all Irishmen and Duchmen. I hear an anvil—perhaps Colorado's—I see a man here and there and there and here a woman. Fort Marcy is the first point that meets the eye on looking out the window which is on the first grade and lowest of the mountains—[mist?] rises high above and far behind the lofty Rockey Mountains. I see a raven flying over the Government corrall. They resort there in great numbers when it snows, and they cannot [find] anything to eat. I took a lesson in the Spanish Reader to day from Vigil[.] both this morning and evening he came in and helped me translate it in English. The old house which stood in front of Squire Collins' is torn down. And which I am glad to see. Howe I wish Sam Dodds was here to enjoy these preasures but Howe is here which is better. Willie has got Mr Christian at work on our table to day but how long he will work at it is a question. A greaser has [Just?] passed—a "lanaso" perhaps. I am not improving in Writing half as much as I [ought] considering the writing I do—I ought by this time to have been a fine writer but I improve it seems to me very slowly. Whiting I believe does not come down to the Office in the afternoon. It looks a little gloomy out and cloudy and is a good time for one to reflect. If father should get here at the time he expected he would be here in the next mail, on Saturday. I think that this is better than lounging round the Fonda playing billiards an expense to father and no good to myself. I will now try writing round hand a little and see how I progress with it[.] Seth Tuley writes the round hand all the time which looks very well I think. I wonder what Bettie is doing now—"Yo no sea"—I would like very well to be by her side talking—I think I could pass an hour very well—at least I should like to try it. I wonder what <u>Mary</u> is doing—I would like to be sitting in the roking Chair in the poarch with her and her mother. I wonder [what] ma and the girls are doing now—perhaps on their road to [New] Mexico—Santa Fe I hope so. I won[der] if Col Menes has gone to see some more of the "señoritas"—he is quite a man for them and wants to learn the Spanish—there goes to "mujeres," "yo no sea a donde." I hear the band playing perhaps in the plaza—I believe I will go up and see. It is now 10 minutes after 10 O'clock—Howe has gone to bed to read. I have read thirty-six pages in Prescott to day. I was up and played backgammon with Willie—four games—he rather beat me. Sallie played two or three songs on the piano for me before I came home. I found Howe at home—he had just come from the Fonda where he had been playing billiards—I have played none to day. I have written rather a long journal for to day. Sallie locked me up in her pa's office this afternoon. Willie and I knocked his solid cake across the plaza for exercise just after supper. I get sleepy very quickly some how—I ought to read until 12. O'clock every night for I sleep late enough in the morning—until 7. O'clock.

Thursday; 28

Well to day as Howe says has been the same old "seven and six." I got the lesson in music and went over and recited it to Mr Bauer and next in order I went up and recited my lesson with Willie to Mr Elison. This afternoon I spent mostly in the pages of Prescott—I read sixty-two pages to day. Howe went over to see the ladies at Squire Collins' and after an introduction has quite a fine chat with them—he gives quite a favorable opinion of them—they are social. I and Col Menes did not go to see any of the "jente" this afternoon—Col is studying the Spanish under Miss Campbell—I do not know whether he went up this afternoon or not. I beat Colorado two games of billiards to night. This distinguished gambler from Washington City is making money I think—he has a bank of "faro" which O'Bannon[31] was betting at to night. It was rather late when I and Colorado came away 11. O'clock I suppose. To day has been very pretty—I went down to see Mrs Bowler with Sallie and Eva Rencher this afternoon, late, about supper time.

I saw the Squire with two of the ladies and another gentleman the husband I suppose of one of them I suppose. We have only one candle—the month will soon be out but father and mother will not be here at its close. I will be glad when the mail comes for then I think and hope to get some letters. But it is time for sleep.

Friday; 29

I am again brought to the end of another day and the week is fast drawing to a close. I went over to recite my music but Bauer was not at home so I came back and will get the same lesson for tomorrow which is a pretty hard one. Cora Whiting was here this morning[,] came down with her father and came in my room and staid a long time—she has taken quite a fancy to Howe and I. I had a miserable lesson in French to day[.] I missed two thirds of the questions I was asked but recieved no reprimands but Willie got scared for missing one. I am getting I seem to myself more no account and worthless every day—now father told me I ought to get a Spanish lesson every day which I do and recite every other day but then in all the intermediate time I ought to employ in reading but to which here of late I cannot concentrate my mind only for a very short time and then I run off to playing—but it is very easy to say and see what I <u>ought</u> to do but I do not put my good resolutions in practice. Howe bought some candy this morning at the bakers[,] very nice clear red horehound and upon giving Mr Howard some he immediately went down and bought all that was in the jar for $1.12 1/2. I have read but twenty-four pages in the whole day of one of the most interesting of histories—Prescott, "Conquest of Mexico"—and with so much time! I have lounged about and played billiards to much. I played one with Don José this morning and he beat me about thirty. I and Howe went up to the Fonda to night and I played two games and Howe four of billiards. Mine was with George Waldo—first game he gave me twenty-five and the second fifteen. I beat both. Howe played with Lieut Jones[32] who beat two and lost two—so they came out even. There is a terrible strong wind blowing to night. Mr Crump I see has returned from Hatches Rancho—I do not know whether Battle got back or not—I shook hands with Crump to night. There is not much gambling going on to night—Clarck[33] I think got beat. I see Gardenhire has a bank of—$50 he told me was the amount. Howe has written and gone to bed to read. I added up my billiard bill and it is $10—tomorrow is the end of the month. I wish father was here with ma and pay or give me a little money and I could square things. The "square inch" question has not subsided entirely yet. Willie was here this morning and so was Hary and Doad Whiting. I and Vigil read some in our Spanish Reader this afternoon. Howe is busy in the Office making a map of [New?] Mexico.

Saturday; 30

I am now at the end of another month at the end of which father expected to be here with ma and the children but we do not find them but will be well pleased if they are here by the end of next month. I rose about my usual hour and went to breakfast. I went up and about half played my lesson to Bauer who talked very cross but gave me the same piece over again. We played the piece together he on the violin and I on the guitar—it was splendid. I played two games and twenty-five points—the two with Hasconne giving him fifteen points—I beat the first and he the second—I played the twenty-five points with Gardenhire. I and Willie recited to Mr Elison this morning for although it was blowing and raining a little still I went—Willie did better than common. I and Willie knocked our ball or his rather across the plaza which is fine exercise. I went in to see if Willie was at home to play again this evening but he had not found the ball which I knocked on top of Johnson's house. Sallie played on the piano a song for me, "Home Again" I believe is the name—she also made some cakes and gave me some. I and Howe went to a baile at Tom Valencia's—I and he danced but once which cost me two bits, and then we came home. It is ten minutes of 10. O'clock by my time. Howe is in bed reading. The mail came in this afternoon but I got nothing. Howe got some letters and papers. We got no word at all from Home by this mail. I have read thirty pages in Prescott—very poor—very poor[.] I do exceedingly little to what I might and ought to do.

End of April.

NOTES: April

1. "Charley Conclin" was Charles M. or "Carlos" Conklin, James Conklin's son.

James Conklin was an old timer in Santa Fe. Born in Canada about 1800, he moved to St. Louis, then to New Mexico about 1821. There he married Juana Ortiz, daughter of Don Pedro Ortiz. Conklin served Col. J. M. Washington as interpreter in the Navajo Campaign of 1849.

J.J. Webb described the area where Conklin lived. "There were but a very few houses north of the Palace on the street now called Palace Avenue," Webb wrote. "Don Augustin Duran, Don Felix Garcia, Don Antonio

Sena y Baca, and James Conklin and one or two others lived not far from where the Presbyterian church now stands and had quite grand houses for the time; and some of them [had] two or three acres cultivated in corn, beans, and red peppers, and a few apricot trees, the only fruit then raised in the town."

See Twitchell, *Leading Facts*, II, p. 102, n. 71; Twitchell, *Old Santa Fe*, p. 403; and Webb, *Adventures in the Santa Fe Trade*, p. 92, n. 127.

2. "Gardenhire," who appears elsewhere in the journal, has not been identified. A family of that name has long resided in Farmington, New Mexico.

3. "Charley" Thayer was Charles L. Thayer, a thirty-five-year-old baker born in Massachusetts. He owned real estate in Santa Fe valued at $5,000. See 1860 U.S. Census.

4. "Jim" Houston may have been the Houston who stabbed Chastine. One James Houston traveled from Santa Fe to Utah in the spring of 1858. See *Gazette*, 3 Apr 58.

5. "Battail" or "Battle" as Watts also spells the name, was J.T. Battaile, in 1860 a twenty-five-year-old Virginia-born surveyor who owned real estate in Santa Fe valued at $2,000. In the spring of 1858 Battaile had been appointed Examiner of Surveys. A surveyor-general's map of 1860 locates "Battail's Rancho" on the Rio Concho, three or four miles northeast of Hatch's Ranch. See 1860 U.S. Census; *Gazette*, 3 Apr 58; and "Sketch of Public Surveys in New Mexico, 1860," (Surveyor-General's Office, Santa Fe, N.M., 1 Sept 1860).

6. A Captain John Chapman led an expedition from Santa Fe against the Utes and Jicarillas in 1849. Reportedly, on May 30, his men killed twenty Apaches who had raided Abiquiu valley, killing ten. Chapman's losses were two killed. A Major William Chapman was the Fort Union commander throughout much of 1861.

See Bancroft, *Arizona and New Mexico*, p. 462; Oliva, *Fort Union*, p. 22; Emmett, *Fort Union*, p. 87; and Robert M. Utley, *Fort Union National Monument, New Mexico* (Washington, 1962), p. 64.

7. Former surveyor-general of Arkansas, William Pelham was appointed New Mexico's first surveyor-general by President Pierce. Arriving in Santa Fe in December 1854, Pelham held the office until he resigned,

angry at his superiors in August 1860. In five years he completed a mountain of work in spite of the fact that he was not a student of Spanish or Mexican law, did not speak or write Spanish, was not a lawyer, that his office was always understaffed, and that his superiors seldom paid any attention to his suggestions.

Responsible for surveying public lands as well as for reporting to Congress on the status of private land claims, Pelham discovered that Santa Fe's land records were a mouldy jumble of bundles and scraps. Adding to these difficulties, private claimants hesitated for various reasons to respond to Pelham's proclamation in January 1855, that they submit written details of their claims so that he could evaluate them.

In spite of the size of his task, Pelham succeeded by 1856, according to the report of the Commissioner of the General Land Office, in arranging alphabetically and classifying "1,014 grants and documents relating to land titles." Historian Victor Westphal notes that "almost all of the 9,019,024.64 acres of land in the forty-seven grants confirmed by Congress in New Mexico and Colorado ... were confirmed upon the recommendation of Pelham and his chief clerk, Alexander P. Wilbar." Thus, it is fair to conclude that Pelham, though serving under conditions that would cause an ordinary workman to revolt, performed an essential job admirably.

Born in Kentucky, Pelham was fifty-seven years old in 1860. That year he owned real estate in Santa Fe valued at $25,000 and personal property valued at $1,500. He may have allowed the strains of his professional duties to influence his private life, for, on an October Sunday morning in 1858, he scandalized Santa Fe by eloping with a local girl who was fresh from the convent.

Marking his letter *"Private,"* Kingsbury wrote Webb on October 17, 1858: "The Town has been full of gossip the last week on a/c of a novel case of Genl. Pelham. Something new for New Mex. No more nor less than an elopement. The Genl. last Sunday morning eloped with Miss Tapia (the girl that Henry O'Neil had some time in the Convent.) He took her in his buggy and started with all possible speed on the road to Vegas ... . It has turned out that they went to Valies (Pigeons) and spent the honey moon, have since returned, and he keeps the bird closely confined in his office.

"I understand the family will present the whole affair to the President and request his removal. Many whom he counted as his friends are opposed to his conduct in this affair and it will probably appear in many of the papers in the States. He has rather overshot the mark and I think it will go bad with him."

Nonetheless, life in Santa Fe quickly returned to hum drum.

By mid-December the *Gazette* reported merely that Pelham would soon leave for the States "on a several months' leave of absence." Describing him as "peculiarly well fitted for the place he holds," the *Gazette* added: "It must be exceedingly gratifying to the General to know that his course as Surveyor General of the Territory has received the fullest approbation of the people of New Mexico, and that all his official acts—as we understand is the fact—have been approved by the Government at Washington."

Pelham's life took another curious turn when he staked his future on the South as the War began. Jailed as a political prisoner, he was released and then appointed Confederate Governor of New Mexico after the Rebels took Santa Fe on March 10, 1862. Shortly afterward, however, Union men re-took Santa Fe, while Sibley's soldiers retreated down the Rio Grande. On the word of a captured Confederate, General Canby reported that "of the 3,800 men and 327 wagons" with the Rebels when they began the invasion, only "1,200 men and 13 wagons remained together" toward the end.

And what of William Pelham? Twitchell notes that he was captured by Canby's Union soldiers during Sibley's retreat. This was certainly hard use for a man who had formerly been an exceptionally able federal official.

See Victor Westphal, *Mercedes Reales: Hispanic Land Grants of the Upper Rio Grande Region* (Albuquerque, 1983), pp. 82, 85-93, 133, and 135-36; Twitchell, *Leading Facts*, II, pp. 323, 458-60, and 387, n. 313; 1860 U.S. Census; Elder and Weber, "Trading in Santa Fe," Ch. 9, pp. 2, 39-40; *Gazette*, 11 Dec 58; Lamar, *Far Southwest*, p. 117; Keleher, *Turmoil*, p. 207, n. 52; and Robert W. Frazer, *Forts and Supplies: the Role of the Army in the Economy of the Southwest, 1846-1861* (Albuquerque, 1983), p. 224, n. 69.

8. "Mr. Howard" may have been the jeweler, W. J. Howard. In 1859 the *Gazette* noted that he had "taken a room in the placita of the Exchange Hotel" for "repairing fine Watches of every description, also clocks, Music Boxes, Jewelry, and other mechanical contrivances." An earlier issue noted that he had worked for Tiffany and Company in New York "from whom he brings to New Mexico a recommendation and certificate quite complimentary to him as a gentleman and as a member of his profession." See *Gazette*, 30 Oct 58, and 5 Feb 59.

He may have been Clement W. Howard, whom Governor Rencher appointed notary public for Taos County, August 3, 1858. See "Executive Record Book I," p. 196, NMRA.

9. Postmaster General Aaron V. Brown of Tennessee, a pro-slavery

member of Buchanan's cabinet, exercised power in choosing overland mail routes and mail contractors after 1857. Morris F. Taylor suggests that Brown was influenced by his southern sympathies. "Brown had regarded [overland mail routes] as part of a system that gave preeminence to the South in Pacific mail connections," he wrote.

Brown died, March 8, 1859, and was replaced by Kentuckian Joseph Holt. In trying to make his department more efficient, Holt ended the Neosho to Albuquerque mail contract, July 1, 1859. Thus ended Tom Bowler and Frank Green's brief venture as U.S. mail contractors. John M. Kingsbury's pessimism about their flyer had proven itself well founded. See Taylor, *First Mail West,* pp. 47, 54, 57.

10. Robert J. Cowart arrived in Santa Fe, Monday, December 6, 1858, as a newly appointed Indian agent. See *Gazette,* 31 Dec 58.

11. "Piper" may have been Capt. Albert H. Pfeiffer of the Ist N. M. Cavalry. Marian Russell called Pfeiffer "one of the most noted Indian fighters of the Southwest." He must have been a fierce looking soldier, for Russell says that he limped from an old arrow wound in the hip. SeeRussell, *Land of Enchantment,* pp. 102, 105-07.

Pfeiffer was also a Ute and Apache Indian agent at Abiquiu from 1859 to 1868. Twitchell wrote that Pfeiffer and Lafayette Head were "the agents at Abiquiu and Tierra Amarilla ... in 1864-65." J.N. Macomb noted that "Mr. Albert H. Pfeiffer, sub-agent for the Utah Indians" had accompanied his 1859 expedition "to about forty-five miles west of the Pagosa or great hot spring." See "Indian Service," *New Mexico Blue Book*, p. 123, NMRA; Keleher, *Turmoil* pp. 307, 317; and 492, n. 50; Twitchell, *Leading Facts*, II, p. 447, n. 367; and J. N. Macomb, *Report of the Exploring Expedition from Santa Fe, New Mexico, to the Junction of the Grand and Green Rivers of the West in 1859* (Washington, 1876), p. 7.

12. Juan Tapia may have been Juan C. Tapia, clerk pro-tem and interpreter of the territorial assembly in 1856. One Juan Tapia, perhaps a different man, was a thirty-nine-year-old shoemaker born in New Mexico. See "Legislative Journal, 1-2 December, 1856, Seventh Assembly," NMRA; and 1860 U.S. Census.

13. Governor Rencher's three daughters were Sarah or "Sallie," Charlotte, and Susan. "Eva" may have been a visiting family member.

14. "Frank" Green was R. Frank Green, sometime overland mail driver and proprietor with Tom Bowler of the Exhange Hotel. By 1860 Green also apparently had an interest in a competing hotel, the El Dorado. Thirty-five years old in 1860, Alabama born Green had real estate in Santa Fe valued at $9,000. Green drove the "Albuquerque and Neosho Mail" from Neosho, via Anton Chico, to Albuquerque and Santa Fe in 1858-59. The *Gazette* described the colorful arrival of the new mail coaches in Santa Fe from Albuquerque: "As they passed our window down Main street they presented quite a handsome appearance. Besides the accompanying baggage wagons, there were four of decidedly the finest passenger coaches we have ever seen in the Territory, each bearing prominently on the side in gold letter the words 'T.F. Bowler, U.S. Mail.' "

Kingsbury and Webb often mentioned Green and Bowler. Kingsbury wrote Webb pessimistically on August 28, 1859: "Tom & Frank I think are manageing [sic] badly. We are safe with them, but it will be a scratch if they do not loose [sic] all they have made before they get through with their mail outfit."

See 1860 U.S. Census; *Gazette,* 8 Jan 59; Taylor, *First Mail West*, pp. 56-57; and Elder and Weber, "Trading in Santa Fe," Ch. 11, p. 32.

15. That is, Surveyor-General Pelham, who had gone to Washington on leave and on government business in December 1858. The "clerks" mentioned here were salaried clerks in Pelham's office.

16. Also spelled "Mantel," this may have been William Mantle, a twenty-five-year-old clerk born in England. See 1860 U.S. Census.

17. "Juan Clamaca" may have been Juan Climaco Tapia, clerk pro-tem and interpreter of the territorial house of representatives in 1856. See "Seventh Legislative Assembly, December 1, 1856-January 29, 1857, House of Representatives Journal," December 1, 1856, NMRA.

18. "McNeill" was probably Harrison McNeil of Bloomington, Indiana, with whom Watts corresponded. See "Letters Written," Watts Journal, p. 407.

19. Since Jim Sabine was a jeweler, this "Mr. Howard" is apparently the jeweler, W.J. Howard.

20. Watts probably means the clerks in the surveyor-general's office.

21. Probably Lt. Craig.

22. An Army "ambulance" was an enclosed vehicle often used to carry passengers.

23. "Miss Campbell" was probably Gertrudes Campbell, an eighteen-year-old woman born in New Mexico. Rosa Campbell, a fifty-three-year-old woman born in Mexico, lived at the same address and was likely Gertrudes' mother or grandmother. Rosa is probably the woman Watts elsewhere in the journal calls "Mrs. Campbell" (see entry for Monday, May 2, for instance). Rosa, who owned real estate in Santa Fe valued at $6,000, could neither read nor write. See 1860 U.S. Census.

24. Henry Mercure was a Santa Fe storekeeper. Kingsbury noted to Webb, September 3, 1859, that Henry Mercure and the trader Henry O'Neil had both closed out their stock, "so we have just at present two less stores. I believe now I will have a pretty fair fall and winter trade."
    Joe Mercure, also a storekeeper, was Henry's brother. Born in Canada, Joe, a forty-one-year-old merchant, had personal property valued at $20,000 in Santa Fe in 1860.
    On August 28, 1863, Joab Houghton wrote Kingsbury from Fort Union: "Jo. Mercure went raving crazy and was taken in three weeks ago to an Assylum [sic] at St. Louis, his brother Henry will wind up his business. It is feared that Jo. is incurable." Later, the *Gazette* reported that Joe had died at the Arkansas crossing and that his body had been brought back to Santa Fe for burial. See *Gazette,* 5 Sept, and 14 Nov 63; and Elder and Weber, "Trading in Santa Fe," Ch. 11, p. 35, and, "Afterword," p. 5.

25. "Barrey" or "Barry" was probably Barry Simpson or W.T.B. Simpson, the clerk.

26. "Mr. Christian" or simply "Christian," memorable for remaining eternally at work on Watts' billiards table, has not been otherwise identified. So far as is known, Christian is still at work on this table.

27. "Jennie" Green may have been Virginia Green, a sixteen-year-old woman born in Virginia. See 1860 U.S. Census.
    "Mrs Rose" has not been identified. Perhaps she was the wife of one L. J. Rose. Kingsbury wrote Webb, September 3, 1859: "1 have received from Doan King & Co. the Mortgage of L. J. Rose all safe & recorded ... . What

did you do with the Billiard Ball you took in for Mr. Rose? Did you make arraingements [sic] for his Grass Seed &c? Don't forget to notify me about these little things, it places me in an unpleasant situation."

A few days later Kingsbury wrote again: "I rec'd by this Mail Stage a box from St. Louis containing Castor Bottles and the Billiard Balls for Mr. Rose but no bill of them. The Bottles suit and he is very much pleased with the Balls."

In the summer of 1858 one J.L. Rose led a California-bound party from Albuquerque. Mojaves atttacked them at the Colorado River; eight were killed, thirteen badly wounded. The survivors straggled back to Albuquerque. See Elder and Weber, "Trading in Santa Fe," Ch.11, pp. 34-35; and Thompson, *Edward F. Beale*, pp. 114, 117.

There was also one Edward Rose, a twenty-year-old clerk born in Iowa. See 1860 U.S. Census.

28. Probably George Beall, a thirty-year-old clerk from the District of Columbia who owned real estate in Santa Fe valued at $800 in 1860. See 1860 U.S. Census.

29. Possibly J.W. Hagar, whom Governor Rencher appointed notary public for Socorro County, August 24, 1858. See "Executive Record Book 1," p. 197, NMRA.

30. Born in Virginia, Brvt. Brig. General John Garland of the 8th Infantry had joined the Army during the War of 1812 and served with distinction in the Mexican War. He took command of the Ninth Military Department on July 20, 1853, relieving Colonel Sumner. Reorganized as the "Military Department of New Mexico" on October 31, the department consisted of the "Territory of New Mexico, except the country West of the 110th degree West Longitude."

Although away on leave from October 1856, to May 1857, Garland retained command for slightly longer than five years—until September 1858. Thoughtful and cooperative, he stamped his years with a military stability previously unknown in New Mexico. With the possible exception of Fort Union, the condition of New Mexico's military posts improved overall. Several posts were relocated or rebuilt. Fort Bliss was established at El Paso, on property rented from James Magoffin.

Garland was responsible for increasing the shipment of Army stores and for improving Army rations. Under his command more officers and soldiers were stationed in New Mexico. Civilians were hired as common laborers, clerks, carpenters, blacksmiths, interpreters, and teamsters. Local goods were purchased whenever practicable, such items as hay, corn, tallow, charcoal, lime, beans, vinegar, and buckskins, which were used for sacks and covers. Roads were improved. This wide variety of improvements made Garland a popular commanding officer with military personel and civilians alike.

Worried about his health, Garland placed Colonel B.L.E. Bonneville in command of the department on September 15, 1858, while he went East on a "temporary' leave. He never recovered his health, and died June 5, 1861.

See Robert W. Frazer, "New Mexico Under General Garland," in *Forts and Supplies* pp. 87-115, 142, 215, n. 26, and 224, n. 75; and Oliva, *Fort Union*, pp. 99-105. For relations with the Navajo during Garland's years, see appropriate pages in Robert M. Utley, *Frontiersmen in Blue: the United States Army and the Indian, 1848-1865* (New York, 1967).

31. Probably Ist Lt. L.W. O'Bannon, of the 3rd Infantry, assigned to Hq. Company, Fort Marcy, on special orders, April 1, 1859. O'Bannon assumed command of the post on July 9, 1859.

From South Carolina, he had been commissioned 2nd Lt., 3rd Infantry in March 1848 and 1st Lt. in September 1855. He remained in Santa Fe as late as May 1860, when John M. Kingsbury mentioned him in a letter. He resigned his commission on March 31, 1861, to join the Confederacy as Lt. Col. of quartermasters.

James Ross Larkin became acquainted with O'Bannon in Santa Fe where he attended at least one party at his home. O'Bannon was a no-nonsense officer, for Larkin wrote on January 11, 1857: "Lt. O'Bannon having meat stolen out of the placita, put arsenic in a piece of mutton, & it was stolen last night. Unlucky thief who eats it." O'Bannon died in June 1882. See Heitman, *Historical Register*, p. 754; and Barbour, ed., *Reluctant Frontiersman*, pp. 104, 109, and 116.

It is unlikely that this was a deserter, one John O'Bannon, Company E, 8th infantry, who had disappeared from Fort Inge, Texas, in January 1859, and who was listed as "Deserted" on the Fort Marcy roster in March of that year. See Fort Marcy Post Rosters; and Elder and Weber, "Trading in Santa Fe," Ch.13, p. 55.

32. This may be the Lt. Jones whom Kingsbury mentioned in a letter to Webb, April 23, 1860: "Lt. Jones (The officer which I introduced to you one day in the Store, you may remember him you liked his appearance & was pleased with him). Lt. Jones rec.d all the corn in a lump, directly was

ordered to send 1,500 Fanegas to Albuquerque. After this was taken out of the store house, it made such a big hole that he was sure that he had receipted for more than the house contained in the first place. This led to a strict examination and it was discovered that 600,000 lbs. of corn or about $22,000 worth missing ... . Now where the swindling was remains to be proven ... and who are the guilty it is not yet known, but the whole crowd Las Vegas, Tecolote, Moro, & and in fact all who had anything to do at the Fort is suspissioned [sic]." Neither Emmett nor Oliva mentions this theft. Possibly the officer Watts named was Captain Llewellyn Jones, commanding Fort Union in 1857.

James Ross Larkin mentions both a "Lt. Jones" and a "Capt. Jones" whom he met at Fort Union in January 1857. On the same visit to Fort Union, he called on one "Miss Freddy Jones." One cannot help wishing there were fewer people named Jones.

See Oliva, *Fort Union*, pp. 143, 467, and 534; Elder and Weber, "Trading in Santa Fe," Ch. 13, pp. 47-48; and Barbour, ed., *Reluctant Frontiersman,* p. 114.

33. "Clarck" may have been Charles B. Clarke, whom Governor Rencher appointed notary public of Bernalillo County in August 1858. See "Executive Record Book I," p. 197, NMRA. He may also have been Elias T. Clark, an old man from Rio Arriba. See Elder and Weber, "Trading in Santa Fe," Ch. 13, p. 57.

Chapter 3

May 1859

Sunday; 1st.

Well I am now to begin both a new week and new month. Father nor ma neither are here as father expected. I rose this morning and washed my neck and ears and then dressed myself in the best I had. I wrote one letter this morning to Bettie and one this afternoon to Grand Pa which are all the letters I have recieved I mean written for I did not recieve any. I went to church this morning and heard Mr Gorman preach—Mrs Edgar and the Squire were out but both of the young ladies staid at home I do not know from what cause. I also went this afternoon and heard the Spanish which I cannot understand but Howe I suppose did who went also—there was scarcely any one there but Howe and I—the man that rings the bell was there with his wife—and then the Parson's son who was there who composed the congregation. The sermon as usual was short. Willie, Sallie and Eva were out this morn-ing. This afternoon Howe and I called around to see the Miss Edgars[1] —but we staid but about five minutes and then went over to see Mrs Jackson's. The oldest one of the girls was the only one I ever saw—I did catch a glimpse of the youngest who is a little the tallest. I met Lola and her mother with another woman[.] I spoke to both and so did Howe. I think the lady I saw was a very fine lady. We had quite a nice little talk with Mrs Jackson who tried to plague me about Sallie Rencher with whom I find a great many think I am sadly in love but they all "slip up" according to the vulgar phrase for she said something which will at least keep me off if no one else which was that, "there was no one in Santa Fe good enough for her!" I ought to have Fannie here to turn up her nose at Sallie. We had an excellent dinner today to which I as usual did ample justice. I bought two shirts at B. and J.'s yester-day which cost $4.00 two dollars apiece. Howe has gone to bed to reading again. We smoked a little to night. Miller has just left[.] he came in and staid a little while and read an anecdote which he and Howe took a good laugh at Saturday.

Monday; 2nd

The room is very warm to night and I feel tired and sleepy. I practiced and had a pretty fair lesson both in music and in French. I recited a good deal better in French to day than I did the last time. I read forty-nine pages this afternoon in Prescott and then about 4. O'clock Col Menes came in to get me to take a little walk with him and we went to see Rosario but she was not home. We next went up to see Miss Campbell whom we found at home with two visitors Chastine and Bois or Bayes[2] or I do not know how to spell his name—they went away shortly after we came—Mrs Campbell said they had been there about two hours. I stopped at the Governor's to night as I came from supper to get the key of Howe who was giving Willie a lesson. Sallie wanted to know why I had on my Sunday coat—wher I had been or where I was going—to which I told her no where. I recieved two letters by the Southern mail—one from Bettie and one from Sam Dodds. Battail came by and he and Howe went over to see the Miss Edgars—they went over about 7 1/2. O'clock and have not returned yet and it is now half past 9. O'clock. I hope they will have a fine time and enjoy themselves which I expect they will do. This has been a pretty fine day—the mountains are covered with snow. I have no key to the door[.] Howe I expect has laid it down as he had it last. I have not played any games of billiards to day. Vigil was in here and I read a little in the Spanish Reader to him. Both of the letters I received were very good and I am glad to get them seeing I did not get any thing in the Eastern Mail. Col and I were around to see Miss Lola Numen but she was not at home—they said she was at church. I heard some one shooting out in the street to night[.] I do not know what about—I heard some man swearing and shoot twice—I have my pistol on my table all the time Howe is gone am thinking it is time they were coming home if they intend to, to night. I passed through Col Streets room to day with Col Menes.

Tuesday; 3rd

Well today is the first time in a long time that I have neglected to post on the events of a day the next—that is I have now to write for yesterday and to day for I neglected it last night for I went to bed very late. I played one game of billiards to night with George Waldo—he gave me fifteen and I think I strung him. Willie and I recited to Mr Elison to day at 11. O'clock as usual, but before we had entirely finished Mr Jackson and Judge Benedict[3] came in and Mr Elison dismissed us. To night one of the longest games of billiards came off I ever beheld—it was a four handed game between Davison and Howe against General Pelham and Col. Clemens.[4] They played from just after supper—about 6. O'clock until 25 minutes of two by the clock. In this time played sixteen games and drank (that is the crowd—I among them—Howe and I took lemonade) twenty-two liquors. Five of the games and five of the liquors were put on to Howe and Davison, while seventeen liquors and eleven games were put on to Col Clemens and the General. I was tired and sleepy when I got home and immediately went to bed.

Wednesday; 4th

I have been troubled most of the day which I am subject to in the States but which I I thought I would be free from out here—and that is headache. I rose this morning about my usual hour and put on a clean shirt and went to breakfast—I am going to break both of my new shirts in this week. I played over my music lesson and then went over to Mr Bauer's and recited or played it rather. I also with the class recited in French at our regular hour 11. O'clock. This afternoon I took a nap to see if I could not sleep off my headache but I awoke with it fully as bad as when I laid down. I have read just fifty pages in Prescott and I think I will finish the second volume tomorrow—I have some seventy-six or seven pages to read. I took all of my piece to day and have it all for tomorrow. Willie is learning a piece to play with Bauer and so am I and Bauer says he would rather play with me now than Willie. I am going to try and beat him—play mine better than he does his. I and Mr Elison and Willie all took a little walk this afternoon late just after supper but it was a short one only being up by the Capitol. Howe is making a map of this Territory which he has been at for a two weeks I suppose already—the clerck have been pretty diligent since the General came out. I learned the step of the polka to night in a minute from Howe and I can now dance all the dances. We had quite a good supper to night and among other delicacies was butter some thing we have not had for—well all winter. Mr Elison was very "tight" last night—very witty and wanting to bet—some one though took him home pretty quick. Howe and Battail have gone around again to night to see the "jente" at Squire Collins'. Willie is quite taken with them and especially the youngest but I think he is <u>too little</u> to make such high pretentions and if he can get in there I would not want to [sure?] I saw the ladies and mother out this afternoon. I have never seen the youngest yet and I think she has not seen me—she told Sallie Rencher she caught a glympse of me and I did the same with her. We have no news from father yet—Howe says he has gone to Europe.

Thursday; 5th

There is one thing which I had intended and ought to commented upon but which like many other things slipped my memory and that is to mention an Italian organ grinder who has been perambulating the streets for the last three or four days. I think some time in the first part of this week or the last of last week he came in Juan Tapia's room and played for a picayune and I see him again to day. It is one of the worst organs I ever heard—it is large and heavy and all out of tune which makes the music miserable—they are bad enough when in good order but when out of order are almost impossible to put up with. I got my music this morning and played it with Bauer—the first page is called the Serenade. I and Bauer play it together as he and Willie do another piece. There are more dogs in Santa Fe than any place I ever was in before—there are two dead over on the side of the road as we go up in Town. I have read some more than usual in Prescott to day. I finished the second volume this afternoon—I had just fifty-four pages to read—and I went up to Hovey's and got the third volume and to night read a chapter in it—twenty-six pages. Howe was up again last night playing billiards with Miller until 1. O'clock—they came out even—played six games. I saw Davison "tight" this evening as was Mr Elison last night. Howe fast the weeks fly away—it is now getting along to the end of the week and the month is fast rolling away—I hope to see ma and pa at its close in Santa Fe. Mr. Mr. Battail: Willie and I all went out and shot at a mark—we shot three shots a piece I think—Willie beat us all—but by a "scratch" for he who made the worse I think. Howe wrote in his journal and then went to bed—at 8. O'clock. Howe gave me some nice clear hoarhound candy which I suppose he got at the Bakers and which I have been dispatching while he is in bed. Mr Crump came in and I gave him some of it which like Mr Howard he immediately asked where I got. Willie and I did not recite to day—Mr Elison was not in his room at the hour and we went up to Mr Jackson's Office and went to scribbling and so did Dametrio—Jackson who was not there could not bother or hinder us—we did as we pleased. I ought answer both of my last letters through the week and not wait until next mail. Howe has written in his journal to night with a quill pen [in] which "Jake Lane" used to say lay the masters skill. I have now eaten every bit of my candy up and of course run out—I am in quite a bad fix. To day's Journal has been quite a long one but not much more than common for I am going to write some thing worth. I got in A guitar string from Joe Mercure's which cost twenty five cents or two bits as they say out here. The bugle has sounded so I will cease.

BUENAS NOCHES.   John Watts

Friday; 6th.

Tomorrow as we say, "Es el dia por el coreo" and which I am always glad of for I look for letters and for word from ma or some one at home so that we may know whether father and ma are on the road or whether they even intend coming or not. I got my music this morning and played it for Bauer and he is going to give me Katty Darling for my next lesson. I got my boots repaired to day by the Soldier Shoemaker. The band played in the plaza this afternoon some very good music and I noticed Bauer among them again although he is going to quit as soon as his time is out—he intends to go to the States in the Fall I think, and I am going to make a desperate attempt to go also. I and Willie went over to see the Miss Edgars about 9. O'clock and as we had discovered before Howe and Battail were there—they went over to take a game of "Eucre" with them but we did not find them playing neither had they been however when we came away Battail intrusted the cards to the oldest one. I have been laboring under quite a mistake[.] while I was there I took the youngest for the oldest and "vice versee" and I think although in opposition to the opinions of all who have seen them that the oldest is the best looking[.] at least I should choose her in preference for a wife—sure. As Howe said they spread out the calico and made quite an imposing appearance. Battail had the youngest for a rarity or change to night or by some mismanagement—Howe prefers the youngest but I take the oldest although the smallest in size and she reminds me of Bettie so much. Willie has been quarreling for the youngest and since I have seen both I am pleased with the oldest. They were serenaded just as we came away by Lieut. Wilkins, George Bell and the two fiddlers who have just come to town. Sallie tried mighty hard to find out where we were going or not to see the Miss Edgars. I commenced a letter to Sam Dodds yesterday but I did not finish it. Willie and I intended to go shooting this afternoon with Battail, to shoot at a mark but did not. I read a chapter in Bancroft or Prescott rather, only to day—recited French.

Saturday; 7th

I am again brought to the close of another week and when I look at it to see what I have accomplished I find it is very little to what it ought. I and Willie did not recite to Mr. Elison this morning as he was busy and the mail had just arrived. Neither Howe nor I got a single letter in the Eastern mail but we got some papers. Howe recieved two letters through the Southern mail—one from ma and one from "Pug" which parts of he could scarcely read for the letter had got wet by some accident I suppose and it was so dim that he could not make out a few parts. Father is still in Washington (April 12th) and ma does not know when he will be home but she said she was looking for him. It sprinkled a little to day and thundered also. I have played only one game this month and that was with George Waldo whom I think

I strung—he gave me fifteen points. I have been reading "Waverly's Magazine" all the afternoon most. Howe took a nap this afternoon[.] while he was at it Whiting came in and woke him up. I wrote one letter to day—an answer to one from Sam Dodds in the mail of last week. I played marbles with Harry Whiting this morning. I and Howe went up to the Governor's to night but I got a little provoked and as I was not enjoying myself I slipped out and came home. Howe, Willie, and Sallie were playing and singing, Sallie on the piano, Willie the guitar and Howe the flute and I was like a dead weight—so I took them unawares and came home. Howe came home in about a half an hour afterwards. I have one more letter to write—that is to Bettie and perhaps one to Grandpa and that is all that I am going to write. We had a game of knocking a solid cake across the plaza—the son of the preacher Gorman. To day has not been a pretty day at all but rather gloomy.

Sunday; 8th.

Again the first day of another week has passed over my head. It has been a fine day and I have enjoyed myself. I wrote one letter to day which was an answer to one I received from Bettie on Saturday—I have begun with a steel pen but I will have to go to my old gold one. I went to church this morning and Parson Gorman as usual preached—Howe and Battail went over and brought the Miss Edgars over although I understand they are catholic's. Mr and Mrs Edgar were there also. Sallie, Willie, Eva and the Governor were also out. I spoke to the oldest of the Miss Edgars who was with Howe. The text was in Psalms, "Wherewith shall a young man cleanse his ways: by taking heed thereof." We had a most excellent dinner and among other delicacies ice cream for desert. It has been quite a pretty day. I borrowed a book of Mr Howard to read to day called, "Lectures to Young Men" —by A.A. Livermore and which I have found to be an excellent book— I have read almost a hundred pages in it. Howe as usual has gone to bed with a book and has a candle on the melodian which is close by. Hovey has a very pretty little girl about five years old named Franciscita—she is a very fair little girl. I read over the French to night.

Monday; 9th.

I am tired to night and sleepy—It has been quite a pretty day. I read ninty-four pages in Prescott this morning and I have not read any more all day. I played two games of billiards to day with Mr Crump—I lost one and won one—I did not wish to play off. I have taken no lesson from Bauer in the last two days he has been so busy. I and Howe went up to the Fonda to night but did not play any billiards. I plagued Editor this afternoon—he mispronounced ridicule—he called it "redecule" and I laughed at him before Barry Simpson and laughed too. George Beall and Battail were over to see the Miss Edgars to night. Barry cleaned Smith in Johnsons store three games of billiards to night. Vigil is not at Santa Fe now but in Las Vegas. We recited in French as usual to day. To day is the first game I have lost this month.

Tuesday; 10th.

Well I have drawn out this day about as all the others. I have done a little good, lost a little money—one game of billiards with Charly Thayer—gave me fifteen and the discount—and have loafed or idled some of it away. I tried printing to day which is seen at the top of the page. I was in a while with Mr Howard who fixed Howe's watch to day—put in a new main spring. I read a hundred pages in Prescott to day—did not recite either in music, or Spanish—two things I do not like a bit. It has been quite a warm day and is also very warm to night. I have practiced on the guitar some to day. Howe finished his big map of the Territory of New Mexico but he has to take a copy of it. Percy Eyre has a box of gutta percha pens—the first I have ever seen and wrote with—they write very smooth and nice. Willie has not been here I believe all day—we intended to go fishing to day but the Governor met with an accident—he mashed his foot. Sallie gave me a very nice ball for which I must give her a nice kiss the first opportunity. We had some jumping up at the Fonda this afternoon just before supper—first one jump and then half [hamman?] where I was third in the ring Howe first, Gardenhire second and then myself. Barry Simpson did not like to see me clean him and I surprised Bill of the Fonda and Manuel Spiegleberg.[5] Howe and Battail have gone over again to see the Miss Edgars—I hope them success. I feel like Juan Tapia said, "muy flojera"—I feel good for nothing—no account.

Wednesday; 11th

Well here I am again to post having gone safely through the day. I have read very little in Bancroft to day—only twenty or thirty pages. We did not get off to day fishing but recited our French at the usual hour. We have been jumping some more at half hamman—I beat Barry Simpson again which plagues him considerable. To day has been a very pleasant day. I, Willie, Sallie and Mrs Rencher all took a ride in the Governor's carriage—a fine ride—down to the race track and back. Dick Simpson and I went around to see the Miss Edgars but they were not at home—over at Mrs Jacksons—so Dick & I "slipped up" but we intend to go around again sure. The Governor is getting adobes made to repair the palace—he has $2,500 from the government to do it with.[6] I am writing with a quill which make good pens but I have a bad one. Howe is reading in bed as usual. Willie was not well[.] he had the headache or he and I would have gone around, but Dick and I are going to try it again, we are not going to give it up. Barry Simpson and George Beall are going over tomorrow night so perhaps Dick and I will go Friday night. To day has been warm and I show strong simptoms of Spring "Fibre." I laid on the bed and read a little this afternoon. But I am tired and will cease for tonight.

Thursday; 12th.

The Fishing Excursion.

I rose this morning about as late as usual and after breakfast Willie came down and said they intended going fishing to day. I immediately dressed myself in the worse suit of clothes I had and went up to the Governor's. They were very slow in motion and on account of this thing and that detaining us we did not get off until 9 1/2. O'clock and on that account as we had six or seven miles to go we did not get there until to late in the day to do much good—you have either to fish early or late if you wish to catch fish for they will not bite in the middle of the day. We got off though at last and our party was composed of Willie, Mrs Rencher, Sam[7] and I. Willie drove some of the way and Sam the rest—he also as a matter of course attended to the ungearing and picketing of the mules. We went up in Mrs Rencher's carriage which is the finest I have seen in this country. It is hansomely finished and has two seats in it. We got up at the place for fishing about 11. O'clock I think. Willie and I climbed one of the mounitans to see if we could see Santa Fe but when we got to the supposed top we found we had a third or fourth of the distance we had traveled still to go so we gave it up and went down. We had a very nice dinner which Mrs Rencher had put up for the occasion—viz. beef tongue, ham, sweet pickle, biscuits and corn bread. I did not catch a single fish neither did Mrs Rencher. Sam caught one and Willie seven or eight. We came home quickly—in half the time we went up in. All went off pleasantly except that Willie caused his ma some anxiety on account of staying so late and keep us waiting and did not come until Sam went for him. With this little exception we had quite a pleasant time. The day has been a delightful one but when we started home it was cloudy and had begun to sprinkle a little. When we arrived at home Willie pressed me to stay until after supper which I did—while there Dick Simpson came and then as Col. Menes says I "vamosed" or "vamused" more properly but neith[er] are corret or have any sense in them. I found no one at home—I expect Howe has gone over to see the

Miss Edgars. I do not know whether Barry Simpson and George Bell are or have gone over or not. I have read thirty-one pages in Prescott to day although away most of the time. I did not as a matter of course say either my Spanish or music lesson. The Governor is in bad health—he has a severe cold has been in bed all day.

Friday; 13th.

Well I am delinquent a little again for I have not posted at my usual time but I can give a very good reason. I went through the scenes of to day with my usual <u>couage</u> and <u>firmness</u>. We did not recite in French the Governor not being well enough to hear us—he has been in bed to day and all of yesterday. It has not been the prettiest day that could be imagined but has been rather windy. But the events of tonight beat us[.] Dick Simpson and I went over to see the beauties of Santa Fe to see the Miss Edgars and we were more fortunate this time we found them at home and spent quite a pleasant evening with them. We got to playing eucher and did not stop until about 12 O'clock. Hoxi and I against Dick and Mary but whom her sister calls Beck. Dick is quite an adept and a very sly fellow at cards—he can stack them and deal them any way to suit himself, but they did not beat us much for we also resorted to stratagem and trickery but we were not a match for Dick. Among other amusements we had our fortunes told—mine came out that I loved the oldest and she me but I was to court and marry Eva Isenhower.[8] The oldest seems the best looking at night and the youngest by far in the day but the youngest is decidely the finest girl I think—she has such lively cheerful disposition and such a joyous countenance—I think most of her but I took a decided preference to the eldest the first night I was there. Dick has better command of language and converses much better than I expected, I am no-where with him in playing eucher or in any game of cards he knows much more but I am learning and if I am behind in that line I am sure I am ahead in the <u>music department</u>—and by the way the young ladies said their pianos would not be here for two months[.] they looked for it I think much sooner[.] Willie has been watching me all the latter part of the afternoon to find out whether I went down to see the ladies with anyone. The older has already claimed Willie as <u>her</u> sweetheart which gets Willie some.

Saturday; 14th.

Well I am now at the close of another week and have as usual to post. I rose this morning perhaps a little later than common on account of not going to bed as early as common. We recited in Spanish this morning to Mr Elison but it was a very poor recite. As it was very doubtful whether I recited or not

I did not more than half get the lesson—Willie did very little if any better. The mail arrived this morning about 12. O'clock—I did not recieve a single letter but one paper from home—the "Republican."⁹ Howe received two letters I think. I recited my music to Bauer this morning at 9. O'clock. He is still writing music for me with seconds for the flute for Howe. There is a baile tonight but I did not go—at Tom Valencia's. I received a treasure in the last mail or Howard for me rather and that was the, "Life of Robert Fulton" bound in turkey green morocco guilt edges and thick backs with my name at the bottom of the book printed. It cost me $5.40—Howard has one just like it only bound in red morocco. There is a terrible wind blowing to night—I went into Miller's room and stole his gold pen with which I am now writing. Miller has been up here to night and he and Crump have been taking "drinks" together. I expect they have gone to the baile. I did not finish Prescott this week as I expected.

Sunday; 15th.

I have gone through the beginning of another week that is I have gone through the first day. We had no church to day for our minister has left Santa Fe to visit other places. I wrote two letters to day—one to Grand Pa and one to Bettie. We had a very fine dinner and ice cream for desert. To day has been a beautiful day. The Mexican Band marched around town playing and dressed in fancy clothes like circus actors. They had a circus this afternoon but I nor Howe did not go—Crump went and came home disgusted with it as did a good many more. I finished "Lectures to Young Men" by A.A. Livermore which I borrowed from Howard and which I think a fine little book. I was in Crump's room to night and I told him I wanted to take lessons from Whiting in writing and he told me to make my letters not less than a half inche long and I would soon learn to write well. I am going to try the plan and see how I get along in it. Howe has gone to bed to read as usual—which he does every night. Howe went over to see the Miss Edgars this afternoon—I believe he wanted to take a walk with one of them—he did not walk but took a chat with them. We did not get any word from pa except through ma who says he is still in Washington—her letter was dated April 18th. Howe and I started to take a walk but we found it too warm and soon returned. I had a talk with Dunn this afternoon who was in my room and with whom I went up town and took a glass of soda with. The Band played in the plaza this afternoon. I saw Hovey "tight" to night for the first time in my life. I borrowed $20 of him this morning. I want to pay Howard and Bauer and other little debts I owe. Crump is married—his wife is in

Philadelphia. I am going to write in this large hand and see what good it will do me.

Monday; 16th.

Well I begun to day remarkable well—better than any I have in a long time—by getting up at 5. O'clock and taking a walk. Howe said the young ladies—the Miss Edgars has said they were going to walk and he said that he would accompany them but after waiting awhile we went on and when we got up on the first peak of the mountains we saw them coming—I walked on but Howe waited until they overtook him and then "shyed" up to the young-est—they walked on and I got away ahead of them and sat down on a piñon bush until they came up l spoke to the young ladies and to Squire Collins and they invited me to join the party which I was not loth to do. We got back about 6. O'clock having been gone about an hour and having walked more than two miles. I had a fine appetite for breakfast. I finished Prescott to day and returned the three volumes and got out one of Maryatt's novels "The Poacher" and one of Bayard Taylor's "Travels"—the "Eldorado" I believe. I commenced "The Poacher" merely but have not worked in the "Eldorado." I, Willie, Sallie[,] Mr and Mrs Rencher and George Beall are going fishing tomorrow up the creek. I have been in the house almost all day reading. I took my lesson from Bauer this afternoon at 4. O'clock. French was recited to day but I had very little of it for I got the lesson we should have recited when the Governor was sick. Miller has not said a word about his pen all day—I have had it the whole day. The elder of the ladies invited me to take a walk with them in the morning which I certainly will do with pleasure. There was a meeting in the Exchange to night to make arrangements for the reception of Mr Phelps of Missouri who is going to make a visit out here. I took a ride on Squire Collins horse this afternoon with Willie—we went out the Taos road about three miles where we had a beautiful view—a splendid landscape—the best I have seen in this country. I borrowed a horse of Doc-tor Kavanaugh to night to go to fish tomorrow. <u>Pero, Buenas noches.</u>

Tuesday; 17th.

Well to day has been occupied on another fishing excursion—but before I went fishing I and Howe took a walk at 5. O'clock with Squire and the ladies who are getting right sociable. After we came from our walk, I went over and borrowed a fine black horse of Dr Kavanaugh—the horse was Hugh or Mayor Smith's[10] I do not know which[.] it is a fine horse and I had a nice ride. Mrs Rencher, Willie, Sam, George Beall and the Governor had gone on and they were just ungearing the mules when I got there. We scattered along up the creek and assembled at 12. O'clock and took a lunch after which we again scattered along the creek and finaly came home about four O'clock and got here at 5. O'clock. The amount of fish caught ranged some how this way. I, George Beall and Mrs Rencher none—Willie one[,] the Governor two and sam four I think which were very fair fish. We had a very pleasant time—nice ride and fun—I could scarcely hold my horse coming home. The Band played in the plaza this evening and as usual the ladies came out and sat on the steps. Howe has gone over there to see them to night but I am going to bed being tired and sore. I read a chapter or two in the, "Poacher." Mr Dunn told me whenever I wanted his horse just to go and get him. To day has been quite a pleasant day.

Wednesday; 18th.

Well I neglected to post tonight when I usually do—but I have a good reason for not for Dick Simpson and I were over to see the "jente"—Miss Hoxie and Mary—I think the most of Hoxie as does Howe. The more I converse with her the more I like her and she is more candid and open than her sister—in fact I think I think more of her than her sister. Their mother calls one of them a <u>flatterer</u> and the other a <u>chatterer</u>—Mary the former and Hoxie the latter. We took a walk this morning and yesterday also. Dick and I had quite a fine time and sat until 11. O'clock when we bid them goodnight. I read some in the Poacher—recited French & music as usual.

Thursday; 19th.

Some one asked me a day or two ago—yes it was George Beall when we were fishing how old I was and I said I would be ninteen the 11th of May which has passed long ago and at which I am provoked. Howe and I rose early this morning but the ladies did not come along—Hoxie came along with her[...?] I suppose Miss Mary staid in bed. I read a hundred pages in the "Poacher" this morning but none this afternoon. I and Crump played two games of billiards this morning and he beat me both and we played again tonight three games two of which I beat and lost one. The Band played in the plaza this afternoon and Howe and I went up and sat before Joe Mercure's store until the[y] finished and then we went over to see Mrs Jackson and had quite a fine chat after which we came up to supper. Last night Cotton[,] Davison, Rogers[11] and a fellow by the name of Howard got on a big bust. Rogers this morning was perfectly crazy—he was insane running about cursing and swearing and bragging that he could whip any body. Willie and I unfortunately did not recite in Spanish to day—I have not seen Mr

Elison for several days. I played my music lesson to Bauer—a waltz and the [...?]. It has been a pretty day and very warm which is also the case with tonight. I put some cold cream on my lips which are chapped.

Friday; 20th.

I am now going to try a gutta percha pen which I am writting with but which I give up for the gold. A good gold pen I think cannot be beat for writing and after a person gets accustomed to them he cannot write with any other to do much good. Howe and I have been rising unusually early this week and walking for our health with the Miss Edgars but they threw us of[f] this morning although we were up waiting for them—we saw them come out but they went down the Southern road towards Alburquerque, but still Howe and I took our walk if it was by ourselves—we went up on the mountains to the North towards Taos. We had quite a nice walk although alone. I played my lesson to Bauer this morning at my usual hour and also recited French. I then went up to the Fonda and played a game of back-gammon with Charly Conclin. I played a game of billiards with Crump and cleaned him but George Beall bothered him so that I beat him and then George gave him the discount and also talked him out of that also when we came home. I finished reading the, "Poacher" this afternoon. I am now ready for the, "Adventures (of Bayard Taylor) in Eldorado." Kingsbury's train of twenty-five or twenty wagons got in yesterday morning and he has been opening them all day. I and Howe are learning to play the guitar and flute together—make music together and we are learning very fast. I wish I was father's private secretary and could get to travel around with him. Howe bought "Nothing to Wear" at B & J's to day for seventy-five cents and I bought some hair oil for the same price. I read "Nothing to Wear" through to night. Crump sat with us a while tonight. Willie and Howe went over to see the Miss Edgars to night but Willie came down late after Howe had been gone almost half an hour. It has been a pretty day but is blowing and bad tonight. Barry Simpson said the next time Dick and I went around to see the ladies he wanted to go around with us. I am getting along in years—I am going on twenty.

Saturday; 21th.

Here I am again a day behind time. Howe and I both went to bed to night without posting. Col. Garretson arrived[12] in the Southern mail and Bean Bois wants to kill [him?]. I received to letters tonight or this afternoon rather in the mail one from <u>Mary</u> and one from Seth Tuley. I did not play any billiards to day—at least lost none. We went over to see Mrs Jackson with our guitar and flute to give them some music but Mrs Jackson was unwell.

Sunday; 22th.

We have had quite a pretty day to day[.] the sun shone out very nice and warm. We arose at 5. O'clock—I took a walk by myself but Howe, Sallie, and Willie Rencher went to the fish pond[13] and took a skift ride—the ladies did not walk with them. Miss Mary does not seem to be in the best health. We had no church to day[.] our minister is away. General Pelham invited me to come up and see his wife which of course will do the first opportunity. The Maromar performed this afternoon as they did yesterday afternoon and last Sunday also but I have not been once yet. I have written three letters to day, one to <u>Mary</u>—one to Seth Tuley, and one to Bettie. The Band played in the plaza this afternoon. I was in Howard's room this afternoon a short time—he was also down to see us—borrowed a pair of saddle bags—he is going to start for Socorro Monday in the mail. I have read the Sunday Times to day—Howe slept a good part of the afternoon. I read some in my Bible to day as usual on Sunday—in "Psalms." Willie was here twice to day—once this morning and once this afternoon[.] he showed us his name in one of the N.E. papers where he lives. We heard that father was at home on the 22nd of April Mary said Fanny had arrived at home. Howe and I will look for Fannie, ma, pa and all the children in the next mail. Harry Whiting was down here a little while this afternoon and I won his knife from him and gave it back. Crump says Bois and Garretson had a little "tusle" to night but were parted before they shed any blood. Howe has gone over to see the young ladies to night. Lola Numan passed by this evening and asked Howe if he was <u>dead,</u> yes he said I am dead. Vigil was over here this afternoon and I read a lesson in Spanish—not a lesson but we read a little in Spanish and then translated it into English. The bells are tolling which makes me feel melancholy. I wrote a pretty hard letter to Bettie—I expect she will think I am getting pretty wild. We have lost the key to our door by some misfortune. I wrote quite a short journal for yesterday. Kelly and family[14] arrived this afternoon late. I have heard no one speak well of Col. Garretson since I have been in Santa Fe.

Monday; 23rd.

To day like many more has slyly and silently passed over my head and fully is the maxim verified, "Whether we work, play or sing, <u>Time</u> is ever on the wing.["] Vigil did not hear me in Spanish this morning[.] neither did I go up to see whether Mr Elison would—I do not know whether Willie went up or not. I recollect now we recited French to day we had quite a long hard lesson. Howe and I rose early this morning and we are getting in the habit of it which is a worthy and useful habit salutary both to the mind and body. We took a walk with the Miss Edgars and Sallie and Willie—we went up by Fort Marcy. We had quite a pleasant walk and just as we got up on the top we had the pleasure of seeing the orb which rolls in its majesty and walks the king of planets appear about the summits of the father of mountains to run its daily course and give light to thousands and warmth to the earth. The hill on which Fort Marcy is situated is stony and the soil is of a reddish color and at a distance looks like clay.[15] I read forty pages in Bayard Taylor's "Eldorado" to day. I commenced to learn again on the violin which I commenced once and then gave up. Howe wishes me to learn to play it and then we can play together. Willie has not been here once to day. Mr Crump was in our room to night a short time. Howe has gone up town to play a game of billiards with Joe Mercure—I played two games of billiards with Vigil and beat both. To day has been quite a terrible windy day—the whole atmosphere was full of dust—we look for father in next mail. I have been in the house a good deal to day. Howe took a "nap" this afternoon. Blanco is out of the corrall for I hear him dragging his log after him. I have not loafed much to day—George Waldo was drunk this afternoon. Crump finished his map a day or two ago. Howard started for Socorro this morning in the hack or stage line of Bowler and Green I believe.

Tuesday; 24th.

Another day has sped and I am now to perform my last duty of the day although I feel very sleepy and tired and feel much inclined to let it go until tomorrow but the maxim is never put off until tomorrow what can be done to day. Howe, Willie, Sallie, Squire and the two young ladies went down to the fish pond and took a ride before breakfast—Howe rowed for them—Willie was too little. Crump and I intended to walk up on Fort Marcy this morning and he intends taking a sketch from it of Santa Fe. We went up this afternoon but it was entirely too hot[.] we could not stand it and so we came down—he begun his sketch at the Baptist Church.[16] I and Willie recited our Spanish for the first time in a long time, Mr Elison told a good tale on Willie—about one of the Miss Edgars calling him Willie and then begging pardon and calling him Mr. Rencher! We had a good laugh over it. I have played no billiards to day. I have read about fifty pages in the "Eldorado" of Bayard Taylor. To night I was in to see Mr Crump a short time. He has four novels he borrowed of Hovey this afternoon one of which he read through this afternoon he said. It has been a pretty fair day. I took my first lesson on the violin in New Mexico this afternoon after I had finished my lesson on the guitar. Howe went over to see the ladies to night—but just as he got there he saw Dr Kavanaugh and Cogwell[17] and then he turned around and came back without going in. Vigil did not come in to hear me to day. I laid down on the bed tonight and came near going to sleep. I have not learned much Spanish to day nor read half as much as I ought. Howe and Willie went down to the pond and took a ride in the boats—Howe is learning to row very fast. I think I am improving in writing since I have commenced writing a large round hand. Howe and I will look for pa in the next mail rather strongly and very in the mail after. But I have written my page and will go to reading in Bayard Taylor.

Wednesday; 25th.

I feel very much like I was attacked by that contagious disease called "Spring Fever" in the States but I have not found out the name it goes by out here. I recited in French to day with the class we had quite a hard lesson and I and Sallie did not have it as well as we might have had it. I recited my lesson in music to Bauer this afternoon both on the violin and guitar. He has written a piece for Willie [and I] both to play together and he has let me have it first. I suppose I have read fifty pages in Bayard Taylor to day which is decidedly better than nothing but when I see how much time I have it seems like I out to read three or four times as much. The days pass away very slowly now I want the mail to come with father in it. I rose early this morning and went up on Fort Marcy with Crump to sketch a picture of Santa Fe. Howe with, Squire, the two Miss Edgars and Sallie Rencher took a walk— Willie was not along. I took good long looks at them with the spy glass. Crump and I played two games of billiards this morning after we came from walking, both of which I beat. Then we went in and took some supper or breakfast rather. To day has been rather warm, but still pleasant. Howe and I went over to see the ladies this evening and intended to go with them down to the fish pond and row them over the pond but it was to windy. However we went down but could not get the oars and therefore had no ride—Willie was with us. Miller came in and got his pen. Howe supports quite a mustacho. We had quite a nice little chat with them though and then went up to supper. I saw Barry Simpson and Davison drunk to night—I never caught Barry before—never saw him drunk—also Don Hovey was tight a few days ago.

Tuesday; 26th.

Well another day is gone. Howe does a great deal of writing now he is

copying the field notes of surveys.[18] I write every night and yet my progress
in penmanship seems very little and exceedingly slow. It is now late at night
being about half past 10. O'clock or 11. I and Dick Simpson spent quite a
pleasant evening with the young ladies (the Miss Edgars). We sat and conversed together on various topics and I as usual talked to Hoxie, the youngest. I told here about the manner in which the sea got salt—from a mill
which is supposed to be still grinding there still, and will always I suppose if
we credit superstition and tradition. I and Willie forgot again to recite to Mr
Elison in Spanish—I never thought of it once. Willie and I played a piece to
Mr Bauer this morning and again this afternoon. I read twenty pages in
"Eldorado" this morning and have read none since. We (I and Mr, Mrs and
Misses Edgar[,] Willie, Sallie, and Howe [and] I rowed Miss "Bec" around
a short time and then took Miss Hoxie and Willie and I took quite a ride.
Miss Bec got a little scared, although she would not acknowledge it. The
wind arose about the time we were starting back 7 1/2 O'clock perhaps.

Friday; 27th.
Well it is now early in the morning—twelve minutes of 11. O'clock. I
had just got a copybook to practice writing but I thought I might as well
write a little in my Journal but I will put it back again. I see to night that
I have written some through the day. To day has been a very lucky day. I and
Howe recited our French to day at the usual hour and as we were reciting the
mail came in from the East. After we finished reciting and started up to the
Fonda—just as we got out the door we espied father walking across the
plaza and we both immediately broke across the plaza towards him, but
found to our sad regret that he had brought none of them whom we longed to
see. Fannie nor none came—he says they will come next Spring. He said
they were all well and ma and Sis came with him as far as Madison.[19] Howe
received a letter from ma by pa in which she says Howe and I must come in
this fall—Howe on a visit and I to go to college. It seems so natural to see
pa—Oh! how much I want to see Bettie—the first thing father did after
sitting down was to sing "The Long, Long, Weary Day." All the fellows at
the Fonda say they are going to tell great "yarns" on me, but Howe and I
have an unimpaired reputation. This I think is fathers eighteenth trip across
the plains—he looks quite ruff when he first arrived but got shaved and put
on a clean shirt and now looks considerably better. I and Willie played together this evening over at Bauer's and Howe went over to see us play. First
I would play one part and then we would change pieces, I play Willie's part
and he mine. I did not take a lesson on the guitar by myself and none at all on
the violin. To night Howe and I stopped in and heard the Band play. Then

after we came home Eddie Edgar came in and staid a while and about 9 1/2. O'clock Howe and Willie made a sally over to see the girls and Eddie went home with them. After they had gone I went up to see pa and found him and Don Hovey talking. Hovey soon left though and then we had a little chat and a song and then he went to bed—he brought us, "The Autocrat at the Breakfast Table," by Holmes. Father wanted to know if I could speak Spanish yet which I told him I could not. I broke one of my guitar strings to night. The wind is blowing to night rather hard—whistling through the door and houses. I am going to do better with my music than I have been here lately. Father wishes me to learn to perform well on some instrument and now is my time. I have so much time. So we will make a new start tomorrow.

Saturday; 28th.

Well to day has passed and as I neglected to post at my usual time my Journal for to day will be short. I did not recite in anything to day except in music. To night I and Howe went over and played with Bauer. We made fine music but I made a botch of the first piece I played which was on the violin —the next I did better on the guitar. I read the papers that came in the mail all the afternoon. I won a treat of candy off of Willie and [watched a] game of billiards between Nat McCrea[20] and Barry Simpson—I bet on Barry. We took a walk I think this morning with the ladies. It seems strange to me that I cannot recollect the events of a day passed from the time in which I ought to have recorded its events.

Sunday; 29th.

Well I am at home now, I am writing in time which had just passed and which I know something about. I arose about twenty minutes before 5. O'clock—washed, dressed myself in clean clothes and then Howe and I went over to walk with the ladies but to our dismay and chagrin they were not going so we came back and Howe went to writing letters and I begun one which I expect I will never finish. There were two Indians to see father this morning—one of them is the interpreter of the Navajos—he was with another Indian and they sat and talked a long time in Spanish. I am trying to write an overly round and high hand. There were more out a[t] church to day than I ever saw before—Col. Menes said he counted them and there was about sixty—there is generally twenty or thirty, Miss "Bec" ma and pa were there—General Pelham and lady—Governor, lady, Willie and Eva. Mrs O'Bannon and Kelly whom I am inclined to think is bordering on to being good looking. We had a very good sermon and short. This afternoon we had a sermon in Spanish and after it a singging lesson. This afternoon late father and I took a long walk after which I sat with him in his room until he went to bed and then I came down home to go to bed but could not Howe having gone over to see the Miss Edgars and taken the key with him. I did not write any letters to day—I begun one to Bettie but did not finish it and I expect never will. I have read a little miscellaneously to day and posted and am now going to bed.

Monday; 30th.

Being very sleepy I went to bed without writing in my Journal and now after breakfast on Tuesday morning I am at what I should have done yesterday or before going to bed last night. I rose this morning at our usual time before 5. O'clock. and went over and went with the ladies down to the fish pond where we gave them a beautiful ride in the boats and then we came back and went up to breakfast where we learned that Doctor Kavanaugh had had his fine horse stolen early this morning—his fine race horse—after breakfast the Doctor with two or three men started after the rogue whom they found asleep near Algodonis and the horse tied to a tree ("<u>dicen</u>") which is about forty miles from here. They brought the fellow up here with horse and every thing he had. I saw the fellow—he was a deserted soldier and looks young—not hardly twenty-one and has quite a boyish face and looks like he did not know how to steal which is certainly true—Lieut. Cogwell took him and put him in the guard house or I expect he would have been hung, whipped to death or killed in some cruel manner. He has got off well so far. I took my lesson on the violin at 2. O'clock this afternoon and Willie and I played together at 10. O'clock. I played a game of billiards with Vigil to day and beat him.

Tuesday; 31st.

This is the last day of the month—tomorrow will commence a new month. I did my daily rotine—recited to Bauer on the violin and guitar this afternoon at 3. O'clock. Howe went over and played with us. I on the violin, also Bauer. Willie the guitar and Howe the flute—"Sounds from Home" was the name of the piece we played together. We all went walking this morning except Miss "Bec" who had the <u>headache</u> (?)! I got my boots half soled to day for $2.00 at the soldier shoemaker. This evening Howe, pa and I all went down to the pond and took a row. Leo. Smiths brother and another fellow were riding together. It has been a tolerable day to day. We all are going to play up at Mrs Rencher's this evening or tomorrow night rather. I woke up with my head at the foot to day or this morning rather. The Miss Edgars took a cry to day their ma says for Booneville—their native place I believe.

NOTES: Chapter 3

1. Elisa Collins Edgar was "Squire" James L. Collins' daughter. She and her family moved to Santa Fe in 1859. Thirty-eight years old in 1860, Elisa was born in Missouri. She owned real estate in Santa Fe valued at $10,000, perhaps property given her by her father. Her daughters, "Hattie" (or "Hoxie" as Watts often calls her) and "Bec," were the talk of the town. Every single man and teenage boy wanted to visit them, among these Barry Simpson, George Beall, Dr. Kavanaugh, Dick Simpson, a stranger from Texas named Violand, and the Watts brothers.

Hattie would marry J. Howe Watts in 1859, when Kingsbury wrote Webb, September 24, 1859: "How[e] [Watts] appears delighted with his young bride. She is Catholic and was married by the Bishop [Lamy]. Several of my friends have made a strong set on me to take the other ["Bec"], I decline the honor. They do not know me."

Collins' son-in-law was James M. Edgar, a forty-nine-year-old clerk, born in Kentucky. Besides their two daughters, the Edgars had two sons, James C. ("Jimmie") and Edwin G. ("Eddie"). In 1860, Jimmie was a sixteen-year-old student; Eddie was thirteen. See 1860 U.S. Census; and Elder and Weber, "Trading in Santa Fe," Ch. 12, p. 6.

2. The identity of "Bois," "Bayes," or "Bean Bois" as Watts calls this fellow is unclear. Possibly this was 2nd Lt. John Van Deusen Du Bois, Company K, Mounted Rifles. Lt. Du Bois, who kept a journal of his travels covering 1857-1862, was stationed at Fort Bliss and Fort Union. In late March and early April 1859, Du Bois passed through Galisteo and Santa Fe. In May or June 1859, he was again in Santa Fe at the time Watts was keeping his journal. See Oliva, *Fort Union,* pp. 220-21, and 234-36.

3. Kirby Benedict was born in Connecticut in 1811. After practicing law in Illinois, he was appointed associate justice of the territorial supreme court by President Pierce in 1853. He became chief justice after presiding over the old Third Judicial District of Rio Arriba and Taos Counties for five years.

Judge Benedict was an independent man of unbending opinion. A life-long Democrat, he was a strong advocate of the Union at a time in New Mexico's history when many powerful members of his party were Southern sympathizers. Although he had loyal friends, he was known for making sharp-tongued remarks in and out of court which offended precious members of the bar and other fussy dignitaries with whom he disagreed politically. He wholeheartedly made lifelong enemies of some of New Mexico's most powerful figures, including military leaders, with whom he feuded ceaselessly.

He became most formidable after acquiring an interest in the *Santa Fe New Mexican*, a rival of the *Gazette*. Indian Agent James L. Collins, editor of the *Gazette,* wrote of him: "He must dabble, dabble, dabble in the dirty pool of politics, which he himself stirs up and from which he constantly bespatters himself with mire the most filthy."

Judge Benedict also had a lifelong attachment to the bottle. The trader Franz Huning recalled seeing him in Albuquerque when he was drunk. Carrying a big walking stick and heading home across the plaza after an evening at "Chato"Armijo's liquor store, the judge found his way, but with difficulty. Huning gave the details: "Sometimes he lost hold of [his walking stick] and dropped it on the ground, and there he was. He knew that if he undertook to recover it he would fall on his face, so he would stand still and wait for help. Anybody, American or Mexican, man, woman or child knew well enough what ailed the Judge ... and promptly rendered him the necessary assistance to recover his club. It was a rudder, he could not navigate without it."

John M. Kingsbury told an amusing story about Judge Benedict and his fellow lawyers, September 8, 1860. "When they started for court at Las Vegas," Kingsbury wrote, "the Judge & all hands were tight, the driver Bully Welch, Houghton & Col. Street [and Samuel Ellison]. They had not reached the rock corral when Ellison got uneasy at the speed, thought they would never get to Pigeon's & took the lines from the driver. Did not drive 500 yards before he hit a stump & upset the whole crowd. The carriage was pretty badly broke but they made out to fix up & go on. In the turn over Judge Benedict fell under the others & hurt his left arm pretty bad. It swelled up directly but they all thought it was not serious as he could move his fingers. Since he has got back & the swelling gone down he finds that the small bone at the elbow was dislocated & is now set itself in the place it was nocked [sic] to, and will be a permanent injury to him. He can use the arm but it will be stiff. The others got off with slight bruises." The moral of this story would seem to be that drunk driving was also dangerous with horses.

Twitchell added one of the many stories about Judge Benedict when he was on the bottle. While presenting a motion before Judge Hubbell in Albuquerque, Benedict made some remarks that Hubbell took as reflecting upon the intelligence of the court.

"Sit down," said Hubbell. "You are drunk!"

"That is true," Benedict fired back. "I am surprised that your honor is enabled to make so correct a decision."

Eventually efforts were made to remove Judge Benedict from the supreme court because of his irregular behavior. He drank excessively. Using the *New Mexican,* he had accused General Carleton and other prominent Army officers of corruption and bad management. Charges against him were formally drawn up and carried all the way to the White House.

"Well, gentlemen," President Lincoln is supposed to have said. "I know Benedict. We have been friends for over thirty years. He may imbibe to excess, but Benedict drunk knows more law than all the others on the bench in New Mexico sober. I shall not disturb him."

Thereafter, Judge Benedict remained safely on the supreme court until after Lincoln's death. In February 1866, President Johnson replaced him with the territorial military hero of the day, John P. Slough. Afterward, Benedict became even more obnoxious and was eventually suspended from practicing law in the courts of New Mexico altogether. His efforts to have himself reinstated were unsuccessful. A saddened and angry old man, he died of a heart attack in 1874.

Albeit known for his tipsy behavior, Judge Benedict, according to a biographer, was "a master of satire, sarcasm and ridicule. He was a man of fine literary taste and ability and some of his opinions are masterpieces of legal literature."

See Franz Huning, *Trader-on the Santa Fe Trail: Memoirs of Franz Huning, with notes by his granddaughter, Lina Fergusson Browne* (Albuquerque, 1973), pp. 58-59. Quotations from the *Gazette* and the *New Mexican* are from this work. Also see Twitchell, *Old Santa Fe*, pp. 348-57; Hunt, *Kirby Benedict*; and Arie W. Poldervaart, "When Benedict Was Chief, 1858-1866," in *Black-Robed Justice* (n. p., 1948), pp. 49-66.

4. Probably the U.S. deputy surveyor, R.E. Clements. In 1858 and 1859 Clements led survey parties down the Canadian River to the Texas line. Because of the hostile Comanche, soldier escorts based at Fort Union and detached to Beck's Ranch or Hatch's Ranch usually accompanied the party. In February 1858, the *Gazette* reported: "Col. Clemens, Deputy Surveyor, who has for two or three months been engaged below, returned, with his party, to Santa Fe this morning, having finished his contract. The Col. is looking well, and reports having had a pleasant and successful trip."

The next year's trip, however, was neither pleasant nor successful. In spite of warnings, Clements led out his survey party in July without the Army escort. Roving Comanche, having sworn to prevent any settlement east of Hatch's Ranch and knowing that settlers would follow the surveyor's chain, captured the entire party, held them for several hours, and threatened the leader.

After Clements promised to give up the survey if the Indians let his party go, the Comanches turned the thankful white men loose. But they helped themselves to the government blankets and provisions. Taking everything but the compass, chains, and horses, the chief warned Clements "that he could call together five hundred warriors 'by one smoke.'"

The survey was not resumed that year. James L. Collins observed that a fort would be needed in the area, after which, he said "it will be time enough to complete the surveys."

See Charles L. Kenner, *A History of New Mexican - Plains Indian Relations* (Norman, 1969), pp. 126-27; Oliva, *Fort Union,* pp. 147, 157, 158; and *Gazette,* 27 Feb 58.

5. The Spiegelbergs were among the most important of the Jewish merchants in territorial New Mexico. The Zeckendorfs, Biernbaums, Beuthners, Staabs, Ilfelds, and Seligmans were other prominent Jewish mercantile families of the day.

Solomon Jacob Spiegelberg, the first of the brothers to arrive, came to Santa Fe possibly as early as 1844. Levi appeared in Santa Fe in 1848, Elias in 1850, and "Manuel" (Emanuel) sometime during the fifties. There were two other Spiegelberg brothers, Lehman and Willi. Bancroft notes that Lehman, "a prominent merchant of Sta. Fe," arrived in 1858 and "another in 1861." The latter would have been Willi. In 1860, Solomon Jacob was the oldest at thirty-five. Levi was twenty-nine, and Emanuel, whom Watts names in the journal, was twenty-three. Elias had died when a roof fell on him while he slept. Solomon Jacob, Elias, and Emanuel had all been born in Prussia; Bancroft notes that Lehman was "a Prussian."

The Spiegelberg family engaged in merchandising, in obtaining government contracts, and in the Indian trade as well as in insurance sales, mining, and banking. After the First National Bank of New Mexico was chartered in 1870 with money from the sale of the Maxwell Grant, the Spiegelbergs chartered a bank of their own in 1872, the "Second National Bank of New Mexico." Lehman, Willi, Solomon, and Levi were major stockholders.

The brothers were active in the Santa Fe trade. In the peak years, Spiegelberg trains arrived regularly from Missouri. Kingsbury noted to Webb, May 28, 1860: "Spiegelbergs first train 26 Wagons unloaded Saturday. He will have a pretty fair run, as he has many strikers dependent upon him for goods." Financial figures for the brothers are impressive. Tobias notes that in 1876 "the Spiegelberg's contracts included orders for 3.5 million lbs. of beef cattle at $5.14 per hundred pounds and 250,000 lbs. of flour for the Mescalero Apaches at $4.45 per hundred."

See Twitchell, *Leading Facts,* V, pp. 258-59; Tobias, *Jews in New Mexico,* pp. 25-26, 29, 37, 39, 64, 65, 66-72; Bancroft, *Arizona and New Mexico,* pp. 791-92, n. 7; and Elder and Weber, "Trading in Santa Fe," Ch. 13, p. 57. Twitchell printed a fine studio photograph of the Spiegelberg brothers in *Leading Facts,* II, facing p. 284.

6. Doctoral dissertations could be written on the eternal state of disrepair and the everlasting patchwork on the governor's palace. Governor Rencher spoke in his "Special Message from the Governor" to the legislature, January 22, 1859—a sort of a period State of the Territory address—of the "impending ruin [of] this Ancient edifice;" and he thanked legislators and Alexander M. Jackson, the territorial secretary, for the funds "to complete the repairs of" and "to rescue" the "Old Palace."

These funds, Rencher said, had "enabled me to complete the repairs, I hope in a satisfactory manner, except the front Portal, which will be done as early in the Spring or Summer as lumber can be obtained." He added: "These repairs have enabled me to place at the disposition of each house a Committee room, if one should be found Necessary." See "Executive Record Book 1," 22 Jan 59, p. 226, NMRA.

7. "Sam" or "Samuel" was Governor Rencher's eighteen-year-old black servant, born in North Carolina. See Chap. 1, note 10.

8. Eva Isenhower was a friend in Bloomington. See original journal, p. 182, entry for 12 Dec. 1859.

9. The *Republican* could have been either a Bloomington, Indiana, newspaper, or a St. Louis newspaper of that title.

10. Hugh N. Smith was a lawyer from Missouri. Described by Keleher as an "intelligent and energetic" man, Smith was politically active in Santa Fe in the late 1840s in what Howard R. Lamar called "a territorial machine" led by Judge Joab Houghton. It included Donaciano Vigil. The issues between this "machine" and the opposition were complex, but among this group were lawyers interested primarily in confirming and selling land grants. Smith, a personal friend of Carlos Beaubien and of the St. Vrains, often represented land grant and mercantile interests.

The opposition favored statehood. Its influential men were Dr. Connelly, Manuel Alvarez (former consul in Santa Fe), Major Richard H. Weightman and others. Spanish speaker, active Catholic, heavy drinker, popular with the local people, Weightman was aiming for Congress. These men were interested not only in home rule, but in the offices statehood would create for New Mexico. Both parties, aware that Texas was prepared to annex New Mexico, wished to prevent this outrage.

President Taylor, a Southerner who favored statehood, complicated things by appointing James S. Calhoun the new Superintendent of Indian Affairs. A wealthy Georgia politician, Calhoun, upon arriving in the territory, began lobbying for statehood. According to Lamar, "the Calhoun forces" began publication of the *Santa Fe New Mexican* in November 1849. The *New Mexican* was a newspaper pledged to statehood.

Following several loud public meetings in Santa Fe, an anti-statehood, pro-territorial convention of nineteen men chose Hugh N. Smith New Mexico's "delegate" to Congress in September 1849. But the House of Representatives, after a long debate in July 1850, decided by a vote of 92 to 86 not to seat him, even though he had traveled all the way to Washington. Smith, in the tradition of a real Congressman, collected, according to Keleher, "$2,000 mileage and $5.00 a day" for a trip which accomplished nothing.

Smith returned to Santa Fe, where, acording to Lamar, he "was concerned with at least ten land grant clients." He was also appointed the first secretary of the territory. But his old political enemies, especially Major Weightman, now New Mexico's Congressional Delegate, wanted this office for Manuel Alvarez. Thus they succeeded in preventing Smith's confirmation. It would seem that Hugh N. Smith had good reason to become embittered, and to embrace the bottle, as he did.

In 1859, while John Watts lived in Santa Fe, Smith died, apparently from drinking too much for too many years.

See Lamar, *Far Southwest*, pp. 73-77, 140-41; Keleher, *Turmoil*, pp. 74, 124, n. 44; Twitchell, *Leading Facts*, II, pp. 269-71, 282-83; and Bancroft, *Arizona and New Mexico*, pp, 445-46.

John Watts also mentions "Mayor" Smith here. Traveling with his civilian clerk, Major Albert J. Smith arrived at Fort Union in January 1857, as paymaster. Major Smith had previously been in Santa Fe in December 1856. However, his whereabouts in May 1859, are not known. See Oliva. *Fort Union*, pp. 213-14.

11. Probably T.M. Rogers, a Georgia born machinist, who would be convicted of homicide in August 1860. "Rogers" had also been involved in a pistol fight at Dr. Kavanaugh's office on March 10, 1859.

Kingsbury described him to Webb on September 8, 1860: "At the court here last month, Rogers, the machinist, I think you know him a short thick set man, perhaps he was with Leitensdorfer when you was here. He was afterwards employed as engineer & Blacksmith at the Gov's. mill. Was convicted of murder for shooting a Mexican in a drunken spree last Christmas day and is to be hung on the 14th this month." It would seem that Rogers was chronically violent when drunk. See Elder and Weber, "Trading in Santa Fe," Ch. 14, p. 32; and n. 12.

It seems doubtful that the drunken "fellow by the name of Howard" mentioned here would have been either W.J. Howard, the jeweler, or Clement W. Howard, the notary public for Taos County.

12. "Col. Garretson" was probably the surveyor who was in the field somewhere south of Santa Fe in the spring of 1858. The *Gazette* noted in April that "his work is progressing finely, meeting with no obstructions from the Indians."

He is probably the same man mentioned by Kingsbury. "Wm. Drew has been drowned," Kingsbury wrote Webb on September 24, 1859. "He was out with Garitson [sic] a surveying trip and in crossing the Rio Del Norte near Santo Domingo while the river was very high. He got in a hole and being unable to swim, was carried down. His body has not been recovered." See *Gazette,* 17 Apr 58; and Elder and Weber, "Trading in Santa Fe," Ch. 12, p. 6.

13. The "fish pond" was a popular gathering place. People went there to row a boat, to picnic, and to bathe. Though this is merely guesswork, it may have been located in the *"cienega,"* a swampy area perhaps two hundred yards generally east of the governor's palace, just below the hill on which the Fort Marcy earthwork was situated. Webb mentions the *"cienega"* and Twitchell describes it. See Webb, *Adventures in the Santa Fe Trade,* p. 92; and Twitchell, *Old Santa Fe,* p. 52.

14. The identity of "Kelly and family" is unclear. Most likely this was R. P. Kelley, the deputy surveyor who in April 1858, was in the field south of Santa Fe. In July he and his assistant left Santa Fe for the Rio Abajo where Kelley had undertaken another surveying contract. It is also possible that this was Lt. Henry Brooke Kelly of the 10th Infantry, one of the many officers and soldiers who left the U. S. Army in New Mexico for the Confederacy in 1861. See *Gazette,* 3 Apr, and 7 Aug 58; and Oliva, *Fort Union,* p. 244.

15. Here Watts is writing of the old Fort Marcy earthwork on a hill northeast of the plaza. This location is not to be confused with the then active military post, Fort Marcy, situated north of the governor's palace and east of the old Baptist Church.

16. From the Baptist Church, Crump and Watts would have had a sweeping view of the entire Fort Marcy installation—the corral, the buildings, the parade ground, with the earthwork on the hill to the east and the Sangre de Cristos in the distance.

17. "Cogwell" was probably 1st Lt. Milton Cogswell, post commander at Fort Marcy in August and September 1858, and for several months in 1859. Lt. Cogswell was in New Mexico until the spring of 1860. "I learn today that Lt. Cogswell has gone to the States on recruiting service," Kingsbury wrote Webb on May 12, 1860. "He owes us five dollars cash balance. He probably forgot it. I have written to him explaining the matter and requested him to enclose the amt. to you."

In charge of a detachment of the 8th Infantry, Lt. Cogswell accompanied Capt. John N. Macomb's topographical expedition from Santa Fe to the Grand and Green Rivers in 1859.

Raised in Indiana, Cogswell had graduated from West Point in 1849, eleventh in his class. During the Civil War he was breveted at the battles of Ball's Bluff and Petersburg. He died in 1882.

See Fort Marcy Post Rosters, NMRA; Elder and Weber, "Trading in Santa Fe," Ch. 13, p. 55; Macomb, *Report of the Exploring Expedition ... in 1859*, p. 7; and Heitman, *Historical Register,* pp. 314-15.

18. Howe Watts may have been working for the surveyor general or for Watts, Sr., since both men would have needed maps and field notes of suveys.

19. Madison, Indiana, a commercial center on the Ohio River, was the southern end of the old "Michigan Road." Here, sending his family back to Bloomington, Watts would have taken steamboat passage to St. Louis and from there to Independence or Kansas City.

20. Captain Nathaniel C. Macrae arrived in New Mexico with Brig. Gen. John Garland. Captain Macrae brought his wife, two daughters, and a piano across the Plains with him to the territory. Briefly commanding officer at Fort Union, Captain Macrae lacked a sense of the military proprieties, for he got into a row with General Garland over the assignment of two soldiers

and then two officers stationed at Fort Union. The result was that Garland reprimanded him in September 1853.

The difference of opinion was over a matter of jurisdiction. Since the soldiers and officers were stationed at Fort Union, Macrae apparently believed they were his to command and assign. But General Garland overruled his orders. Since the officers in question were "chiefs of their respective departments," Garland wrote Macrae, "they should not be subject to detail in matters relating to the post of Fort Union."

Governor Rencher appointed one N.M. Macrae notary public for Valencia County on May 31, 1859. One "Nat" Macrae engaged in mercantile business in Valencia County, for John M. Kingsbury noted on May 6, 1860, that "Nat" had gone broke. "I went as far as Los Lunes [sic]," Kingsbury wrote Webb. "Saw Macrae. Nat is broke, we may get something but the show is very slim. He has behaved badly, and would have been able to pay everyone in full but has gambled off and paid about $3,500 or $4,000 ... . As near as I could learn he must owe about $7,000 ... ." By September, Kingsbury had lost hope of collecting anything. "The Macrae debt I count a total loss," he wrote Webb on September 8. "It will be a scratch if we ever recover a cent there. He is laying about Albuquerque & living like a lofer."

N.M. Macrae was a member of the Santa Fe Literary Club that had censured W.W.H. Davis in 1856.

See Olivia, *Fort Union*, pp. 100, 204, 205, 207, and 573; "Executive Record Book 1," p. 217, NMRA; Elder and Weber, "Trading in Santa Fe," Ch. 13, p. 51, Ch. 14, p. 30; and *Gazette*, 20 Dec 56.

above: Santa Fe Plaza, looking east. McNitt Collection.
Courtesy NM State Records Center & Archives, Neg. #6852.

below: Santa Fe in 1859 looking west from near Fort Marcy.
1-Baptist Church, 2-Fort Marcy, 3-old adobe house, 4-home later occupied by
Senator Elkins and Judge Waldo, 5-federal building under construction,
6-officer's quarters, 7-soldier's quarters, 8-lower part of Santa Fe. McNitt
Collection. *Courtesy NM State Records Center & Archives, Neg # 6845.*

Pigeon's Ranch, Glorieta, New Mexico, June 1880. A major stop
when going east on the Santa Fe Trail. Surveyor-General Pelham
spent his honeymoon here. Photo by Ben Wittich.
Courtesy Museum of New Mexico, Neg. # 15781.

Mary Josephine Blackwood Otero (Judge William G. Blackwood's
sister), and Miguel Antonio Otero, Sr., her husband, with a slave
girl. c. 1860.

Courtesy McCain Library & Archives. University Libraries.
University of Southern Mississippi., Hattiesburg.

Augustine De Marle *(left)* and Charles P. Clever.
Courtesy Museum of New Mexico, Neg. # 7131.

"The Great Lord Hovey," Oliver Perry Hovey.
Courtesy Museum of New Mexico, Neg. # 20622.

Abraham Rencher, Governor of New Mexico Territory, 1857-1861.
Courtesy Museum of New Mexico, Neg. # 10758.

Pen and ink sketch of Exchange Hotel and Seligman Brothers store. Loomis Collection.

Courtesy NM State Records Center & Archives, Neg. # 21959.

"The Fonda" corral is in front of the buildings with cathedral in center back. Present day Water Street runs across the center foreground. c. 1860s.

Courtesy Museum of New Mexico, Neg. # 15171.

The Baptist Church, later the First Presbyterian Church, Santa Fe, New Mexico. Fort Marcy corral in foreground. Watts and his friends lived and played in this area. c. 1868. Photo by Nicholas Brown.

Courtesy Museum of New Mexico, Neg. # 37895.

Southeast corner of Santa Fe Plaza with The Exchange Hotel *(center)* and Seligman & Clever Store *(right)*. Watts calls The Exchange Hotel, "The Fonda." c. 1855.

Courtesy Museum of New Mexico, Neg. # 10685.

The Elsberg-Amberg wagon train on the Santa Fe Plaza, October 1861.
The portal behind is that of the Palace of the Governors.
Courtesy Museum of New Mexico, Neg. # 11254.

A Santa Fe Trail wagon train on San Francisco Street at the Plaza. c. 1868.
Courtesy Museum of New Mexico, Neg. # 11329.

John and Sue Barnes Watts' home in Newton, Kansas, 228 W. Eighth Street. The corners of the front porch are handsomely rounded. It is said that John, in his later years, enjoyed sitting on this porch and chatting with neighbors who might pass by.

Courtesy David Remley.

Samuel Ellison.
Courtesy Museum of New Mexico, Neg. # 9869.

Dr. Finis E. Kavanaugh. c. 1863.
Courtesy McCain Library & Archives. University Libraries.
University of Southern Mississippi, Hattiesburg.

Alexander Melvorne Jackson,
Secretary, New Mexico Territory - 1857-1861. c. 1875.

Cordelia Kavanaugh Jackson. c. 1870.

Photos courtesy McCain Library & Archives. University Libraries. University of Southern Mississippi, Hattiesburg.

End of Santa Fe Trail   Arrival in Pioneer Days of Stage Coach in Santa Fe, New Mexico, the oldest City in the United States. Reproduced from an old original photograph.
EXCHANGE HOTEL
SELIGMAN & CLEVER

"End of the Santa Fe Trail," an antique postcard.
Courtesy of Richard Levy, Albuquerque, New Mexico.

Book II

SUMMER 1859

"We had lettuce for dinner to day at the Fonda." — *Friday, 3 June 1859*

"Howe and I rose early in time to wash and get ready for breakfast—I only washed my neck but Howe washed all over I believe—I wish I could get a tub[.] I would wash myself all over once a week at least." — *Sunday, 24 July 1859*

"I took a walk with Howe, Jim, Hattie and Mr. Edgar—we went up to Fort Marcy and sat a while[,] looked through an opera glass, gathered flowers and made a boquette and threw with a sling on Sunday at that!" — *Sunday, 14 August 1859*

"The piano ... came today—arrived at last ... . They went out to meet the wagons this morning but it commenced raining and they came back. I went over to night and had the exquisite treate of hearing some fine music." — *Thursday, 18 August 1859*

"Howe does not write in his journal anymore—it seems wrong and sad." — *Sunday, 28 August 1859*

June : 1859.

Wednesday : 1.

"Well now the day is over and night passed I feel quite relieved for I had some forebodings as to how I would come out. We rose at our usual hour and went over to Squire Collins and then in company with the ladies went by for Sallie and Willie; who was down to see us at 4 1/2 o'clock but had to go back — I told Bauer of his coming down so early this morning and Mr & Mrs Bauer both plagued him about it — he was decidedly gposh, he does not know how to account for Bauer's knowledge. I got my French lesson this morning so did Howe and then we took the book up to Willie and Sallie. We had the good luck to get both an "Ollendorff" and a "Telemaque" of our own at the least the latter which was a present from Squire & Charles to father. I did not read no Spanish to Vigil any to day. I have not looked in Bayard Taylor to day. Joe Jackson and José Armijo had a fight in the Fonda to day — the former being drunk — and the dispute was originally about a game of pool they had yesterday or a day or two ago. I did not see it but they say José threw him down two or three times but was afraid to hit him for fear some of the Americans would jump in and take his part and it was so for I heard a fellow say (Sandusky) that for one would. I got shaved this afternoon and after supper I and Howe and father went over by the Governor's and had some fine music. First Sallie & Bauer in the piano then Kezer, I, Howe, Willie and Bauer the "Sounds from Home" which they played so until they had it over again. The first, second & the first violins — third flute, fourth guitar. We got through quite full — better than I expected. Howe and I played our Waltzes together — two of them. I made a rather foul out in a waltz I & Bauer played by ourselves but quite I got through it — we had plenty of music — they retardes mine very fast came. And now it's all over and I am glad. I feel considerably better. And this is the manner in which I have begun the first of the month of June 1859

Chapter 4

JUNE 1859

Wednesday; 1.

Well now the day is over and night passed I feel quite relieved for I had some forebodings as to how I would come out: We rose at our usual hour and went over to Squire Collins' and then in company with the ladies went by for Sallie and Willie, who was down to see us at 4 1/2 O'clock but had to go back—I told Bauer of his coming down so early this morning and Mr & Mrs Bauer both plagued him about it—he was decidedly gotton, he does not know how to account for Bauer's knowledge. I got my French lesson this morning so did Howe and then we took the book up to Willie and Sallie. We had the good luck to get both an "Ollendorff" and a "Telamaque" of our own at the least the latter which was a present from Squire De Marle[1] to father. I did not read in Spanish to Vigil any to day. I have not looked in Bayard Taylor to day. Joe Jackson and José Armijo[2] had a fight in the Fonda to day —the former being drunk—and the dispute was originally about a game of pool they had yesterday or a day or two ago. I did not see it but they say José threw him down two or three times but was afraid to hit him for fear some of the Americans would jump in and take his part and it was so for I heard a fellow say (Gardenhire) that [he] for one would. I got shaved this afternoon and after supper I and Howe and father went over to the Governor's and had some fine music. First Sallie & Bauer on the piano—then Rider, I, Howe, Willie and Bauer the "Sounds from Home" which they fancied so that they had it over again. The first, second & the last violins—third flute, fourth guitar. We got through quite well—better than I expected—Willie and I played our Waltzes together—two of them: I made a rather bad out in a waltz I & Bauer played by ourselves but still I got through it—we had plenty of music—they also had wine and cake. And now it is all over and I am glad—I feel considerably better. And this is the manner in which I have begun the first of the month of June 1859:

Thursday; 2.

I do not know but I do not feel much like writing to night but it is a task if I neglect once I will I will again and I do not want to become as I did once I, "let her slide" as they say. I do not see that I am improving much in writing although I write regularly every night. I, Howe, Squire and Hoxie all took a walk this morning out over the mountains and when we were on one of the peaks we saw some one else over on and ajoining one and when we went down he also went down and came towards us and it proved to be father who was out looking for a rare bush which he discovered a year before but he could not find it. We walked on together and when we came to the Baptist Church we met Sallie and Eva and I went back with them until we met Hoxie and Howe who had lagged behind and then we came on together until we came to Squire and then I and Howe went up to breakfast and we walked along with Sallie who gets teased a great deal about <u>me</u> and I about <u>her</u>. Barry Simpson was teasing her in regard to me this morning whom he over-took walking. I bought two bits worth of candy at the Bakers this evening. I did not recite in music for I had no guitar[.] Willie did not send mine down to me. Neither did we recite in Spanish—which we are making quite a poor out at. I and Dick Simpson went round to see the young ladies tonight, and we were just commencing when George Beall, and Nat McCrea came in which rather broke up our private arrangement for Dick wanted to talk with the youngest to night but that knocked it all in the head. We came away quite early—at 25 min. after 9. O'clock. Howe, father and I were all down to row tonight but we could not get the key to the lock of the boats. The ladies are not going in the morning they told me. I got my bill at the Fonda to day and I am going to settle up if pa gives me the "concave"! But I must yield myself into the hands of "Murphy"!![3]

Friday; 3.

It is now just twenty-five minutes of 9. O'clock by my watch—Howe has just left to go and see the Miss Edgars—father told him he thought he would be rushing them but he slipped off when father went up to his room. I write exceedingly poorly for a person that has had as much practice in writing as I have—I seem to myself to be getting worse instead of better. We have quite a lesson in French now it is getting very heavy or soon will be[.] we commenced reading "Telemaque" this morning[.] we read about a page in our book which I expect is [right on?]. I have not read any in Bayard Taylor for two or three days—as yet none in it to day. Eddie and Jimmie or as they call him "Bud" were over here to see us this afternoon and we went down and took quite a row in the boats together. Howe and I rose rather later than usual but went down to the pond and took a row. Willie was down here early this morning to go down to the pond and take a ride but they ladies did not go—they told me they could not go last night and so Howe and I did not get up this morning—but Willie now declares nothing can get him up after being sadly fooled twice. It has been quite a pretty day but a little windy. I played two games of billiards with Crump [this] morning and beat him both. We had lettuce for dinner to day at the Fonda. We have not recited a Spanish lesson to Mr Elison. I and Howe have candy nearly all the time to eat. I feel very good for nothing to night from some cause perhaps it is so hot—so warm and sultry. I took my violin and guitar lesson to day from Mr Bauer as usual. I have been drinking a great deal of water to night. I find that the Spring fever is prevalent out here as among other countries. I expect Howe and I will go to the States, this fall perhaps but it is "quien sabe."

Saturday; 4.

Another week has closed over my head and I am now paying my last tribute to its memory. I and Howe did not rise early to walk this morning with the ladies—it was entirely too windy and blustery so we laid in bed and had quite a fine nap. I recited on the guitar this morning and evening both— at 9 1/2, O'clock this morning and two in the afternoon. Willie and I did not recite this morning in Spanish. The mail arrived this morning and I received one letter which was from Sam Dodds and a good long letter it was. Howe received an exceedingly fine present to day from some of the Edgar family he does not know whom. I did not recite in Spanish to day as I have once said. I am getting so I cannot bear Willie—I get disgusted with him—he is somewhat egotistic in manner and conversation—he is what Fannie would call conceited or in common terms has the "big head"! I have not seen the girls the whole day. Howe received as common any amount of news papers. I have read a little in Bayard Taylor to day for a rarity. Father settled my bill at the Fonda to day which I think was $122. for three months board $105. and billiards $17. everything is settled up now I am glad to say. Howe has gone to bed and I think I will follow suit very shortly.

Sunday; 5

Well I have not passed the day as pleasantly as I could have wished. I washed and put on clean clothes as usual and answered Sam Dodds' letter which is the only one I have written. I went to church and Mr Gorman finished the second topic of last Sundays text. Howe wrote five letters. I bought a pair of kids [gloves]of Johnson yesterday for $1.50. We had quite a respectable attendance to day although not so many as last Sabbath. I have felt bad all day—pain in my stomach—I eat little dinner and still less supper. I read some in my Bible and in news papers also today. I and Howe took a good sleep this afternoon. We heard some nice music to night at Bauer's. The "Maramaras" showed as usual to day. I think I shall go to bed early for I do not expect to get along well at all. Howe says he is going to the States this fall <u>sure</u> and he says he will go <u>too</u>. <u>Pues Buenas Noches.</u>

Monday; 6.

Well I intend to write in my Journal to night before I give up to sleep however much I may have. Tis a good maxim never put off until tomorrow what you can do tomorrow [sic]. I rose with Howe at our usual hour and went walking with the young ladies. Willie and Sallie went along too. I and the rest of the class recited in French to day but we did not get through "Telemaque" and the lesson in "Ollendorff" let alone the grammar before the bell or gong rather rang. I had a very bad lesson for Bauer and the consequence was I got well scolded the first he has ever given me—but I have been unwell for two days now which was the cause of it—I have had quite a soreness in my bowels all day, and yesterday. I have read a little in Bayard Taylor and have managed to fiddle away the day in some manner. Howe has written in his Journal and gone to bed—I laid down on the bed a while but I know its no use for me to go to bed for I cannot sleep. We had quite a pleasant walk this morning I think. Oh yes! it rained a little to day for the first time in a long time if not before—I think the first since I have been in Santa Fe. The Office has been full of mexicans all day—some to see Whiting. But I have written as much as I feel like writing now.

Tuesday; 7.

I am not in the best of health at present neither have I been for the whole of this week. "<u>Yo estoy malo, en mi cabaza, y mi estomago</u>," but still I was not idle to day but I did not recite in Spanish or music—the first time I have missed since I have been taking lessons. I read sixty-six pages in Bayard Taylor. I took the usual walk this morning[.] we went down to the "Lake" as the <u>ladies</u> call alias fish pond. I did not recite to Vigil to tampaco in the the reader. We have not had a baile for a long time. It rained a little this morning or afternoon rather. I scarcely know what I am about. I beat "Old Man Jones" three games of backgammon before supper. I eat very little breakfast, also dinner and took a cup of tea with crackers for supper. They have been gambling the whole day with intermission for dinner. Eddie Edgar was over here for about an hour this afternoon and straightened up the books and papers on both tables and then we talked a while. Crump is drawing a plan of Speigleberg's store which he is going to have insured. It is now by my watch just eleven minutes after 7. O'clock and I am preparing to go to bed for my bowels are very sore my throat also and I have a slight headache— I hope I will not be unwell on Thursday night for I want to go to the concert with one of the ladies and Howe with the other. Mrs Bauer is a little suspicious of my going there for I asked how much [it] would be for <u>two</u> and she looked me in the eye and laughed. Bauer thinks he will leave next Saturday, Sunday and Monday—he is going in Amberg's⁴ train which has not arrived yet. I felt this evening a little chilly—I hope I will not have any more of the chills for they are bad enough and a taste is enough for any one I think. I got shaved the other day by John our barber. By reading Bayard Taylor's Trave[l]s and noting carefully how he writes and what he writes as he passed along I will be able to describe my trip from the States here and back also as I shall have to compose if I return to college. If I return the overland route I pass so rapidly as not to be able to take ma[n]y notes but I [am] neither certain as to going neither which route if I do. Hoxie, Eddie and Mr Edgar all took a walk about 6. O'clock this morning and then Hoxie and her "mama" went up to see Mrs. O'Bannon who I and Howe with others think is a fine lady. I borrowed some matches of "Uncle Tom" to night to light the candle. He is not the fellow in "Uncle Tom's Cabin" I think who plays so conspicuous a part. But I have written enough for a sick fellow I think. <u>Buenas Noches</u>. "<u>Vaya Con Dias</u>."

Wednesday; 8.

Howe and I agreed that when either of us went off at night and the other was out to put the key over the door and piece of the frame which sticks out and I to night came home and found the door locked and a candle lit and I call for Howe but he was not there and so I thought he had gone off and taken the key so I went in Mr Crump's room and staid until a few minutes ago when I thought of our place of hiding the key when I came out found it and came in. It is now a little past 9. O'clock and I have come in to write in my Journal. I thought to day that when I should write in my Journal that I would write every thing I could think [of]. I and Howe rose at our usual hour and took our accustomed walk with the ladies—Willie and Sallie also were along. I recited in French and in music both—Bauer is <u>very</u> kind to me and I ought to get him better lessons. Some one of the Band (Blake he told me confidently) posted some in regard to Bauer this morning which was sarcastic a little but of low origin and shows a bad disposition for its author. He was very much provoked about it—so much that he could not give Sallie her lesson on the piano. I played three games of billards to night with Crump two of which I won and lost one. Father immediately paid for it. I read some in Bayard Taylor to day—I will finish his "Eldorado" this week I think and I have already been two weeks on it and this is the third. Howe has read "Charles IV" in two volumes and [a] novel in the mean time. He has gone over to see the ladies I expect. It thundered, lightened, and rained to night. I put a wet cloth around my neck last night to cure a sore throat but it did not do it and I will try it again to night and see if I do not succeed better. Mr Crump will leave for the States in about a week he thinks. Tomorrow is the night of the great concert which I hope to attend.

Thursday; 9.

Well here I am a day behind which is something I do not exactly relish. But I went through the day with my usual gait. There will be some fine times here this fall I'll bet. Father I expect will run against Otero[5] who has scandalously mistreated him as also many other of his friends. Otero has represented the Territory twice and father himself has done more for its good than he. Mr O'Brin[6] has been elected by a convention at Mora but it is thought he will decline running and then father will take the field. I recited in music but not in Spanish—[nor?] in music since I have come to think. Bauer was getting ready for his concert. I went to the concert to night—admittance one dollar. Howe took Miss Hoxie[,] Doctor Kavanaugh Miss "Bec." The concert was a pretty fine one but too long—there were twenty pieces and they did not get through until 11 1/4. O'clock. I walked along down with the boys and spoke to the ladies and their "<u>Mama</u>"! There is considerable gambling going on in the Fonda—they are not content with gambling at night but continue also in the day. I went over to recite my music but lay down on the bed and talked with Bauer and his wife and played with "Pinto & Lola" — Willie came in soon and also took his "gain."

Friday; 10

The most fortunate thing that has happened to me this week was pa gave me two dollars to go to the show. I slept late this morning from being out late last night. The ladies said last night that they would not walk this morning so Howe and I did not get up. I played one game of billiards to day with George Waldo just after breakfast. I went to work this morning and translated the French and got the grammar and Ollendorff [why?] Howe said the Governor had gone to the [Plains?]. I also did not recite in music. I finished Bayard Taylor's "Eldorado" and commenced "El Gringo," by Davis. We had quite a nice singing school to night at the Governor's. Mrs Edgar and

O'Bannon were there, "Bec," Howe, the Squire[,] Mrs Gorman and Son and I with the family [were] there. Hoxie is sick I was sorry to learn. Howe has gone to bed. Wilbar[7] won twenty-one hundred in gold and has lost it again though. Smith and Kavanaugh both have lost.

Saturday; 11.

Like on many other occassions I neglected to post at my usual time and now it is a pleasant Sunday morning and I have just come from breakfast. I believe we did not walk this morning. I did not recite in Spanish but did in music on the violin and guitar to Mr Bauer at 2. O'clock in the afternoon. Sallie Rencher gave me a nice bouquet last night after singing. The mail arrived this afternoon but I received no letter—Howe received one with a raft of papers. Father and I went over to the baile to night at ["Tom's?] which was a very nice one too. I have commenced reading El Gringo which I will finish this next week. I and Jimmie and Eddie all played ball out in the commons, and then Jimmie and I came in sat down and had a talk.

Sunday; 12.

Well the first day of another week has passed and gone, Howe and I and father all will go in the States this fall I expect. I rose and washed my neck this morning and put on as clean clothes as I could raise and then went up to breakfast. I did not write a single letter to day—Howe wrote two or three. I read a little in my Bible and then some of the newspapers. I went to church this morning and had quite an excellent sermon although some of [it] was rather bitter against the Catholics. This afternoon we laid down to go to sleep but Eddie came over and staid a while and one and another so we did not get to sleep any. Mr Howard came down to get a draft of $150. but father had none but soon after got one of Squire Collins. Mr Howard is going to order a fine lot of jewelry and then I will get a set of sleeve buttons and some studs. Father is going to let me have the rent of the house of Doctor [Gonberth?] and Henry Mercure—so that I will have a little spending money after I have paid my board. We met this afternoon and organized a Sunday school. Miss Hoxie and her ma were there. Mr Gorman was appointed Superintendent—the Governor Assistant and I secretary and librarian. I took two books out myself which I am doubtful whether I will read through. We walked over home with Hoxie and her ma and spent a very pleasant hour with them and then went to supper. Bauer and wife called over to see us and staid a short time.

Monday; 13.

<u>The Hunt.</u>

Well all of to day has been occupied in hunting. This morning I and Howe, Eddie, Jim (alias "Bud") and his pa all went hunting. We went about three miles South—down the creek and stopped by three large trees under which Howe sat all the time and killed the most birds which was four but we soon run out of ammunition and then we came home. I did not kill a single one this morning but all the rest did. This afternoon we went again though— Howe walked this morning down and some of the way back. We got back in time to say our French this morning. We all rode this afternoon and we had four guns in the crowd. I was on Squire Collins' little gray pony.—Howe Whitings horse. Jim and Eddie on a mule and their pa on another. We killed eight birds this morning six doves and two snipes. This afternoon we killed twenty-seven more four of which I killed—all were doves but two snipes which Mr Edgar killed, I cannot kill a snipe I tried several times. In the whole day therefore we killed thirty-five—Howe killed the most—Jim the least. We had quite a nice day of it and when we came home nothing would do but that we should go over and eat supper with them—then we had a nice talk in the parlor—played two or three games of eucher—then Howe came over and got the guitar and went over and played on the guitar for them[.] I played one time—Howe several. We both came home about 10. O'clock and went to bed without posting. I read none to day neither did I recite in music to Bauer.

Tuesday; 14.

Well although I have posted once to day still I have not yet for today. I rose in time for breakfast this morning but did not get up to walk as the ladies gave us due notice last night that it would be <u>too warm</u> to walk this morning and therefore we did not rise. Willie I believe was fooled again for he not only rose but came down to us to see what was the reason we did not come and walk. I have made a full days work with the exception of the Spanish—Mr Elison is away from town. I have read some in "El Gringo" to day. Our Bugler has a new bugle I noticed a night or two ago but forgot to say anything about it. I recited in music this afternoon on the guitar none but my lesson on the violin was laid aside for another Mr Bauer gave me and a part also for Howe on the flute and Willie on the violin. Howe says the more he writes with the pen I am now writing with, which is his own—the more he likes it. I like it myself also. We had some very fine music over at Bauer's this afternoon—he called in an old german and he and Howe and Bauer all played together—there goes our bugle again. I went up to Mr Gorman's this afternoon to get him to give me lessons in Spanish which he consented to if I would instruct James his son in music on the violin or flute I am not sure which. They shewed me the likeness of one of their children—a girl who is going to school in the States—they say she will graduate in two years. She is quite a nice looking girl. Charly Thayer told me to night that he was going to leave for the States in about two weeks—his relations live in Boston whither he is going—he has a girl of twelve years old he says—his wife is dead. I went down to the fish pond to night or this afternoon rather and washed myself and put on clean socks. It sprinkled a little while I was there. Miller and Battaile are both back and the latter and Howe went over to see the young ladies. Willie was down to find out whether Howe and Battaile went over there to night. He says, George Beall is up at their house playing on the guitar. The day has been warm an exceedingly good one to catch the Spring "<u>Febre</u>"! We arranged to recite every day at four O'clock in Spanish but I think it will be different from Col Menes reciting at 4. O'clock. This is a beautiful moonlight night—just the kind to walk out with the ladies and a very fine time to "pop the question." I am going to be busier now I have taken up the Spanish under Mr Gorman but I wish to know Spanish thouroughly and correctly. I expect I will have some little beard when I go back to the States. I bought a bits worth of candy to day. I have not received a letter in a long time[.] I do not know whether the friend[s] have forgotten me or not—I am not going to write all the time and get no answers. Father bought Sis a watch and chain at Tiffany's New York of which she is very proud.

Wednesday; 15.

Well to day I have turned over a new leaf in my book of information or in my mind. This morning we did not walk with the ladies. I read in "El Gringo" some—recited in French to the Governor at 11. O'clock, we did not have time for the grammar and Ollendorff but got through with "Telemaque" in time for dinner. I got my boots repaired which cost three bits and also some candles at Joe Mercure's for four bits. I recited to Bauer in music at 2. O'clock and my first lesson in Spanish to Mr Gorman's at 4. O'clock. We are studying Coke's Grammar and Ollendorff also. I think I will learn Spanish now if I continue at it with perseverance. This afternoon I read. We called over to see Mrs O'Bannon but she was not at home so we came back. I went with Mrs Rencher, Sallie, Eva and Judge Benedict's little girl over to Mrs Jackson's who is not very well[.] she has the toothache. I saw a most disgusting spectacle this afternoon—a woman letting a young bear [sock ?] her. But the finest and most useful thing is yet to be told which was that I, Sallie, Willie and his ma all went up to Captain Macomb's[8] and looked through his telescope at the stars—the first one I ever looked through. It was an exceedingly fine treat to me and Mrs Rencher—Willie [and] Sallie laughed some and so did I. He also shewed us a sextant he had to measure the distance between the stars. Howe and Battail took the ladies down to row at the pond—he said they inquired for me but I was nowhere to be found or I might have had some fun rowing them also. The pond I think is not very full now or I would go in bathing. We looked at Saturn—the moon and several other of the stars—looking time about. I noticed a broken uneven [edge?] on the lower portion of the moon which the Captain says are mountains. But it is late and time for me to retire.

Thursday; 16.

Here I [aim?] and made a blot on the first line—a bad beginning but I am glad it is not on my character—it looks bad on a piece of paper but how much worse on a person's character. Well now as I have moralized some I will try and recount the events of the day. I rose this morning as usual in time for breakfast but took no walk with the ladies. I read this morning in "El Gringo" and have read seventy-four pages in all to day. This afternoon I got my lesson on the violin and went over and recited it to Mr Bauer but did not get any on the guitar. I intended to have gone around to see the ladies tonight but in the first place Dick could not go for he was going to row the ladies Miss Jennie & and Mrs General in the boats to night. Father and Judge Beard[9] arrived from Alburqueque in time to get some dinner—he has got things pretty well fixed I believe. I recited as usual this afternoon at 4. O'clock in Spanish with James and Mrs Gorman. I wanted to go down to the lake with Jennie and Eddie but I could not find either of them at home and therefore did not go. I read some this afternoon. I was down to see Dick after supper when I found he could not go and so I tried to get Battaile and then George Beall but he and Cogswell are going off now to play eucher with them and so I am out. It has been very warm to day, the thermometer was to 102 in the shade so Howard says who was down to see me this afternoon. The days slip away very rapidly to me. Pa is going to Taos on Monday next and I would like to go with him if I can get a mule or horse. It is now just 11. O'clock—Howe's in bed.

Friday; 17.

As I can write much faster with a quill I believe I will use it or a quill pen to night—one which Howe has made. I rose this morning as late as usual I believe and went to breakfast to begin the day with. I got and recited in French this morning at the hour as usual. It has been very warm—Bauer told me he gave me my last lesson tomorrow for he looks for the train Tuesday or Wednesday when he will leave for the States. The mail for a rarity came in to day and [I] think there was a passenger by the name of Webb[10] of whom father brought some property—that where Kingsburry keeps his store. Mr Phelps[11] has not arrived yet. Father is going to Taos Monday and I expect I will go with him—I want to. I recited this afternoon to Mr Bauer on the violin[.] I have not done anything with the guitar for two or three days. I received a letter from Seth Tuley in the mail which was all I received. I, Jimmie, Harrie and Doad Whiting all went down to the pond rowing—While there Allen with another man came and went in swimming or washing rather for they could not swim a bit it is too shallow. To night I went over to the singing at Mrs Rencher's and We had quite a house full—among new comers was George Beall, Jennie Green, Battaile and Dick Simpson. Miss Hoxie was also up for the first I expect. This is not very plain writing but sufficient for me to read and I suppose no one will ever get hold of this Journal or any of the others that I have written. I have not heard from Bettie now for two months it seems to me but perhaps it is no more than one if that. It has been very warm to day—the thermometer was as high as one hundred and twenty at 6. O'clock this afternoon. I have read a little in "El Gringo" to day. I went home with Jennie Green from the singing and she seems to be on very friendly terms with me now. I played a game of billiards to day or yesterday I have forgotten which[.] I gave gave him twenty and beat him. But I believe I will go to reading the papers I have written enough.

Saturday; 18.

Well, here I am again a day behind which I do not like the least bit. Bauer was going to hear me to day but the news by Amberg that his train would soon be in knocked my lesson in the middle of next week.[12] Bauer has been busy getting ready all day. He gave me my bill which was pretty large $55. for three months and a half. I and Jimmie, Eddie and Howe all went hunting this afternoon about 4. O'clock down the creek and after killing twenty-five birds we came back but in the night and had the fun of going to bed without any supper. Howe's horse broke loose and run about three miles (to Agua Fria) before he caught it. And then we came home fast. Harrie, Doad, Eddie, Jim—and I all went in bathing in the pond this morning which was very nice.

Sunday; 19.

And, another day has passed silently away but still not in vain for I have employed most of it profitably. I answered two letters, one this morning—to

Seth W. Tuley and one this afternoon to Mary E. Miner. I went to church this morning and the parson preached a pretty fair sermon. He gave me a Spanish and English testament—the one on one side and the other on the other. We had Sabbath School this morning at 9. O'clock and quite a fair one to for Santa Fe I think. Mrs Edgar and Bec were out this morning to church and the former to Sabbath School. I went in the afternoon also to the Spanish sermon which was short. I read some in the "American Messenger" and clear through the "Child's Paper." "Bud" was over here a short time this afternoon of two hours and a half or three. To night Howe and I went over to see the ladies and I staid about an hour and then came home and left him there talking and I suppose he will come when he gets ready. Tomorrow is the race to which I think I shall go. Father and I are not going to Taos tomorrow as we expected. There are a great many strangers here now. Pointer is here from Taos. I am not going to wait for thoughts, those that come into my head I will put down and when they cease coming then it is time to stop.

Monday; 20.

We have quit walking with the ladies or they have rather quit walking and we do not walk by ourselves. I and Howe both slept late. After breakfast we all got ready and about 9. O'clock we went out to the race that is Howe, Battaile and I and we overtook Jimmie and Eddie going down to the race.[13] We also passed the ladies going down with Squire Collins and Mr & and Mrs Edgar. I rode one of Mr Hovey's mules down. I bet $2.50 cts on the race which I won but expected to ride in some other fellow's pocket. I bet with Bill at the Fonda—I bet on O'Bannon's horse and he came throw alone for from some cause the rider of Gilchrist horse turned off the track but the judges decided that it was a fair start and that O'Bannon's won—Bill did not like to lose his two & a half but it was "a whack," as Barry Simpson says. Cotton has been training O'Bannon's horse for a long time so that he would not fly the track for if he should take a notion to the fellow who was riding him who was a mere boy could never have rode him nor held him on the track. Well here I have made my first and perhaps last bet. Father nor Howe neither bet a cent. There was quite a crowd there and every body was betting on "Don Santiago's" horse and the[y] sliped up. Barry Simpson won $75. he had a pocket full of gold and some silver dollars. We had a "fist and skull" fight this afternoon in the Fonda between Charly Thayer and Joe Jackson neither of them fortunately had their pistols on. It arose about Joe wanted to bet Charley that Howe could beat him playing a hundred points for a $100 but Charly would bet no less than $500. so Jackson could not come up to him. Charly said there were but two men in town who could beat

Cotton and Kader[.] Jackson said there were four, Howe and Clark besides the above—and Charley said they could not and so they went from word to word until they got at it. It commenced out side but came off in the bar room. Stephens[14] pulled out his pistol and said the first man that interfered was a dead man. I think Charly got the worse of it—they finaly parted them. I was over to see Mrs Jackson this afternoon and I found Howe and Hoxie both there and so I did not stay long. I and pa were both down to see Mrs O'Brin and she is quite a fine lady speaks Spanish well but is an American lady. I played four games of billiards to day and lost two of them. One with Louie Felsenthorf which I won also one with Mantel which I won and an other with Mantel and with Vigil which [I] lost. It is very warm to night and the wind blows terribly. I recited in Spanish at 4. O'clock "solo" except the last part when his son came in. Mr Phelps is in Alburqueque, and will be up here this week I suppose.

Tuesday; 21.

The Pic-nic.

We arose this morning about our usual hour and after breakfast we looked around to see if we could find horse, mule or conveyance in any method. We all had some kind of conveyance except Howe and I, and we tried to get mules of Hovey which finally he said we could have but they had saved Howe a mule at Squire Collins but which he let me have to ride so I went over and I, Jim and Mr Edgar mounted and started for the long before arranged pic-nic. The weather did not look favorable at all but foreboding of a bad day for when we started it was blowing hard. before I started I purchased a pair of kid gloves at B. & J.'s[15] for '$1.50 which I paid down. It was some time before I could manage my mule but he went along very well with Jim on a pony. The place selected for the pic-nic was the Rio Hondo—a dry creek which is about six miles from Santa Fe which is a nice ride—we turned out of the road a short distance and went up the bed of the creek for a short way where we found two nice tall pine trees with a cool spring close by. Here the ladies got out and seated themselves in the cool refreshing shade—and now while the ladies are resting themselves and "Sam" and the other drivers are tying the horses we will see who compose the party. In one ambulance came Squire Collins with "Hoxie," "Bec" and Mrs Edgar with a fine assortment of eatables and also a number of bottels and demijohns which the Governor and others thought excellent from the number of "todies" they drunk. In another ambulance came Mrs Whiting with Doad and also eatables. The third was composed [of] gentlemen only—viz—Messers O'Bannon, Edgar, Doc. Kavanaugh and Lieut Cogwell. The fourth was the

Governor and lady and Sallie which was the last. Those who came a horse or mule back are the following, Willie R.[,] Harry W.[,] Jimmie E.[,] I and Howe—the first three on horses and the last two on mules. We staid until 3. O'clock from the appearance of a terrible storm we came home. We employed the time in playing eucher, chatting taking walk[s] and rambling on the mountain sides. We had a very nice dinner but without anything to mar or interrupt [it]. It was concluded by rolling a huge stone down the mountain side. George bel came home by his watch in twenty minutes—the wagons were strung along at considerable distances apart and the horsemen along with them. We got a little sprinkled but it was all wind and no rain. We hurried home helter skelter each one breaking for home. And so ended the pic-nic which was enjoyed and complimented by all.

Wednesday; 22.

Well to day again I went through with my various duties as usual. We arose as late as usual and went to breakfast. This morning we could not find our "Telemaque" and recited in French only in "Ollendorff" and the grammar. I have read some in "El Gringo" today—a book which I ought to have finished last week but did not. We recited at 11. O'clock this morning as usual. It seems to me that I write worse and worse instead of improving any. I shaved this afternoon for the first time in considerable time—I have always got John to do my shaving when I needed any which is very seldom. It rained to day some in the afternoon. I recited my Spanish as usual to Mr Gorman this afternoon. I have played no billiards to day. To night Dick Simpson and I thought we would step over and see the ladies but we had not more than got fairly commenced before in came Hugh Smith and Doctor Kavanaugh but still I and Dick stuck to our position but soon found ourselves but mere cyphers and we very politely withdrew and left the field to the Lawyer and Doctor and I think it will be some time before we go again. Doctor engaged Miss "Bec" to go riding in the morning to select a place for the pic-nic on the Fourth of July when we will have quite a fine one—there will be music and they will have a dance. I think Dick has been slighted and as his "compadre" I feel slighted too. I do not believe Dick was invited at all to the last pic-nic. Well such is life they say. I have not read a great deal. Bauer did not get off[.] I will read more before I go to bed though.

Thursday; 23.

Reception of Hon. John S. Phelps in Santa Fe New Mexico.

To day has been quite a day in Santa Fe—one of excitement and interest to all for on to day was received the noted statesman and patriot John W.

Phelps. He has been wakeful ever to the interest of New Mexico and from the [time] he entered the Territory (he said) he [was] warmly greeted by all. We received word this morning that he would be in this afternoon at 4. O'clock Whereupon an ambulance of with four men (Judge Benedict, pa) [went out] to meet him and this afternoon at 2 1/2 O'clock the band with three, four, five or six ambulances went out to meet him with many on horse back. I procured a horse of Hovey (Major Smith's)[16] and went out with the rest. We went down the road to Alburqueque about six miles and then halted and soon Mr Phelps came up with Doctor Connelly driving him in a carriage —he spoke to all he knew and had an introduction to most of those that had gone out. Otero did not come up with him. We came along to town the horsemen riding two and two—then the Band and then Mr Phelps and behind the other ambulances. The Band played as they came along at intervals, and when we got in town they got out of the wagon and walked in before him while they played. When we had entered we went around the plaza and under the portal near the door of the Governor was a platform nicely carpeted on which was the committee who came and conducted him thither. We met the bishop[17] and one of the padres whom Mr Phelps spoke to very politely. The Governor introduced Mr Phelps to the audience when Judge Houghton[18] made a short speech—the[n] Mr Phelps in a clear, distinct and natural voice returned thanks for his warm reception which Doctor Connelly I think translated into Spanish. I then came away but when I came back he was still translating—after he finished he set down[.] the Band played and Mr Phelps was conducted to his apartments in Mr Hovey's house where father stays also. He came with pa after which I suppose he went to his room. He is quite a sensible, unassuming man and many were disappointed with his personal appearance—but the giant mind is concealed within. Hovey treated the Band and a house full of Mexicans to liquor at Rose's. I played four games of billiards to day with Vigil and lost three of them. And so the day has passed away. Tomorrow is a big day with the Mexicans.

Friday; 24.

Saint John's Day.

To day I believe is considered the biggest or at least one of the biggest days with the Mexicans and on to day they ride all do who can possible get a horse. This afternoon but stop—the morning comes first. This morning the Masons marched from their lodge to the Baptist Church where Wilbar made a very good speech. Mr Howard was very much pleased with it and said it ought to be published. There were some ladies—father with Mrs Bowler and Mr and Mrs O'Brin, Sallie and "Bec"—Jimmie Green and some others. I have played several games of billiards with different persons. Two games of billiards with Vigil lost one and won one—one with Louie Felsenthorf—two with George Waldo both of which I beat. Mr Hatch[19] is here: came in from his ranche. Kit Karson is here from Taos but is going up tomorrow, he says. The mail came in while we were taking supper—I received no letters[.] Howe got several and quite a number of papers. Father also received some papers and letters. I and Howe went over to see Misses & Mrs Edgar as singing met there. We had quite a nice time and when Mr Gorman went away we had a little dance—quadrille and eat candy. I came over for my guitar and George Beall played for the ladies. We had quite a nice time. I recited in Spanish this afternoon as usual but we have changed it to 2 1/2 O'clock. Jimmie and Eddie I expect will join the class. But I want to read the papers etc. etc.

Saturday; 25.

I have passed through another week and now on the evening of the last day I am performing the last memorial to its departed hours which if not improved as well perhaps as I might, have not passed away unimproved nor been idly squandered. I rose this morning about my usual hour and went to breakfast. We did not recite in Spanish at the appointed hour for I had forgotten the new arrangement to recite at 2 1/2 O'clock and I did not get there until 3, O'clock. We did not recite in French to day at all. Willie and Sallie both told me last night that they did not intend to recite and I did not get it— Howe read it over with all of the former which he and I had not read but missed. I finished "El Gringo" this morning and comenced a "Manual of Billiards" by Phelan the great billiard player of America. Jimmie came over and staid a while with me to night. After we had read a while we heard the Band of the Maramaras playing and we went up town and found the cause to be the arrival of Miguil Otero was the cause. I do not think he had quite as warm a reception this time as last. While up town I got in a game of billiards with Mantel—we played two games and I beat both. I then came down home and it is now about 11 1/4 O'clock. Howe went up in town to night and he has not come home yet—I do not know where he is—perhaps over talking with Hoxie. I [have] some notion of going with Battaile out to his rancho but I cannot say. Father went to Taos this morning on short notice and I did not get to go. Father and Mr Phelps danced at the baile last night until 12. O'clock I believe.

Sunday; 26.

Well to day has been a long day to me for I have been sick and in bed the most of the time. Last night about 3. O'clock I got up out of bed for I felt as though I was going to vomit but before I could get to the fire place away she went all over the carpet but which I had Uncle Tom to clean up this morning. Howe and I think of going to the States more and more every day—I expect we will go in a month and a-half or two months—and perhaps with Parker's train.[20] I am going out with Battaile tomorrow morning to his ranche—on or near Red River. I washed myself and put on a clean shirt and at 9. O'clock went over to Sunday School and acted as Librarian. I have been so unwell that I eat no breakfast nor dinner and very little supper. Jimmie has been over here a good deal this afternoon. I have not read any—I sent up for a glass of lemonade which they sent down with a little wine in it which I did not ask for but I drank it nevertheless. Howe and Battaile have gone over to see the ladies to night. Hoxie (an excellent girl) sent me over some custard and cake for dinner and although I eat but little I thank her for the kindness — she reminds me of Bettie. This is not the best pen in the world. It rained very hard this afternoon. But as I do not feel the best in the world I believe I will go to bed. One of the children of the Parson poisoned himself this evening and they were much scared. Doctor Kavanaugh says he will not die he thinks.

[Note: Pages 90 and 91, June 27 - July 17 are blank.]

NOTES: Chapter 4
June 1859

1. Born in Prussia in 1816, Augustine De Marle came to Santa Fe in 1846 as a 2nd Lt. in the Army. Governor Rencher appointed him auditor of public accounts in January 1858. He served as clerk of the territorial supreme court from 1856 to 1859. For some months in 1859 he printed the *Santa Fe Gazette*. Elected curator and librarian of the Historical Society of New Mexico in 1860, he died in Santa Fe in 1861.

An impressive looking fellow, De Marle was photographed with the attorney Charles P. Clever about 1860. Franz Huning recalled that "Aug.DeMarle" and a couple of other men "were prominent monte and faro dealers" when Huning first arrived in Santa Fe, December 1849.

See Mary Jean Cook Research, Santa Fe, 1 Apr 95; Huning, *Trader on the Santa Fe Trail*, p. 23; and *Gazette*, 16 Jan 58.

2. Neither "Joe Jackson" nor "José Armijo" has been identified.

The Armijos were a controversial family. Brothers Manuel and Rafael were Albuquerque merchants who sympathized with the South and were financially ruined at the time of the Texan invasion. Franz Huning recalled that the Confederate commanding officer, Sibley, "made his headquarters at the house of Manuel and Rafael Armijo, who were deep in the plot of the invasion, and who furnished him with all the goods he wanted, also loaned him much money, and on his retreat from the Territory went to Texas with him. Afterwards all their property was confiscated and sold at public auction."

The most famous, of course, was Governor Manuel Armijo, whose home was at Lemitar. Armijo served three terms as governor during the Mexican Period, between 1827 and 1846. For historians he remains controversial. Noting that his unsavory reputation depends largely upon the accounts of Anglo Americans whom he treated badly, Marc Simmons nonetheless remarks that Armijo "earned a reputation for dishonesty, vindictiveness, and cruelty unmatched by any of his contemporaries on the southwestern frontier."

Other members of the family who made positive contributions to New Mexico's history had unsullied reputations. For example Luis Armijo served honorably many years as judge of the Fourth Judicial District in Las Vegas. George Washington Armijo rode with Roosevelt's "Rough Riders"and later held various public offices in New Mexico from 1900 until his death in 1947. Keleher remarked of George Washington Armijo: "For decades he was a vital, colorful, picturesque figure in New Mexico politics."

See Marc Simmons, "Manuel Armijo," in Howard R. Lamar, ed., *The Reader's Encyclopedia of the American West* (New York, 1977), p. 48; Keleher, *Turmoil*, pp. 132, n. 70, 203-204, n. 38, 481, n. 1, and 504, n. 17; and Huning, *Trader on the Santa Fe Trail*, p. 69.

3. It is possible that Watts means "... into the hands of Morpheus."

4. Born in Prussia, merchant Jacob Amberg was thirty-four years old in 1860. That year he listed real property in Santa Fe valued at $1,000 and personal property at $25,000. James Ross Larkin met him in Santa Fe in November 1856, while Amberg and Dr. Connelley were business partners on the plaza. Amberg was, wrote Larkin, "a very polite German gent, with whom I supped." Thereafter, Larkin and Amberg dined together several times.

After engaging in business with Dr. Connelly, Amberg formed a partnership with his first cousin, Gustav Elsberg. The two soon moved the operation from Westport, Kansas, to Santa Fe where they rented the old Messervy store adjoining Webb and Kingsbury's on the plaza. On August 31, 1857, Kingsbury wrote Webb: "I have found a customer for Messervey's store. Amberg & Elsberg take it as it is for one year at $35.+ per month. I had to clean the store and repair the roof." Besides his business activities, Amberg, along with several other local Jewish merchants, became an early member of the Santa Fe Masonic Lodge.

Gustave Elsberg was also born in Prussia. He came to America about 1849. After living in Philadelphia and New York, he arrived in New Mexico at least as early as 1855. The partners operated far and wide in the territory as wholesalers. Franz Huning recalled: "In the summer or fall of 1857 I bought a small stock of goods from Elsberg and Amberg at Santa Fe to open a little store in Albuquerque."

In 1861, twenty-two-year-old Hermann Elsberg, Gustave's brother, clerked for a branch of the business at the copper mines near the Mimbres River. When a band of Apaches ran off the horses and mules, a party rode in pursuit. All of them including Hermann rode into an ambush and were killed.

The *New Mexican* described the firm of Elsberg and Amberg as "one of the wealthiest and most influential firms in the country" engaged in "the general merchandise business and in many other enterprises of a commercial nature." One of the other enterprises was operating a stage line between Santa Fe and El Paso. This operation became a financial loss when it was interrupted by the Civil War and Navajo raids on the coaches.

Amberg and Elsberg took in Herman Ilfeld and also helped Adolph Letcher open a store in Taos. Herman Ilfeld's brother Charles would develop one of the largest mercantile businesses in the territory. All the brothers and cousins received help, a practice of mutual support customary for Jewish mercantile families in New Mexico.

At the time of the Texan occupation of Santa Fe, the firm lost heavily. Gustave Elsberg himself lost merchandise valued at $4,300. After the War, suspicion and ill feeling destroyed the basis of the old partnership. In 1869 Gustave Elsberg sued Jacob Amberg and Herman Ilfeld; Adolph Letcher and Charles Ilfeld were also implicated. Apparently, Amberg ran away to Mexico.

Elsberg eventually lost most of his fortune and returned to clerking for various businesses in Santa Fe and for the Army at Fort Marcy. According to the *New Mexican*, he died in 1880 beloved by his friends but "reduced to comparative poverty."

See 1860 U.S. Census; Tobias, *Jews in New Mexico*, pp. 29, 46, 48, 53, 73, 74, 75; Elder and Weber, "Trading in Santa Fe," Ch. 7, p. 4, n. 10; the

New Mexican, 16 June 65, and 19 July 80; and Barbour, ed., *Reluctant Frontiersman*, pp. 101-102.

5. Miguel Antonio Otero (senior) was born in Valencia County in 1829. Both his parents were natives of Spain. He graduated from St. Louis University, then taught briefly at a college in New York State. Returning to Missouri, he studied law and was admitted to the bar.

A lifelong Democrat, Otero served as an alcalde and judge in Valencia County. He was first elected delegate to Congress in 1855 over Padre José Manuel Gallegos. Serving three successive terms, he won reelection in 1857 and again in 1859. "Everything is in a state of excitement about the election," John M. Kingsbury wrote. "The returns are not all in yet but the probability is that Otero is elected, and as a matter of course the Territory is saved."

In spite of Otero's southern sympathies, Lincoln appointed him secretary of New Mexico in 1861. Thereafter he and Judge John S. Watts, a rock-ribbed Republican, became bitter political enemies. In 1859 they fought a duel with pistols, presumably because of remarks Watts had made about Otero's family in a speech at Mesilla. In 1861 Judge Watts replaced Otero as New Mexico's Congressional Delegate.

Otero was a partner in the very successful mercantile firm of Otero, Sellar and Company which operated along the railroads throughout the Southwest. He was the president of the San Miguel National Bank of Las Vegas until his death in 1882, and was always a promoter of railroad interests, especially the Atchison, Topeka, and Santa Fe and the Southern Pacific.

He was also, it must be said, largely responsible for the passage of the New Mexico Assembly's slave code in 1859. Called by some "the Otero Slave Code," this ill-conceived law represented one of the darkest aspects of New Mexico's history.

Many New Mexicans favored the "peculiar institution," and a bill to repeal the "code" apparently brought ridicule to its sponsor. "The Hon. Legislature have got through their labors for this session," wrote John M. Kingsbury on February 5, 1860. "Keithly was speaker of the House. He introduced a bill to repeal the Slave law which was past the session before, & it kicked up a big fuss. There was strong talk of Tar & feathers &c. Turned him out of his chair and finally compeled [sic] him to resign altogether and leave town."

Otero (senior) must not be confused with his distinguished son, a Republican, also named Miguel Antonio Otero. Otero (junior) served as Governor of New Mexico for nine years as well as territorial treasurer from 1909 until 1911.

See Twitchell, *Leading Facts*, II, pp. 309-310, n. 234, and n. 441; Lamar, *Far Southwest*, pp. 104-105; and Elder and Weber, "Trading in Santa Fe," Ch. 11, p. 36, and Ch. 13, p. 14.

6. "O'Brin" has not been identified. This is clearly not the same as Judge James O'Brien, who was appointed chief justice of the territorial supreme court by President Harrison and served in that position from 1889 to 1993. See Twitchell, *Leading Facts*, II, p. 505, n. 423.

7. After being William Pelham's chief clerk, Alexander P. Wilbar was appointed New Mexico's second surveyor general, August 29, 1860. Serving until October 1861, Wilbar was eased out on charges of extravagance and replaced by John A. Clark, the political appointee of Lincoln's Republican administration.

Like Pelham, Wilbar was overworked and underfunded. His office was perpetually short of clerks, whose salaries were reduced during his year in office from $1,800 to $1,400 and then to $1,330 and even in some cases to $1,200 per year.

He also inherited all of Pelham's other problems. Not only was the surveyor general expected to evaluate the legal claims of applicants for land grant confirmation, but he was responsible for surveying and laying out the boundaries. Both of these were complicated tasks, the first requiring some legal knowledge, and the second requiring extensive field work. With over 1,000 claims on the docket awaiting decisions, Wilbar, like Pelham, was exasperated by the failure of many claimants to file. The vague descriptions of boundaries found in the Spanish and Mexican records and the hazy memories of the claimants and their neighbors added to the confusion.

To make matters worse, Congress refused to listen to Wilbar's suggestions. They ignored his requests that boundary disputes be settled in court, that a board of commissioners be established to look into conflicting claims, and that claimants be given a deadline for filing. Nor would Congress separate the responsibility of the legal examinations and adjudications from that of surveying the land. As a result of all these unresolved difficulties, Wilbar's daily life must have resembled Don Quixote's flailing away at windmills. Meaning well and working hard, Wilbar accomplished but little.

A.P. Wilbar was a member of the Santa Fe Literary Club in 1856. With L. Smith and N.M. Macrae, he served on a committee which censured territorial secretary W.W.H. Davis "in reference to the objectionable language used by him upon a previous occasion in regard to the Santa Fe Literary Club." The Club described Davis' remarks as "insulting, dirty, and intensely vulgar language" which "placed himself beyond the pale of an association with gentlemen, and by his bilingsgate slang has forfeited all claims to *any* association with the Santa Fe Literary Club." The *Gazette* agreed that Davis' remarks had been "unwarrantable" and "undeserved" and added that while "the President and Senate may confer an office upon a man, ... they cannot confer with it talents, dignity, or respectability."

Precisely what Davis' remarks were is unclear, but they were considered so offensive that the censuring committee believed "it unnecessary and indelicate to convey upon paper the foul language used by the gentleman in question." Barbour indicates that Davis had merely "ridiculed" the club when they "petitioned" him as territorial secretary for "incorporation."

From Massachusetts, Davis could treat men whom he did not consider his equals in education and ability with disdain. He looked down upon the people of New Mexico as "sunk in ignorance" and as a "people" who "love darkness rather than light." It is not surprising that he offended members of the local literary club whom he probably considered pretentious.

See Westphal, *Mercedes Reales*, pp. 93-95; Twitchell, *Leading Facts*, II, p. 314, n. 241; Horn, *Troubled Years*, p. 60; Barbour, *Reluctant Frontiersman*, p. 176, n. 109; and *Gazette*, 20 Dec 56, and 8 Jan 59.

8. Captain John N. Macomb was one of many literate and intellectually curious officers who graced the U.S. Army in the West during the 19th century. Chief of the Corps of Topographical Engineers in New Mexico, Capt. Macomb was placed in charge of developing military roads in the territory in 1857. His duties included locating, widening, and grading roads and constructing bridges. In 1859, he improved the road from Fort Union to Santa Fe. "Travel for army freight wagons as well as for civilian freighters and travelers was made easier by these improvements," wrote Leo Oliva. In addition, mail service was more often on time because of improved roads.

Macomb—a popular man whose work the *Santa Fe Gazette* and Governor Rencher praised—also improved the roads between Santa Fe and Taos, and Albuquerque and Tecolote. His development of the Albuquerque-Tecolote road was, wrote historian Robert W. Frazer, "probably the most useful wagon-road construction undertaken by the army in New Mexico prior to the Civil War."

In 1859 Macomb received a $20,000 appropriation to locate a military route from Santa Fe to Utah across the Colorado plateau to the junction of the Green and Colorado Rivers. Lt. Milton Cogswell of the 8th Infantry provided protection for the expedition which was accompanied by geologist and paleontologist, John Strong Newberry. Macomb's report ranks with a handful of superior topographical reports by military and scientific men in the West during the last century. According to historian William H. Goetzmann, Newberry himself "introduced a new level of sophistication into the study of western geology."

With the beginning of the Civil War, the Corps of Topographical Engineers dissolved, its officers drained off by other Union services, while other officers resigned to join the Confederacy. Macomb for a time commanded a balloon reconnaisance unit. By legislative act of March 3, 1863, the Topographical Corps was merged with the Corps of Engineers.

See "Executive Record Book 1," p. 211, NMRA; Oliva, *Fort Union*, p. 107; Frazer, *Forts and Supplies*, pp. 114-15; Macomb, *Report of the Exploring Expedition ... in 1859*; William H. Goetzmann, *Army Exploration in the American West, 1803-1863* (New Haven, 1959), pp. 318, 362-63, 394-97, and 431-32; and William H. Goetzmann, *Exploration and Empire: the Explorer and the Scientist in the Winning of the American West* (New York, 1966), p. 308.

9. "Judge Beard" was undoubtedly Spruce M. Baird, an old hand in the territory by 1859. A redhead known as "Colorado," Baird was described by Howard R. Lamar as "a burly Texan rancher and lawyer." He had been sent to New Mexico in November 1848 as the representative of Texas when that state claimed New Mexico to the Rio Grande. Having passed laws establishing New Mexico as a county, Texas sent Baird to supervise the organization. The new county was to have one judicial district—Baird was to be its judge—and was to send one representative to the Texas house of representatives. President Polk, a Texas sympathizer, endorsed the bogus claim.

Baird was not well received in Santa Fe. Interested in statehood, New Mexicans had no desire to be residents of merely another county in Texas. Fortunately, the military establishment sided with the local people, and the Texas efforts went awry. "There is not a citizen, either American or Mexican, that will ever acknowledge themselves as citizens of Texas," stoutly affirmed a Santa Fe newspaper.

Undaunted, Baird decided to stay on. In 1853 he and Dr. Michael Steck were appointed agents for the "Southern Apache" ("Chiricahua or Mogollon Bands" they were labelled in the *New Mexico Blue Book*). At some point, Baird hung out a shingle and began to practice law.

Among that early wave of lawyers grasping for land grants, Baird was one of the owners of the Las Animas Grant. He was also an influential member of the first territorial assembly and a territorial attorney general. He ran for Congress, but was defeated by Miguel Antonio Otero (senior). For a time he owned a printing press, purchased from R.H. Weightman, which Don Miguel E. Pino rented to print *El Democrata*, a newpaper supporting Baird's run for Congress in 1857. In 1861, Baird fervently, though unsuccessfully, defended Paula Angel, the first woman to be convicted of murder and hanged in the territory.

Though a hard worker, Baird was an unlucky man. Because of his southern sympathies, the Government confiscated his property in Albuquerque during the Civil War.

See Warren A. Beck, *New Mexico: a History of Four Centuries* (Norman, 1962), p. 142; Lamar, *Far Southwest*, pp. 88, 104, 140, and 268; Keleher, *Turmoil*, pp. 203, n. 38, 397-99, and 503, n. 108; Poldervaart, *Black-Robed Justice*, pp. 54-55; and "Indian Agents,"*New Mexico Blue Book*, p. 124, NMRA.

10. Watts is referring to the merchants Webb and Kingsbury whose store was on the plaza. Judge Watts had agreed to purchase property from Webb and Kingsbury. Chronically land rich and cash poor, however, he did not make the payment. His failure to meet this obligation caused very hard feelings, especially on the part of Kingsbury, who described the whole affair in great detail with considerable bitterness in letters to Webb. See appropriate pages in Elder and Weber, "Trading in Santa Fe."

11. Every businessman and politician in Santa Fe was looking forward to the visit of Congressman John S. Phelps of Missouri. Phelps was the type of politician who viewed the territory as a golden land of infinite investment potential. See Lamar, *Far Southwest*, p. 108.

12. The arrival of a "train" of freight wagons from Missouri over the Santa Fe Trail was always exciting news in the usually sleepy village.

13. A matched horse race was an event of unusual anticipation in a sleepy town. Everyone turned out, either to place bets or simply to cheer and to feel the crowd's pulsing blood.

There were no starting gates as there are in horse racing today. One way of starting was the "ask and answer." One rider would ask, "Ready?" and the other would answer, "Yes." Instantly the race was on.

Another way was the "lap and tap." A starting judge would "lap" the two horses then "tap" a drum or a bell or sometimes fire a pistol to alert the finish line judges that the race was on.

Typically, one owner would offer to "match" a race with another owner, that is, he would offer to bet so much—say $500—that his horse could beat the other man's horse at a certain distance. If the challenged owner agreed, then the race was "matched," and the date, time, and place would be set. The spectators were free to place their own bets on the horses. Usually a lot of drinking, bragging, and ballyhoo went on. An excellent discussion of racing in America may be found in Robert Moorman Denhardt, *The Quarter Running Horse: America's Oldest Breed* (Norman, 1979), p. 47, ff.

14. "Stephens" may have been R.M. Stephens, a thirty-five-year-old carpenter born in Tennessee. See 1860 U.S. Census.

15. Beck and Johnson's store.

16. Perhaps Major Albert J. Smith, an Army paymaster, who was in Santa Fe with James Ross Larkin in late 1856. Major Smith was at Fort Union in January, 1857. Watts mentions him elsewhere in the journal. See Oliva, *Fort Union*, p. 213.

17. Bishop Jean Baptiste Lamy, a French priest who arrived in Santa Fe in 1852, was sent to reform New Mexico's antiquated Church. Over the years, Lamy made many enemies, but also had loyal friends. Much has been written about him. See Lamar, *Far Southwest*, pp. 102-103; Twitchell, *Leading Facts*, II, p. 329, ff; and Paul Horgan, *Lamy of Santa Fe: His Life and Times* (New York, 1975).

18. Born in New York in 1811, Joab Houghton was trained as a civil engineer. He arrived in New Mexico about 1843 and went into the mercantile business with Eugene Leitensdorfer and his brother Thomas, operating from 1844 to 1848 as E. Leitensdorfer and Co. Twitchell says that the firm, its store located at the corner of Galisteo Road and San Francisco Street, "was one of the leading mercantile houses west of the Missouri River." Interested in politics as well as business, Houghton was appointed U.S. Consul in Santa Fe in 1845.

In the 1850's he got himself appointed one of three building commissioners to draw up plans for a territorial capitol. Congress then appropriated funds year after year to construct this building, a project which required twenty-five years and was finally completed and put to use as Santa Fe's "Federal Building."

Soon after arriving in Santa Fe in 1846, General Kearney appointed Houghton one of three judges of a provisional territorial superior court, along with Carlos Beaubien and Don Antonio José Otero. Bold and shrewd, though untrained in the law, Houghton presided over the court in Santa Fe County from 1846 until retiring from the bench in 1852. His lack of legal training caused a "decidedly peculiar and irregular method of entering orders, judgments, and decrees," Twitchell wrote. Thus there was endless dissatisfaction with his court's work.

Judges Beaubien and Houghton presided over the trial of the accused murderers of Governor Charles Bent at Taos, a grim affair described graphically by a spectator, Lewis H. Garrard. "American judges sat on the bench, New Mexicans and Americans filled the jury box, and an American soldiery guarded the halls. Verily, a strange mixture of violence and justice," wrote Garrard.

Like other Santa Fe lawyers of the day, Houghton coveted land grants, and served twelve grant claimants, including Cerán St. Vrain. He was firmly opposed to the extension of slavery into the territory, and was a vocal opponent of the notion that Texas owned New Mexico to the Rio Grande. He was a solid Union man,

Reappointed to the court in 1865 as presiding judge of the Third Judicial District, Houghton stirred up "the severest criticism" by his rulings to confiscate the property of well known men who had supported the Rebel cause. So great was the wrath against him, the U.S. Attorney, and the U.S. Marshal, that "on December 5, 1865, they were denounced to their faces as unmitigated scoundrels," wrote Twitchell.

In 1876, Houghton married one of Captain William R. Shoemaker's daughters.

See Hammond, *Alexander Barclay*, pp. 208-209; Twitchell, *Leading Facts*, II, pp. 272-73, n. 197; Poldervaart, *Black-Robed Justice*, pp. 21-35; Lamar, *Far Southwest*, pp. 64, 90-91, and 140; and Lewis H. Garrard, *Wah-To-Yah and the Taos Trail* (Philadelphia, 1974), pp. 238-40.

19. Alexander Hatch was one of those enterprising men who settled along New Mexico's eastern frontier in the 1840s and 1850s. There were Lucien B. Maxwell in the Rayado and Cimarron country, Samuel B. Watrous along the Mora and Sapello Rivers, and James M. Giddings, Preston Beck, and Alexander Hatch to the east of Anton Chico. A fearless man who established a farm and ranch in the heart of Comanche and Kiowa country on the northern end of the Antonio Ortiz Grant, Hatch prospered after the Army decided to use his "ranch" as an outpost. Not only was there protection for his crops and belongings, but the Army provided a ready market for his corn and hay.

Like other bold men of the day, Hatch was not above taking things that did not belong to him. John M. Kingsbury wrote his partner Webb on September 8, 1860: "At the court old man Hatch was indited [sic] for putting his brand on cattle that were proved to be stolen, 9 head and all fresh branded."

Located about thirteen miles northeast of Anton Chico along the Rio Gallinas several miles above its junction with the Pecos, "Hatch's Ranch" already had substantial buildings and a cornfield by 1856 when Captain W. L. Elliott surveyed the area for a suitable location for a military post. Elliott reported to his superiors that Hatch's buildings would give "comfortable shelter" for a company of soldiers and their horses, that there was plenty of firewood and water as well as corn enough to last the winter. The new post was established in November 1856, briefly named "Fort Biddle," but, after that name was rejected, called simply "Hatch's Ranch." Soon the village of Chaparito sprang up about three miles to the north.

Captain Elliott and his company of mounted rifles completed additional construction at Hatch's in December 1856, then stayed on until March 1857, occasionally scouting for Indians. Two Army wives, one of them with a baby daughter, spent that winter at Hatch's. They were Valeria Elliott, wife of Captain Elliott, and Lydia Spencer Lane, wife of Lt. William B. Lane. Mrs. Lane's baby was only one year old. Struggling to keep off loneliness, Mrs. Lane noted that "when we saw the ranch we felt somewhat melancholy at the prospect of spending the winter in such an isolated spot, so far from everywhere." She added that the Lanes and the Elliotts lived together in the same house with the Hatches, "a long, low, adobe house, with a high wall around it, except in front."

Occasionally occupied by up to four companies of soldiers, Hatch's Ranch was a satellite of Fort Union. It protected settlers on the plains and travelers on the important road down Conchas Creek and the Canadian River. Lt. Beale, who visited the post in 1858 and 1859, wrote of it: "When we arrived [Hatch] had already collected some ten thousand bushels of corn which he was selling at over one dollar a bushel *to the government* and others ... and being a shrewd man makes large profits by taking contracts or the delivery of grain or selling it at his house." Hatch's Ranch was abandoned as an Army post during the Civil War.

See Kenner, *New Mexican-Plains Indian Relations*, pp. 120, and 122-23; Oliva, *Fort Union*, pp. 109, and 137-39;.Lydia Spencer Lane, *I Married a Soldier*, repr., (Albuquerque, 1987), pp. 5, 53; and Elder and Weber, "Trading in Santa Fe," Ch. 14, p. 32.

20. It seems probable that "Parker's train" was in charge of one Preston Parker, born in 1840 in Independence, Missouri. Preston Parker made six

trips across the Plains between 1862 and 1865. He was in charge of wagons hauling corn to Fort Union. John M. Kingsbury mentioned Parker the freighter in a letter to Webb on May 12, 1860: "Joe Hersch ... has bought out the stock of the Jew House which I told you had started here last fall with a new stock which Parker freighted out for them." See Mary Jean Cook Research, Santa Fe, 1 April 1995; and Elder and Weber, "Trading in Santa Fe," Ch. 13, p. 55.

Joshua O. Howe, John Watts' Grandfather.
Courtesy Indiana University Archives.
Bloomington, Indiana

Chapter 5

July 1859

Monday; 18.

There is now quite a blank in my Journal of three weeks exactly. During this blank I have taken a trip to Battaile's ranche where I have had quite a fine time. I kept a journal all the time I was out there but unfortunately lost it yesterday when I was coming to Santa Fe and within ten miles of San José. I met several persons going that way and I presume it has been found but whether I will ever see or hear of it again is quite a doubtful case. I left Battaile's Ranche[1] on Friday last and came to Hatche's Ranche—I left Walkers[2] about 6 and got to Hatche's about 8. O'clock. I had received a letter from Howe saying that he would leave for the States on the 18th—I received it on the 13th and came <u>post haste</u> to Santa Fe. In my journal was a letter to David J. Miller from Walker and my own letter from Howe and I lost it on <u>Sunday</u>.

I came to San José Saturday and home to Santa Fe on Sunday. I found out a thousand things already and every thing is new and I am clear behind the <u>times</u>. The first, most important and surprising thing is in regard to Howe who has given up going to the States <u>at all</u>—has bought Doctor Kavanaugh's house for $1800. He also tells me he is going to get married to Miss Hoxie Edgar who he says was about to <u>go dead</u> when he told her he was going to the States.

He told her on Saturday night that he would leave on Monday morning for the States—and from that time she would neither eat nor sleep and he says Mrs. Edgar called him up and wanted to know, <u>what he done to Hoxie</u> to make her act so—and he laughed at her until he made her mad.

And he told her he had done nothing but he saw what was in <u>the wind</u> so went over on Sunday night and <u>proposed</u>, got her consent, her mother's and fathers and grandpa's and father's consent to the marriage which is to come off in the Catholic ceremony and on the 20th of October next when she will be seventeen and Howe is past twenty-one. He has invested his money in property and will not go to the States but after he gets married will settle down here and go to work. Squire says they can live over there—he will give them two or three rooms. The first and most important item being given I will now go to the minor ones. I find they have been having fine times since I left. A large pic-nic on the fourth of July out at the Rio Jondo where we had our first.

This morning the first thing I did was to put on some decent clothes which I [...?] up among the old clothes. I could not find my cloth coat but took one of Howe's which was a good deal better.

I played three games of billiards to day with George Waldo—I beat the first—he the second and then I put the whole three on him. I had not played a game for three or four weeks. I got some supper at Mrs Gorman's where Howe is now boarding and where I will—he charges six dollars a month. We will quit the Fonda. I and Howe do not play billiards much now. Father says he will go to the States the 15th of next month and if I wish I can go but ma says if I do not—I mean if Howe does not come in for me to stay for company for him but he will have enough company. He and Hoxie are both the best pleased folks I have seen in a long time. I have not done much to day. I went up though and said a lesson in Spanish with Jimmie, Eddie and Jimmie who while I have been gone have got a little ahead of me.

I went over to see the folks at the Squire's twice to day and with Howe both times. He has been going over there two or three times a day since I have been gone and nothing is the talk but his marrying Hoxie and George Beall "Mary" alias "Bec" whom he has given a fine gold dimond ring and with Howe has been sitting up until 12 and 1. O'clock with Bec along with Howe and Hoxie. Howe said he was afraid he could not get her but Battaile told me that Hoxie was half dead after him and they both love each other to death.

To day I eat the first apricot I ever saw and tasted. There was a little Mexican boy with some for, twenty for a picaune. Howe had a picaune and we had some—they taste something like a peach and half a little fuz on them like a peach and they are some thing also like a plum—between the peach and the plum. I found a collection of letters for me from the following persons—Bettie, Sam Dodds, Seth Tuley, Grandpa, and Mary Miner.

They tell me over at Mrs. Edgar's that I am larger—have grown while I have been gone and am also hansomer which I never in my life claimed to be. I and "Bec"[are] "muchas amigas" and she thinks a great deal of me it appears from observation. I went to see Mr. Howard to day. I judge from a sentence or two in Bettie's letter that she is going to be married before long, for she says she is going to be married or hints that she is at least I think so.

I am very well pleased with Howe's intend[ed] and do not believe he could have done better.

I wonder what Fannie and ma will think when they get the news and all the old sweethearts of Howe? I expect they will not be the best pleased in the world and especially as Hoxie is a <u>Catholic,</u> but that he thinks adds to her worth and I am sure it takes nothing away.

I had an introduction to a gentleman from San Antonio this evening over at Mrs Edgar's by the name of Violand. We had quite a nice little game of cards there to night—eucher—I and Howe were partners.

I got John to shave me and cut my hair to day[.] They have elected as Delegate for New Mexico Padre Gallegos[3] to run against Otero—father did not get nominated.

Tuesday; 19

Well this is the second whole day that I spent in Santa Fe since my return from the Rio Conchas. I rose this morning at the same time Howe did and just at breakfast time. We hurried and dressed, washed and combed our heads and then went to breakfast which was just ready. I like to board up with Mrs Gorman who I think is a fine woman—she has for borders General Pelham and wife, Col. Hopkins[4] and Howe and I—also Mr. Shaw who is some relation of theirs I think and who is a minister is also staying but for a short time. I recited in Spanish this morning with the boys and also went further than they did. Mr Gorman says I can get as much as I wish and he will hear me. I have not been to see Mrs Edgar to day whom Howe familiarly calls "<u>mamma</u>" and will be some day, soon at that. We have but one candle and that is a borrowed one but long enough for two. This afternoon late I read a little in Shakespeare's "Othello, The Moor of Venice" which is pretty good as are all his plays. I played three games of billiards to night with Phil Smith.[5] The first game I gave him thirty—the second forty and the third fifty—I won the first two and he the last. I paid down the cash. I bought a plain gold ring of Howard to day for nine dollars which weighs $5. It is twenty-one carots fine—made of the pure gold—he made it himself. I did not pay him but got it on "<u>tick</u>." Howe is over to see the ladies to night I expect—he and Mr Violand went over in the afternoon but they had company which they did not find out until after they had bolted in on them for they did not come to the door when they knocked. Howard is going to cut "J.W." or "John" in this ring tomorrow which ever I wish. I called on Mrs Rencher and Sallie this afternoon and found Mrs General there making them a call. Sallie played me "Ellen Bane" which I have been humming a great deal out at Battaile's Ranche. I am letting my mustacho grow a little before I cut it off.

Wednesday; 20.

I rose this morning about my usual hour although I read in Shakespeare until 11. O'clock—after coming home from the Fonda which was about 10. O'clock.

I learned another thing about Mr Violand—his object in coming here—which was to marry Hoxie—Howe told me this for he asked "Bec" last night or night before I believe it was whether Hoxie was engaged or not and "Bec" told him she was and he sat down under the portal of the Surveyor's Office for there is where we came for the Band was serenading Major Phelps who rooms in Hovey's "brick," house—and said he had the blues—he was melancholy and thinking about Hoxie's being gone and from him forever. He said over there in the parlor that he was going to write down to San Antonio that Hoxie was a gone case. He says he will leave shortly now.

After breakfast I studied a Spanish lesson in Ollendorff and recited to Mr Gorman at 10 1/2. O'clock.

Howe is also studying Spanish but at 5. O'clock instead of four like the Col was going at it. He is studying [Coke's?] Grammar and taking forty pages a day or at a lesson. I read some in "Othello The Moore of Venice."

I was down to see Dick Simpson who is all right and tomorrow night he and I are going to give the ladies a call. To night I played one game of billiards with George Waldo and two with Mantel one of which I beat and lost the other with the one I played George Waldo.

I have passed the day as best I knew how. Howe has passed it quite pleasantly I expect for he went over to Mrs. Edgar's this morning at 9. O'clock and did not come home until three or two O'clock and now again to night I expect he is over there—he is getting quite familiar and I do not wonder that the people talk about their getting married for Howe goes there three or four times every day. I have and am now wearing Howe's coat for I have none and cannot find one to suit me. I paid Mr Howard four dollars on my ring. He made it out of Fort Uma [Yuma] gold and I know the ring is pure gold—twenty-one carots fine he says.

Thursday; 21.

Well another day has passed and I through it—last night I finished "Othello, The Moor of Venice." I rose and went to breakfast about the usual hour. After breakfast I studied the lesson in "Ollendorff" but when the time came I was too busy to recite—Howe and I have been moving this morning out of the Office to Mr Hovey's brick so farewell old room in the Office where I have spent many a happy day. Uncle Tom helped us and father also—it took us all to carry the wardrobe. We finished moving about 12.

O'clock. We here have three bed steads & beds on two of them so that Howe and I have a bed a piece. I have played considerably at billiards to day.

This morning I beat George Waldo and then Willie and I got into a double handed game with Juan Clamaca and another Mexican and the first game they almost strung us—then they gave us twenty and we strung them—and they then gave us ten and we played off and fortunately we beat them which surprised them as much as us. I have bought a lot of things to day. At Beck and Johnson's two pairs of fancy socks at three bits a pair—two pairs of white at Henry Mercure's at two bits a pair—two pairs of drawers at Louie Staab's—I do not know how much and a pair of dancing pumps at Spiegleberg and also a broad cloth coat at $16. and a pair of kid gloves at $1.50 I expect.

To night there was a little dance at Mrs. Edgar's and I, Howe and father all went over well "rigged"—in dancing pumps. There was two ladies there who are strangers to me from Texas I believe and both married. They introduced a dance very new to me which they call, "The Lancer" and which I never danced nor saw danced before. The party was small but quite pleasant. The Band gave us music— "The Lancer" have six parts to it. The party broke up about 1. O'clock but I did not get home until 2. O'clock and Howe a half an hour later. I dropped off to sleep very soon but remember when Howe came home. Mr Violand was the most popular man with the ladies last night or this night rather. He danced the best of any fellow I ever saw and Hoxie just swung on his arm. They think a great deal of him over there. He is quite down hearted because Hoxie is engaged and got on a "tight" the first night he found it out, and he is going to leave for San Antonio in two or three days. Hoxie was with him nearly all the time last night. We had quite a fine time and I enjoyed myself very well and I think all the rest did also.

But Mr Violand came up here after Hoxie a little too late—the bird was gone and Howe is quite a fortunate fellow I think for there was a great many who wanted her. I have been reading a book to day called "Etiquette and Guide," which father purchased at Washington City I think.

This afternoon I laid on the bed and read—it is quite a nice thing to have two beds—one a piece so that we need not disturb each other.

Friday; 22.

Well I have made out to keep straight through the day. I felt some what tired when I arose this morning but [still?] I made out to get up to breakfast and took my share with grace.

I studied my Spanish lesson this morning and while I was at it Willie came over and staid about fifteen minutes.

Howe has slept nearly all day—he was asleep when Willie was here and slept until dinner time and after dinner again he went to sleep and I left him here—I do not know how long he slept. The mail came in this morning fortunately early—time for a person to answer their letters but I did not receive any so I will not be bothered with answering more than five which have been waiting for me while out at Battaile's. I have read some miscellaneously—in newspapers to night. We had apricots for dinner and supper to day. I played one game of billiards to day with Vigil—he gave me twenty-five and beat me and also Willie the same number and beat him. It rained a little this afternoon. I, Sallie[,] Willie and "Bec" intended to take a ride if it had not been so bad, but we post=poned it on account of the "inclemency of the weather!" I went up to see Sallie and she took me into the parlor and played a piece[,] then into the kitchen and showed me some preserves some of which are for me. I bought fifty cents of candles at Louie's to night. I answered Sam Dodd's letter to day but no more.

Saturday; 23.

Well I have lost no billiards to day but played two four handed games—I and "Boone" against Willie and Phil Smith we giving them twenty points. I finished "Etiquette and Guide["] to day and wrote the answers to four letters and I have one more before I am done which is to Bettie. I read some tonight in "Phelan." This morning I got and recited my lesson in Spanish to Mr Gorman. This afternoon I was writing all the time as I have said but at 5 1/2 O'clock I, Sallie, Willie and Miss "Bec" took quite a ride—we had a nice time. I rode with Sallie and Willie with "Bec." It seems to me that very little has happen[ed] to day for me to fill up my journal with.

I suppose it is because I have been in the house all day. Howe has played just a dozen games and lost two to day. Miss Edgar said I was not sociable—they think I am very sparing of myself especially when compared with Howe but then he has a right to go there as much as he pleases for he has there quite an attraction.

Howe says I am quite a favorite of Miss "Bec's" which I am glad to hear. I think I shall have to go and pay "Bec" a visit before long. I think also a good deal of her and Hoxie also.

Willie is quite in love with Hoxie or Hattie as Howe calls her and I think he thinks Hattie thinks a great deal of him, but he may slip up there. I expect to sleep nicely to night for I am tired and sleepy.

Sunday; 24.

Well the first Sabbath since my return to Santa Fe has passed over my head and a pleasant day it has been. Howe and I rose early in time to wash and get ready before breakfast—I only washed my neck but Howe washed all over I believe—I wish I could get a tub[.] I I would wash myself all over once a week at least. I wrote one letter this morning and one this afternoon—the first an answer to Bettie Ruter's and the second to sister Fannie whom I told all about things that were going on here and how we were all getting along.

I went to Sunday School today at 9. O'clock. I believe is the hour and I taught Willie's class—Jimmie Gorman. I also went to preaching and so did Howe and father. I went in the afternoon but Howe nor pa did not go—we had very few in attendance. I learned one or two new words but did not look at but two of them. Willie R. was here twice to day—once by himself this morning and once this afternoon with Howard whom Howe tell[s] me has his wedding ring made out of placer gold.

Jimmie Edgar has been over here twice or three times to day. Once this afternoon a little before Willie and Mr Howard. Father and Mrs Bowler came in while they were all in here and stayed and talked a while to Howe in Spanish, and then her and father went away again. I have eight letters for the mail but two of which I am sorry to say laid here all the time I was gone. For next mail then I have two for Seth W. Tuley, two Mary Miner[,] one to Bettie, Fannie, Grandpa and to Sam Dodds one. I have the largest mail I have ever written yet. I read some in a Sunday school book and so did Jimmie E. for he came over and staid with [me] just as Howe went over there. Howe says he is going to be more study next week and is not going over there so often. He and I went over there today for dinner and they had a dinner just to suite Howe and I—it was plain and good and substantial—we talked to each other in Spanish which the girls did not like a bit but wanted us, to, "stop it"!!! This is their great word. The band played in the plaza this afternoon and I went over and sat on the step of the front step with Jimmie and Mrs Edgar. I took Hoxie over some envelopes this afternoon. As Howe was going to supper a little white dog run out and bit him just before the eyes of some women to whom he had politely bowed. But I [have] certainly written enough for to night. I have not heard from my journal nor Miller's letter which I lost not far from San José.

Monday; 25.

Well the first day of another week has passed and now at the close let me see what I have done. I got my Spanish lesson this morning and recited it as usual.

Howe's shooting last evening was rather a more serious affair in the end than anticipated for he shot a man—Mexican I believe in the nose and the surgeon of the Hospital took it out[.] of course the shot was done accidently and I do not suppose there will be anything done by the Mexican or his friends. Father went over I believe and saw both the man and the bullet that came out of his nose. It was reported up in town that I had shot at a dog and hit a child which was not expected to live long. Father came down from up in town in quite a hurry to learn the straight of the matter and he looked all he could when he told us what he had heard up in town about the matter.

Having settled this matter now we can proceed to the rest of the gossip, if we have nothing else to fill up the paper with. Last night's journal I wrote with a stell pen and to night I am writing with Howe's fountain pen. I rad some in a new paper this afternoon, "The Times" and also began the, "Life of Fulton," by Reigart. The book which Mr Howard sent to New York for— he has one just like it only the cover or back is of a different color.

I read some forty or fifty pages in it this afternoon and think I shall read some in it to night.

I was over to see the ladies this afternoon but did not get to see them[.] they were dressing to go out shopping to Mr Kingsburry's I believe is where they were going and I did not get to see any one but that paragon of a woman (in Howe's eye) Mrs Edgar with whom I had a talk of a half an hour when I left. "Bec" and I and Jimmie had intended to have gone riding this afternoon but it rained—quite a rain it was too. I and father eat together to night for the first time in a long time—he went with General Pelham I think or at least he went to see Mrs. Pelham and staid to supper with us.

I have played two games of billiards today with George Waldo even and one with Charly Thayer which I lost, at the discount. I beat George one and he me one.

Jimmie Edgar has been over here two or three times and Harry Whiting twice. Doad and Cora once who were here this morning. Howe brought down some candy which they "pitched into" with considerable "gusto."

I will close with a maxim I read the other day —
    "He that in writing would improve,
    Must first with writing fall in love."

Tuesday; 26.

"The day has passed and gone"—I think I have heard that before. I rose this morning in time for breakfast. Howe stayed all night over at Mrs. Edgar's—there was quite a number of Indians there and she wanted some man in the house.

Last night Hovey had a meeting at his house for Otero I suppose—they were most all drunk and some were talking and some speaking and the Mexican Band at intervals would strike up and then Clever[6] would go to dancing.

After they had had a speaking the band marched up town and when they came near the Fonda, Baca the Sheriff and Minks commenced shooting in the crowd and shot Andrew Tapia[7] I think in the leg and hand and he and two or three more cleaned the crowd out. Minks he run like a fine fellow they said for if they had caught him they would have given him a good lynching. I read considerable in "Life of Fulton["] last night after I went to bed, but I must employ some time on to day with my Journal. Howe and I went up to the Fonda early this morning and played a game of billiards and then he played with Armstrong. He gave me this discount but I cleaned him at it.

I got and recited my lesson in Spanish this morning as usual. I read some in "Fulton" to day and for dinner we were invited to Mrs Edgar's where we had a nice dinner where we had the pleasure of seeing Hattie officiate at the head of the table. Among other delicacies we had oyster pie for supper. We went with Hattie, "Bec" and Mrs Edgar this afternoon at 2 1/2 O'clock over to see Mrs Jackson whom we found I believe in good health but Mr Jackson she said had not good health at present.

The girls bought some candy at Louie Stabb's which we were constantly eating. They asked us to stay to supper but we very politely declined, but got some at the Parson's.

Father has gone over there to night to see the folks. Howe is snoring in bed but I think I will read some yet before I go to bed. The wind is blowing hard tonight. We had a beautiful sun set to night—Howe and I were out looking at it a long time.

Wednesday; 27.

To day has passed and pretty much the same old "seven and six." I studied and recited the Spanish for the Parson. I generally recite two of the lessons in "Ollendorff" at one lesson. I am ahead of the class which consists of Mrs Gorman, Mrs Pelham, Jimmie Gorman, Eddie and Jimmie Edgar. They I believe take but one lesson at a lesson and consequently do not get along as fast as I do. I play a little on the guitar every day. I have read some in Fulton every day for the whole week I think and I expect to finish it this week.

I have not been over to see the ladies to day but I cannot think and say the same for Howe.

I have played two and a half games of billiards to day—one with father this morning at the discount a half of a game with Willie Rencher and one game to night with George Waldo. I lost all but the last game.

I took a little "nap" this afternoon which did not do me any good that I know of. I got caught to night—while I was at the Fonda playing billiards. It rained quite hard and thundered and lightninged terribly—more than I ever heard in the States. But it did not last long for in a half an hour I came home and now it is no more than 10. O'clock.

Howe has gone to bed and it will not be so terrible long before he will have a companion and what then will become of John—or more familiarly Johnnie! Howe and I have always eat together slept together and been together nearly all of our lives.

My heart almost fails me when I think of leaving Howe perhaps forever but still I will not think of that now. I feel some what melancholy to night, but I do not know why. Bettie is going to be married to and I do not know how many more[.] perhaps Mary may be married by the time I get back home but it all goes in a life time they say.

Eddie and Jimmie were both over here a little while to day. Jimmie wanted to buy—I mean borrow our horse but it rained so he and "Bec" did not go riding.

Thursday; 28.
I think the rainy season has set in for it has rained every evening this [week] I believe and now again to night it is raining. I rose about my usual hour this morning—we take breakfast at 6 1/2 O'clock if we are there in time. I studied and recited my lesson this morning to the Parson. I put on a clean shirt this afternoon and went up in town. I played checkers with Ed Rose[8] —three games—I beat two of them and the third was a draw game. about 4 1/2, O'clock Vigil came up and he and I took quite a spree with billiards—we played four games and I lost one of them—he gave me twenty-five—we played on the upper table with the big balls but I can do better I think with the small balls and on the lower table. I have played some on the guitar to day and also read some in "Fulton" which is good and which I expect to finish this week—"sin duda." We have some very mean candles which we bought at Louie Stabb's but to night we got some at Frank O'Bren's store.[9] Howe played two games of billiards or three rather to night with Charly Thayer who beat him and always has "playing off."

Howe, father, and I, all came down from the Fonda together but Howe did not get all the way[.] he stopped to see his sweetheart. I called up to see Sallie this afternoon[.] her ma has the neuralgy in her face I think but is getting better. They intended to have a dance tomorrow night for tomorrow is Willie's birth Day but cannot on account of Mrs Rencher's illness. Sallie played me "Ellen Bane," "We have lived and loved together" and, "Thou hast learned to love another."

While I was at the front door talking, for Willie and [I] had intended coming down to see the girls—Mrs. E.[,] Hattie and Mr Violand and Bec and Howe all came along down the portal. "Bec" she said for me to come and go down home with her and I said I would in a moment and she stopped and asked Mrs O'Bannon about Mrs Rencher—I said a word or two to Willie and then I walked along down home with "Bec," where Howe, Hattie[,] Mr V. and Mrs E. were all standing. Howe and I bid them good by and came on up to supper. I will read some I expect to night in "Fulton."

Friday; 29.   **Son las doce menos cuarto**

I have just come from the Fonda where I have been playing billiards with Louie Felzendorf. We played three games[.] he beat the first I the second and he beat me playing off.

My billiard bill for this week is $3.50 or 75 I think some where near that. I expect to go to Alburquerque on next Monday—I told Willie Rencher that We were all going to leave Santa Fe on next Monday and <u>he</u> supposes for the States. I finished "Fulton" to day—read eighty-seven pages. Howe and I eat supper over at Mrs Edgar's to night and there was introduced [to] Mr Boogdan whom they call "Dick" and Mr Violand was there whom they call "Nick." We had quite a fine supper and oysters among other delicacies. I took a ride this evening on father['s] $150. horse[.] I rode out on the Taos road to the pole set up in honor of Col McComb who by aid of the government greatly improved the road. I loped all the [way], most, there and back. I have played some on the guitar to day and played to night for Mrs Edgar on the guitar a little and botched things up rather badly. But as I am tired, sleepy and it is late I will cease.

Saturday; 30.   **Son las doce menos ses minutos.**

Here I have come home later than I did last night but I did not come out so badly. I played two games with Mantel both of which I won. I rose about my usual hour. Howe and pa said that night before last I hollowed in my sleep—so loud that it woke both of them up instantly. I studied and recited my lesson to the parson although Saturday. Howe did not recite—the mail came in yesterday and ever since Howe has been answering letters. I have been reading in newspapers all day.

I have been over to the ladies none to day but I stopped this afternoon for they beconed for me to come over. Willie wanted me to ride this afternoon with him but I got off from [it] for I took a ride only two days ago. I commenced a letter to ma this afternoon which I think I will copy before I send. Howe played three games to night—with Smith—beat two. Doctor

Kavanaugh won a race on his horse and sold him for $500. He has returned. But it is bed time I begin to think.

Sunday; 31.

I cannot write with a pen in the house to suit me although there are three gold pens and a box of Gillots 303.'s, which are considered the best stell pen in the United States and I am now writing with one of them. I rose this morning five minutes before breakfast time and in that time washed my neck and ears—face and hands and put on clean clothes. Howe had got up before me and was half dressed when he awoke me. I went to Sabbath School this morning and had two scholars—Willie's class namely Jimmie Gorman and Eddie Edgar. I also went to church and on account of the parson having a bad cold Howe started the hymns, and he took his flute to be sure to be of the right pitch. The Parson preached from Job. 14. chap. 14 verse "If a man die shall he live again"—he has divided it and is going to make two sermons from it. We were invited over to Mrs Edgar's for dinner, and a very fine one we had. I and Bec are going to be "muchas amigas"—in fact we are now. Howe, father, and I, are all going down to Alburquerque tomorrow—I and Howe in the mail.

I read some in "Learning to Feel." To night Jimmie was over here and I amused him by printing and writing fancy with the pen. He carried off three or four sentences I wrote in spite of me which had the following written on them, "Beck is a mighty poor girl!!" "Hattie is worth nothing!!" "Mrs Edgar is worth all of Santa Fe," and "Sallie is my Sweetheart—(signed) John Watts (L.S.)." Jimmie is tickled to death almost over the last which he snatched out of my fingers. It is now 10 1/2, O'clock and Howe has not put an end to his stay yet. Father says he wants to get up early in the morning but I think it is time I was getting to bed myself.

NOTES: Chapter 5

1. Battaile had a ranch in the Rio Conchas-Canadian River country of eastern New Mexico.

2. "Walker's" has not been identified. It may have been a privately settled ranch on the eastern frontier, like Hatch's, Beck's, or Giddings' Ranch. See Kenner, *New Mexican-Plains Indian Relations*, pp. 120, 121, 122, and 123-24.

Possibly the "Walker" who wrote the lost letter was Captain John G.

Walker, Regiment of Mounted Rifles, who had arrived at Fort Union in November 1858. Captain Walker was commanding officer of Fort Union for a time in 1859. See Oliva, *Fort Union*, pp. 105, 157, 229, 230, and 574.

Perhaps this was John Walker, an Indian agent in 1857. See *Register of Officers and Agents ... of the United States* (1857), p. 82.

3. Padre José Manuel Gallegos, a defrocked priest from Albuquerque, had entered politics and was elected Delegate to Congress in 1853. Hubert Howe Bancroft described him as a leader of the provincial faction in the Catholic Church which opposed the cosmopolitan faction of Bishop Lamy and his French priests. "The struggle was largely one between two factions of the catholic church," wrote Bancroft, "one headed by Bishop Lamy—of French origin—and his new clergy, and the other by the Mexican priests, who regarded the new-comers as intruders." Opposed by ex-Governor William Carr Lane in a cliff hanger, Padre Gallegos won the election of 1853 by 4,971 votes to Lane's 4,526.

Although Gallegos had nativist appeal and influence in New Mexico, he was not prepared to serve territorial interests in Congress. Not only did he have no grasp of the political labyrinths of Washington, but he knew little English. Thus his service was limited, and he was replaced in 1855 by the St. Louis educated Miguel Antonio Otero (senior), a merchant-politician much better equipped to serve in Congress.

See Bancroft, *Arizona and New Mexico*, p. 650; Twitchell, *Leading Facts*, II, p. 295; Lamar, *Far Southwest*, pp. 102-106; and Beck, *New Mexico*, pp. 215-16.

4. "Col. Hopkins" has not been identified. Apparently he was a merchant, for Kingsbury noted in a letter to Webb, May 28, 1860, that "Magruder ... has since sold his little stock to Col. Hopkins, who will carry on the same store. His sale amts. to near $1,500.+." See Elder and Weber, "Trading in Santa Fe," Ch. 13, p. 57.

5. "Phil" Smith was probably Philip Smith, born in Virginia, a twenty-year-old clerk in the surveyor general's office. See 1860 U.S. Census.

6. Howard R. Lamar described lawyer Charles P. Clever with one adjective—"wily." Governor Edmund G. Ross characterized the Santa Fe lawyers of Clever's day as "Americans possessed of some legal lore with a large amount of cheek and an unusual quantity of low cunning and astuteness that always had an inclination to run in a crooked direction."

In about 1860 Clever was photographed with Augustine De Marle. Clever does not have the look of a man one would want to trade horses with, although in fairness to Clever, no sensible man would have dared trade horses with *any* New Mexico lawyer of that day.

Born in Cologne in 1827, Charles P. Clever immigrated to America in 1848. He then traveled the Santa Fe Trail with the same government train that brought Franz Huning out from Fort Leavenworth in the fall of 1849. Both Huning and Clever had signed on as bullwhackers. The train had thirty-two wagons, most of them with six-yoke teams. Huning recalled of Clever, however, that "the train had not been on the road more than an hour when my companion Clever was found to be so utterly worthless as a whacker that I had to take his team."

Arriving in Santa Fe about Christmas Day 1849, Huning found Clever, who had left the train several days back, "already installed as barkeeper in a beerhouse kept by Peter Deus." Since work was hard to find, "it was therefor [sic] necessary," Huning wrote, "that we should live with the greatest economy, so we clubbed together and rented a room, three or four of us, and cooked our own meals." Clever worked for Eugene Leitensdorfer, then became a business partner of Sigmund Seligman. According to Twitchell, the firm of "Seligman and Clever" operated from sometime in the fifties until 1862 (Tobias dates the partnership from 1854 to 1861). A photograph taken possibly as early as 1860 from the southeast corner of the plaza shows the Exchange Hotel on the left, and, across the street, the "Seligman - Clever" store. During these years, Clever was also a member of the Santa Fe Literary Club.

After reading law, Clever passed the exam in 1861. Having served as Clerk of Santa Fe County, he was appointed U.S. Marshal in July 1858. In 1861, Governor Connelly appointed him adjutant general. Loyal to the Union, he was Colonel Canby's adjutant at the Battle of Valverde. Later, he was appointed territorial attorney general under Governor Robert B. Mitchell. In 1862 he was appointed, along with Facundo Pino and Kirby Benedict, to a board of commissioners to codify the territorial laws.

Politically ambitious if not savvy, Clever provided the legal backing for Governor Mitchell's attempt to declare the laws passed by the legislature and signed into law by acting governor Arny in Mitchell's absence "illegal and invalid." As Mitchell's attorney general, Clever declared Arny's laws "null and void." Although he may have had a point, there could not have been a way more certain to create lifelong political enemies. When Mitchell was fried by his opponents and by the *New Mexican,* Clever also got blistered.

Enemies acquired during this political power struggle stalked Clever for the rest of his days. He was elected Delegate to Congress in 1857 by a ninety-seven vote majority. The Governor as well as H.H. Heath, the territorial secretary, certified that he was the winner. However, Heath also signed a certificate indicating that the election was fraudulent, and the legislature passed a supporting resolution. Thus Clever, who had already been seated in Washington, found himself turned out in February 1869, by his opponent, Colonel J. Francisco Chaves. He got no help from his old enemies back home. As late as October 1872, disbarment proceedings were held against him in the district court of Bernalillo County.

Described by Twitchell as "a man of great strength of character" who "had many friends and many enemies," Clever died in 1874.

See Lamar, *Far Southwest*, p. 105; Twitchell, *Leading Facts*, II, p. 411, n. 337; Huning, *Trader on the Santa Fe Trail*, pp. 10, 20; Bancroft, *Arizona and New Mexico*, pp. 716, 719; Remley, *Bell Ranch*, pp. 39, 50, 316, n. 59; Tobias, *Jews in New Mexico*, pp. 46, 86; Horn, *Troubled Years*, pp. 119-20, 124, 125-26, 129-30; *Gazette*, 20 Dec 56, and 24 July 58; and Elder and Weber, "Trading in Santa Fe," Ch. 13, pp. 2, 3, n. 10. Elder and Weber indicate that the firm of Seligman and Clever leased this property on the plaza from Colonel Fauntleroy in February 1860, effective June 1 of that year. This building had previously housed the Webb and Kingsbury store.

7. "Andrew Tapia" has not been identified. "Minks" was probably Prussian born John H. Mink. A probate court clerk in Santa Fe, he was one of several men calling themselves "Democrats" appointed to attend a convention to nominate a candidate for Delegate to Congress in 1853. In July 1858, he was appointed county attorney for Santa Fe County. The *Gazette* announced that Mink was "competent for the position ... and we expect will give satisfaction in his official acts." In 1860, at age forty-one, he owned real property in Santa Fe valued at $2,000 and was a clerk in the surveyor general's office.

Mink was short on luck, or courage. In 1853 Joe Collins soundly thrashed him on the streets of Santa Fe, after which he spent the night guarded by twenty Mexican friends because he was afraid, according to John M. Kingsbury, that "the Americans wanted to kill him and he expected them that night."

On September 25, 1861, as a captain of New Mexico mounted volunteers, Mink surrendered his entire command to a Confederate force of about 115 men in a skirmish at Cañada Alamosa near Fort Craig. Although the Rebels paroled the enlisted men, they held Mink and Lt. Medina prisoners.

See 1860 U.S. Census; Tobias, *Jews in New Mexico*, p. 47; Twitchell,

Leading Facts, II, p. 371; Elder and Weber, "Trading in Santa Fe," Ch. 1, p. 8, n. 28, and p. 9, n. 34; Lamar, *Far Southwest*, pp. 100-101; and "Executive Record Book 1," p. 196, 3 Aug 1858, NMRA.

8. Probably Edward Rose, in 1860 a twenty-year-old clerk, born in Iowa. See 1860 U.S. Census.

9. Mentioned elsewhere in the Watts journal, Frank "O'Bren" was probably Frank O'Brien, who kept a store in Santa Fe.

Chapter 6

August 1859

Monday; 1.

I did not go to Alburquerque to day as I expected although I got ready and went up where the stage was and thought I was going but things turned out as follows. Father had intended to ride his horse down and let me go down in the stage and ride him back but when the stage was ready to go he saw the stage was almost full of passengers so he said he would go down in the stage and consequently I did not go. I did not recite in Spanish to day to the Parson on account of my thinking that I was going to Alburquerque.

This is the kind of a hand Seth Tuley writes a large round hand which is almost straight at least as much so as possible. I borrowed a book of Mr Hovey this morning after I came back, "New York Boarding Houses" which Mantel says is not worth the paper it is written on while Howard says it is a good thing and what I have read I think is pretty fair. I played some on the guitar to day.

Willie was over here this morning and sat a while—no it was this evening I believe—Jimmie Edgar was over here also. I fooled Willie the best though—I told him two or three days ago that I, Howe, and pa were going to leave these parts on to day and he thought that I was going to the States and he told his ma so and she said she was very sorry that I was going away and that she had intended to make me a cake before I went but was sorry that she was unwell and could not fulfill her desire but she will have an opportunity yet if she wishes. I am sorry that Willie told his ma for it I find has got like every other secret scattered all over town. Mr Jackson asked me this after-noon if I had not intended to go to the States to day—he said he had heard it but I soon explained it to him. I took a ride this afternoon with Bec down the Alburquerque road with Eddie also. To night about 9 1/2 or 10 O'clock Bec sent over for me[.] she said Howe and Hattie had gone to Mrs Jackson's and she was alone. I went over and there was nobody but Mrs E. and Bec and I went in and had a fine talk until Hattie came when some strawberries were [handed?]. When I came home I went in and told Mrs E. good by and there was H. and Howe on the sofa together and [I] immediately walked out but she run after and caught me at the door and said I must tell her good by and what a smack I gave and received from both girls?! The subject is so interesting that I cannot stop yet. I went out and sat on the front step with Bec for a half an hour I suppose and I asked her to let me kiss her and she said she would when I went to the States for then I would be her brother but I did not like to be put off in that kind of a style and when I had kissed Hattie she did not want me to go home without first kissing her which I did—both of them were real busses for Howe and Mrs Edgar both heard both kisses I expect for Howe he broke out in a big laugh.

They were kisses on both sides for I kissed Hattie and Bec's cheek and they made mine pop. I think I will be able to live off of those two kisses for the next week or two. Howe was tickled and Mrs E. too I expect. Jimmie and Eddie had both gone to bed. Although the subject is engrossing and exceedingly interesting yet I can talk of it always and although Howe has not yet come home I at least will go to bed. I lost three games of billiards to day[.] Charly Thayer beat me playing off three games.

Tuesday; 2.
I believe I will write a little more of the round hand order. Every thing went off I believe as usual to day and one good thing I have played no billiards today. Howe collected rent off of Doctor [Guberth?] to day $20 dollars all of which I did not get for father had a little there that the Doctor said he had charged to either Howe or I and so he took that out. I am going to have things better arranged than that if I can. I studied and recited to the Parson this morning in Spanish as usual. Jimmie, I, and Eddie went hunting this afternoon in one crowd and Howe with Mr Howard in another. I do not know whether they killed any thing or not. I killed eleven doves and one snipe and Jimmie one dove—his gun was dirty and he could not get it to go good was the reason I killed so many more than he did. I sat down under a bank and killed most of mine. The first shot I made I believe was the best shot I ever made. I killed a crow or raven flying—he tumbled down so pretty. When we got ready to go home Eddie['s] horse got away and we could not catch him but drove him (John Wards pony), along the road but he soon got to running at random through the fields of corn, wheat, etc., of the "rancheros" at which they got very mad and came out hollowing at us and wanting to know why we did not go in the road to which I told them as well as I could that the horse had broken loose and we could not catch him[.] at

last though we got him in one of the Mexican's corralls and bridled him and then Eddie had no mercy on him from there home.

There was a Mexican with us all the afternoon while we were shooting. When we first went down it was windy and sprinkling in the bargain but it soon cleared off and along toward night the doves got thick which I killed almost every shot. We shot with pistols out there—I with my little five and Eddie with a six shooter—he beat but I believe it was a big "scratch" for he "plugged" center a hole in the side of a bank which we were shooting at— I struck in the edge of it. We came home in a gallop. Squire Collins came home this evening or morning rather I believe[.] when he approached the Indians they all run and he came back without doing any thing. Howe is over there now and has been a great deal of to day. I did not get any supper to night but that is not going to hurt me I guess. Howe told me last night that Brogden told H-e that he was dead in love with her and wanted to marry her—also that Lieut Cogwell wanted her and told her that if she would have him he would throw up his commission and go to the States but she would not do it and Howe has got her at last and a good wife she will make no doubt. I suppose I might as well finish out this page now I am so near. We got sprinkled a little before we came to the hunting ground. I cannot keep thinking of the two nice kisses which I got last night. Jimmie is going to the States with me to go to college and board at home with me at least he says so that his Grand pa said he could go and he says his word is law, Jimmie is almost tickled to death over it. I do not know when we will go—after the wedding I suppose.

Wednesday; 3.

Well I did not write at my usual time for this reason[.] Howe and Mr Howard went to San Domingo to see a dance of the Indians—the "Green Corn" dance I believe and Jimmie E came over and staid all night with me and therefore I postponed writing. I studied my Spanish but forgot entirely to recite and in this manner I had a little time to spare and I thought I would go up in town and I went to the Fonda and found George Waldo and we went at it[.] the first game he put on me with two liquors—the second [he] also beat[.] I cleaned him the third and then we played off everything and I beat him. When I got through it was just <u>dinner time</u>! My lesson consequently suffered and the Parson said he would have to put a black mark for to day and I said I guessed we would. Every thing I believe went on as usual and the same as if Howe had been here himself. I went up to see the Governor in regard to reciting French and he said I could continue it as soon as Mrs Rencher recovered and then he would have the class every day. I also called to see Mrs Jackson and sat a while and about dark came down to Mrs E-s and sat and talked to H- and Bec—while we were talking Doctor Kavanaugh came in and Bec showed him a book she had as a present from her father to [...?] —not [...?] on!! I came home about 9 1/2, O'clock and Jim with me. H-e came out and down to the end of the portal with us and kissed and told us both good night as brothers!! Jim and I sat and talked a long time—then undressed and talked on the bed with our heads at the foot and the candle burning—and finally we blew out the candle and after talking a little went to sleep and were free from the noise, bustle, and trouble of life.

Thursday; 4.

Oh! NO! we did not go hunting to day—this sentence was suggested by "compadrito Santiago" or Jim who is now sitting by my side and chatting—he is going to stay all night with me. This morning I rose in time for breakfast and wakened Jim tambien. Well I commenced writing in my Journal to night but, it was not altogether right nor polite for me to write so much with company for I had just written for yesterday for which I was behind so I put off writing until tomorrow. I have played no billiards to day nor done much of any thing. This afternoon Jim, Eddie and I all went hunting and in the rain at that and after we got down to the trees three miles below it commenced raining pretty hard so we got off and hitched our horses and went to the trees which sheltered us but it soon stopped and we went on down to our accustomed place. It was quite a pretty evening but we all but Eddie had bad luck for we could not get our birds[.] we would cripple them and they would fly a little [way?] off and fall but we could not find them. I got two that flew off and dropped and killed two that never flew. I killed four, Jim two I believe and Eddie seven or eight. I have got in quite a way for writing this back round hand—Jim says he likes it and I do too pretty well. We got back about dark and Howe and Howard came in from San Domingo a little before us—Eddie shot and hallooed at him but they would not stop for us. I rode "Lucy"—a large fine mare mule—with Eddie on behind me and Jim rode John Wards pony. Howe went over there immediately and kissed them all around I believe that were concealed from public observation. H-e as soon as she saw Howe coming ran back in the parlor for we were all there in the front door and on the steps[.] so Howe told them good evening and went on in the parlor where he kissed and told H-e good evening—"you bet"! I went up with Bec to Mrs Renchers and Willie and Sallie were sitting out playing on the guitar. We sat there a while (Howe went up with H-E) and then came down to Mrs E-s. W & Sallie sat there "a while" and then went home[.] then I sat there a while with Bec and Mrs E. and Jim—we all came over then and went through our rooms and the whole house. Mrs E. took "Etiquet at Washington" home with her. "A Dios."

Friday; 5.

Well here we are again and Jim to stay all night with me "otra vez." I studied and recited my lesson to the Parson this morning at 11; O'clock. I have played no billiards to day nor did much of anything it seems to me. The morning passed away quite rapidly it seemed to me. I went up in town this afternoon and played three game of checkers with Ed Rose and he cleaned me for the first time in his life I think. The mail came in this afternoon late but I received no letters from any one and I was not very badly disappointed. Howe received two letters -- one from Belle [Ryans ?] and one from "Pug." I and Bec and Eddie all took a ride this afternoon and I rode our $150. horse "Kit Carson," and the way he goes along nice is a sight. I made some [...?] which Howard gave me [a] long time ago and Jim gave me the bottle to put it in. We had quite a nice ride and we all enjoyed it—Bec rode Kingsbury's horse and Eddie John Wards Pony. I went over to night to see Bec—Ht-e is not well she has the headache—Howe did not go over there to night. Bec, Jim and I all had a nice little chat together and then Jim came over to stay all night with me and as he is wating for me I will be short to night.

Saturday; 6.

Well I feel rather like if I was in bed I could sleep. I studied and recited in Spanish to the Parson this morning at the usual hour. I played billiards with Juan Tapia this afternoon four games[.] he lost two and I two so we came out even. Howard has received some fine jewelry of which I have had my pick and I expect I will have more jewelry than I can pay for. I picked out sleeve buttons, studs and a ring but I am as yet doubtful whether I will take all of them or not[.] I have no thirty dollars about my old clothes. I wrote a letter to Sam Dodds to day in this back hand style like Seth Tuley's writing. I have been reading to night. Jim E- was here but would not stay all night. Howe has gone to bed without posting and I am going to be very moderate, for I am tired and want to go to bed.

Sunday; 7.

Well my journal for last night seems to have been quite slim and as for tonight I do not know how it will turn out. I rose this morning but not in time to wash off and Howe did not either so we dressed and went to breakfast. After breakfast Howe had Uncle Tom pour six or seven buckets full of water into Hovey's bathing tub—which is a nice long one about seven feet and three feet wide at the bottom. In this he took a good wash and after he had finished I took one also which was splendid although the water was very cold—drawn up out of the well. I went to Sabbath School this morning and taught Jimmie Gorman and Eddie Edgar.

I also went to church with "Bec" and when I went to come home with her Doctor Kavanaugh stepped up and she put off with him and I was left behind but still I fell back on Mrs Edgar who was going home. I plagued Bec about [it] considerably before I let her off about it. Docter and Hugh Smith are both candidates from the democrat party and the other is called the "National Democrat Party," which met this afternoon in the court house.[1] I eat dinner at the Edgar's this day as I did last Sunday. I and Jim went over to hear the Spanish and the Parson had two new members to his Spanish audience—it is now increased to three. When I went to supper to night Louie Staab told me that Jim Houston had stabbed Chastine and he was not expected to die or live rather. I went up to see him after supper but did not see the wound. He was stabbed in the right side and in the lungs. The cause of the affair was politics. Jim was strong for Otero. Jim was a little tight they say and stabbed Chas. without provocation and if Chas. dies I expect they will hang Jim sure.[2]

Howe is over at Hatties to night as he is every night. I sat and talked with Howard to night and then came home. I finished a letter to ma and one this morning to Sam Dodds. Jim came over here in a very good humor (good boy) and I drove him off by my sour mood that I was in. I have had the blues very badly to night from Some cause or other—Yes, Jim he has gone off home and I will go to bed—I miss Howe's company so much and I have on me now one of the most indifferent careless moods I have had in a long time.

Monday; 8.

Well to day has passed and I believe instead of the round and back hand I will take a running hand or one at least leaning the other way. I studied and recited a lesson in Spanish to the Parson this morning at the usual hour. He has now removed into his study which is a neat and cozy little room. He is teaching school now begun this morning—he has three little Mexican boys counting the little boy who waits on the table, the son of the Parson's peon.

After recitation I came down to my room and comminced reading in a Spanish book after which I went up to the Parson's and bought the, "Pilgrim's Progress"—in Spanish which is called "Viador." I read half of the first chapter most [of] which was a very short one. I staid in the house and read in it until almost supper time but not all the time when Jim came over and said that Bec wanted me to come over and stay and take supper with them so I brushed my hair and went to put on my coat when I turned to Jim and told him I had eaten onions for dinner and could not come so he broke and went and told them what I had said and so I did not go over but went up to Mrs Gorman's for supper where I had quite a nice one. After supper I went up and town and played three games of billiards with Mantel whom I beat playing off.

I then came down home and as I passed by Mrs Edgar's I heard them singing and playing on the guitar—they were playing, "The Long Long Weary Day" which was a beutiful song when Bettie used to sing it and it sounded very nicely to night. I came down and found Jim and Howe sitting here and they said there was a house full of company. I joked with Jim a while when Howe and he went over about 10. O'clock—the former to tell the folks "Good Night" and the latter home. I am pretty well over my "blues" now, I had such hearty laughing at Jim.Chastine is some better this evening they moved him down to his ranche.

Tuesday: 9.

The most important transaction of the day I suppose is my purchasing two new shirts at Beck and Johnson's. I rose this morning later than usual— a half an hour after supper or rather breakfast hour. Howe bought three shirts at B. & J.'s too to day. I put on one of my new shirts to night and went up to the Fonda and played three games of billiards with Dick Simpson two of which I beat—he giving me twenty-five. I recited in Spanish to the Parson as usual to day. I believe I can write a back hand again. Jimmie E-r has not been over here to day I believe. Willie was down to day and he asked Howe the foolish question, "When are you going to get married"—any body that had much sense would not ask the question for if he <u>was</u> he would not let it be known and if he was <u>not</u> it is nobody's business but his own, but he told Willie a "fib" in order to satisfy his curious mind[.] he told him he was going to get married on the 20th of this month when he has not the least idea of it or, <u>I would have known it</u>. but it is a good deal better to let the <u>little big man</u> find out that he does not know more than twice as much as he thinks he does. But such talk as this is all foolishness so I will "<u>stop it</u>!!" I have not seen the girls since Sunday. Mr and Mrs Edgar were over to look at the house we live in and they think it is a very fine house I expect. I was putting on my shirt when they came but they run me out in the corral where they soon followed me but I give them the slip and came back and finished dressing. I wore my $12 sleeve buttons this evening for the first time since I bought them. My shirts cost me $2.50.

Wednesday; 10.

Well I let this day pass by without posting at the proper time on account of Jim who came over and staid all night with me for Eddie had gone up to stay with Harry and Doad Whiting, but we have got to considering Jim as one of the family for he knows us well and knows every thing that is going on. I studied and recited a lesson in Spanish as usual to Mr Gorman in his study. I read in "New York Boarding Houses" some also which I think is pretty good although Mantel told me it was not worth the paper it was written on. I think I improve more by writing a round or back hand such as this sentence is written in. I have played no billiards to day although I drank lemonade three times on George Waldo and Dick Simpson's playing. They played seven games of billiards that I know of with a great many lemonades and whiskys. The last two games they played they bet on—the first $2.50 and the second $5. George won the first but I did not stay until they finished the game. I played four games of checkers with Ed Rose and he beat me three out of the four. I went over to see the folks to night for I had not been there since Sunday.

They had a house full of company to night all of it unexpected I presume. Mr and Mrs Houton,[3] Doctor Steck[4] (who was there and took supper with them) Doctor Kavanaugh and Hugh Smith. We had quite a nice chat and after they all went away we had a nicer time. Howe and I went over together but when Smith and the Doctor came he broke but about the time they were going away he slipped back and went into the placita and after all had gone he had a nice time I suppose with Hattie. Beck had curls to night and looked right well. Hattie kissed me to night before Howe, "ma" and Beck and Jim when I left to go to home. I learned the accompaniment to, "Don't be angry Mother." Bec borrowed the music and I learned the accompaniment from her.

Thursday; 11.   **Son las once V cuatro minutos.**

Well now before I go to bed I think I had best play or write some in my Journal. I have just come from the Fonda where I played four games of billiards with Dick Simpson he giving me twenty-five—I beat him three out of the four. The commencement of this page shows that I was playing some thing for I rather mixed up the first sentence. I studied well and recited my lesson to Mr Gorman this morning at my usual hour 11. O'clock. I have employed most of the day in running about. I have played on the guitar a great deal. Howe and I went up to see Sallie and the rest of the folks. I made two unsuccessful attempts to kiss to night, one of Eva and the other of Sallie— Eva was in the parler and it was almost dark—before the candle was brought in—Sallie and I were playing out under the portal "Pon Honor" and Willie he stepped in for something and I "gushered" Sallie but I would not force her. Howe I believe has been over to see the folks but I have not. Jim borrowed our horse this afternoon and he, Sallie, Willie and Bec all took a ride and Ed too I believe, But it is late and I am sleepy.

Friday; 12.

Well I expect my Journal for tonight will be rather on the "curtailed["] order (a la Col. Means). I have just got permission from Jim's ma for him to stay all night with me. Howe, Willie, Doctor Fulkenson, and Clem Howard[5] were all over at Mrs Edgar's tonight—they pressed me (the girls) to stop and sing one tune or accompany with the bass rather which I did without further solicitations. I studied and recited a Spanish lesson as usual—one every day and sometimes two lessons a day. I played one game of billiards to day with a fellow by the name of Black giving him twenty-five and beat him. I read to night and cut pieces out of papers for my Scrap-Book into which I pasted some pieces to day. I read some this afternoon in "Viador"—I have not finished the first chapter yet. Jimmie is over here and patiently waiting for me to finish my writing. I just this moment asked him the Spanish word for, "yet" but he could not tell me until I asked him the Duch word for, "yes" which is pronounced like the, Spanish, "ya" or "yet." But good night. Mrs Edgar whom I saw to night was not in a very pleasant mood from some reason—was crying—"parece."

Saturday; 13.

Well I believe I will try a steel pen for to night. To day I believe has passed off without much interest—no more than usual. I studied and recited my Spanish as usual to day—I believe since I come to think about it that I did not recite. The mail from the South came in some time this afternoon I believe—I received one letter and Howe one—mine was from Sam Dodds and [a] good long one at that[.] Howe's was from ma which I have not read yet but will as soon as possible. I read some in Spanish to day and in the newspapers. In Sam's letter were also two programmes, of the Commencement. There were two books—Official Documents which came for father to day. I have hummed on the guitar some to day. There was an election or a "junta" of the "National Democracy" or Otero party who elected O.P. Hovey for the house of Representatives and Ashurst[6] for the Senate I suppose and then some Mexicans for the inferior offices. I have been in the house nearly the whole day until to night I went over to see "the folks" as Howe calls them and I had quite a nice time, but before we—Howe was already there—had been talking long in came Doctor Kavanaugh which increased the entertainment very much. About 9 1/2 O'clock the Doctor left and I too but Howe is there yet having a <u>full</u> and <u>good</u> "<u>go in</u>" I suppose. Jimmie E-r borrowed our horse this afternoon to go with Jimmie Gorman to Tzucia and the[y] got lost coming back and did not get home before dark. I played one game of billiards to day with Juan C. Tapia which I beat[.] he did not want to play any more. Howe played four games this afternoon four quite tight games, two of which he won and lost two.

Sunday; 14.

Ah! Well! Another day has passed and I have <u>passed</u> with it more like an irrational animal than a man. I rose this morning in time for breakfast which I procured before I dressed myself for the day. After breakfast I came home and after Uncle Tom had cleaned the room up I had him pour five [warm?] buckets full of water in the bathing tub into which I soon jumped and had quite a nice wash <u>all over</u>. After I had been dressed a short time the Sabbath School bell rung and Howe and I went over. This morning when Howe and I went to breakfast the Parson placed the number and page of the tunes before Howe to start—Howe has lately been starting the tunes for the Parson and he wants to get Howe to start them all the time which Howe does not like and told him that he was going to hear the Catholic service this morning and would not be on hand and there fore could not be expected to start the tunes.

I answered Sam Dodds' letter to day and a pretty long one too like his—"tit for tat." I read a chapter to night in my Spanish Testament. Howe has been laying on the bed reading to night. I went to church this morning and to the services in Spanish also in the afternoon. I took a walk with Howe, Jim[,] Hattie and Mr Edgar—we went up to Fort Marcy and sat a while looked through an opera glass, gathered flowers and made a boquette and threw with a sling <u>on Sunday</u> at that! The last was, "<u>una cosa muy mala</u>." I took dinner with Mrs Edgar and we had quite a nice one at that after which I came home—these Gillotts' pens write very nicely if you press on the pen lightly. "Flos"[,] Hovey's watch dog[,] has ten pups which she had this afternoon. Jimmie was over here this afternoon and sat and read for some time. I like to write with a good steel pen very well but I cannot make much headway with most of them. Howe has quite fine times with Hattie who he loves and in her it is fully responded to I think. Bec still wears her curls which she looks right nice in—she does so <u>I think</u>. I have been I expect an hour writing this page. Mr Edgar told Howe, "if you want to catch the calf

give the cow a milking" but I put the tail end first and <u>vice versa</u>.
<u>Good Night.</u>

<u>John Watts.</u>

Monday; 15.

Well to day begun a new week and the way I played billiards to day was a sight—I played six games with the following persons, first two games with Col. Menes giving him twenty then with Mantel two games—then two with Juan Tapia—I lost all but the two with Mantel. I think I can <u>hold off</u> a while now. Gardenhire tried to plague me about <u>my mustacho</u>—if I have one which is quite a doubtful case. I recited a good long lesson for the Parson this morning—the fortieth in "Ollendorff"—the Parson seemed pleased too which I like. A month from to night and Howe and Hattie I think will be married. As I said most of the day has been passed with playing billiards. I and Howe went over to see the folks to night and we Howe, Hattie, Bec, and I all walked up to see the Governor and folks—we sat out doors and played on the steps or rather under the portal—we soon came home though for it looked as though it was going to rain and we did not want to be caught in it. Hattie kissed me <u>twice</u> to night once of her own free will and once I and she both kissed, good, loud, kisses—when I came home—Jim came with me—he is nearly dead to go [to] the States. I will let this suffice for to day as Jim is here.

Tuesday; 16.

Here we are again Jim and I and him full of mischief as usual. I recited in Spanish as usual and played two games of billiards, one with Juan Tapia which I won and one with Tasker[7] or Boone which I lost—we played even. I and Jim are full of fun and frolic and so is many other good fellows. I and Jim sat in or under the portal until after dark when we went over to Mrs Edgar's where we found Willie with his guitar and Sallie with her best looking face on. We stayed there a while and talked while Willie played on the guitar and after a little while we went out and down to the window to serenade Hoxie which I turned into burlesque—not so much honor to do it either—we started over home when we concluded we would go back and back we put and told them good night when Willie and Sallie went away. Jim is now sitting reading waiting for me to write. I wrote August on the other page very well I think[.] I never tried those kind of letters before I believe.

Buenas Noches

<u>John Watts.</u>

Santa Fe

N.M.

Wednesday; 17.

And now I am come to the middle of the week and still I have done very little. I commenced the day as usual by getting a Spanish lesson. Jimmie and I rose at 6. O'clock this morning and Howe got up when Uncle Tom came to open the window shutters and black our boots. Nothing strange or unusual has happened to day I believe at least nothing that I now recollect. I read in, "New York Boarding Houses" some to day a great deal more than usual.

Howe went over to see his "Duck" but she was sick in bed and has been all day and was yesterday. Howe is rather disappointed in not seeing Hoxie.

I went over and staid a short time and brought Jim over home to stay all night with me. I am writing with different ink, inkstand and holding my pen in quite a different style. Jim is seated on the table by me whittling and waiting for me to finish writing. Howe was laying on the bed but now he has got up and is undressing to go to bed. I feel quite easier in using my hand with my second finger under the pen instead of by the side of it—but Jim looks impatient.

Thursday; 18.

Well I have heard some thing out of the ordinary rotine today which I will mention in its order. I studied and recited Spanish as usual today to the Parson. I and Howe played three games of billiards to day for we could find no one to play with us.

I beat him "playing off"—he gave me the discount.

Well the piano and other things came to day—arrived at last—Howe has been over there this morning and to night also. They went out to meet the wagons this morning but it commenced raining and they came back. I went over to night and had the exquisite treate of hearing some fine music. Bec played some and Doctor Kavanaugh and Judge Blackwood[8] came in and the Judge commenced played—after having been invited—and they kept him at it a long time—he plays very well and almost as good as Bauer. We have some new boarders at the Parson's—Mrs and Mr Kelly[9] who has returned from surveying, also Mayhall and Hager and they look quite rough. Hoxie is well and gave me a nice kiss when I came home. The parlor looks quite changed and smaller from the many pictures, books[,] ornaments, etc. in it. Willie and Sallie were both down to night to see if the piano had come but when Doctor and the Judge came they both broke for home I suppose[.] at least I did not see them any more. Hattie is well and up and looked quite nice when she came out. Sallie played a tune or two but not without much insisting. I saw many likenesses of both gentlemen and women. Howe still writes ["A page to a Sage"?] very quick—in half the time I have been writing and I am not done yet but I think will conclude shortly. I finished "New York Boarding Houses" this afternoon.

Friday; 19.

Well now another week is drawing to a close where I expect to get a letter from some one—no sea de quien. I recited my Spanish as usual at 11. O'clock to the Parson. We have our table lengthened now so we are not crowded. They tried to plague me this morning at dinner and pump me in regard to Howe's getting married but they could not make any thing off of me.

I took my book into Hovey and exchanged it for Rogers Works in which I read more than a hundred pages—I have been reading all afternoon. I also read a page in the, "Viador" which I finished just about supper time. I and Howe have both been playing billiards to night. Howe and Quintana—three games—Howe won playing off[.] I beat George Waldo two games and then he went to the baile. I suppose pa will be home tomorrow. Howe is going with Col. Hopkins to San Miguel. He has been over to see the folks. I have not been there to day. I gave Jim two of my old vests which were too short for me. I read in Rogers Works, The Pleasures of Memory, Human Life, and An Epistle to A Friend.

It seems to me that I ought to finish out this page and even that is little enough. Howe went to bed to night without writing but, "Never put off until tomorrow what can be done to day"—de veras. I am getting along slowly in Spanish but still, "slow but sure." I think from present appearances that Mr Kelly will have an increase in the family before many days. I wonder when "Bec" will get married! I saw their likenesses taken when there were young and very small for they in hight are not very important but still they are both "seen and heard"—like Bettie R—small[.]

Saturday; 20.   **Eleven minutes of 11, O'clock.**

Well this is the first Saturday which the mail has missed in a long time —often it comes in on Friday.

I did not get any Spanish to day it being Saturday[.] I thought the Parson ought to have one day out of the week to himself—for recreation or in what ever way he chooses to spend it—for Sunday which is the world's Day of Rest, is the ministers hardest working day.

I read in "Rogers Works" this morning and also read four pages in the, "Viador." This afternoon I beat Col. Means this afternoon playing off— it was the first time for that I had ever beat him a game in my life—I gave him twenty-five. I was in fine play—the first game I run the first or second lick[.] I got twenty odd which put me even with him and then you see it was on even ground.

I was waiting at the Fonda all afternoon and until 9. O'clock or more to night for the Eastern Mail—the Southern has arrived and I received neither a letter nor paper—Howe received one letter from Gus Lynch. We heard by some passengers that came up in the Southern Mail that father was in Socorro and I suppose will not be up here until next mail. Chastine died this morning some time I do not know exactly when—Mr Johnson said he lived just four hours longer than Mr Preston Beck—Chas has lived until the thirteenth morning since he was stabbed. They have Jim Houston chained down and they say he cries like a child, but that will not help the case any. I also heard of two more men getting killed down below—one at El Paso and one on the road bet[w]een here and there. I shaved off my mustacho this morning when Howe had left and now I look clean and I think better. Howe is answering Gus' letter to night.

The ladies sent over for me to go riding with them but I was up at the Fonda and so they let me slide but Bec, Eddie, Willie, Sallie and Howe all went. Howe and Quintana played two games to night one and one[.] Quintana did not wish to play off[.] he told Howe that when they played off he always beat and therefore was a little afraid.

Sunday; 21.

Well another day has passed and a new week commenced[.] I dressed myself this morning in clean clothes as usual but did not wash all over only my neck for I did not have time—the bell for Sunday School rung before I commenced to dress—After I dressed I went over to Sunday Shool and while I was there Howe who had got ready and was waiting for Col. Hopkins with whom he went to San Miguel where court commences on Monday; he will be gone until the last of the week or first of next—I promised to kiss Hattie for him while he was gone every night. I finished a Sunday School book to day called "Learning to feel." Chastine was buried this morning at 10. O'clock in the Mason and Odd Fellow's burying ground. Parson Gorman officiated. I wrote one letter to day—to Fannie and put one in it to mother from Howe. I expect he caught a ducking for it rained here very hard. I went over to tell Hattie good night and found Clem Howard there—he is going to leave for San Antonio tomorrow—going to stop in Alburquerque two or three day[s],—he quoted, "Full many a gem of purest ray serene" from "Pope"! I said I thought it was in "Grays Elegy." Jim came over to night just after the rain and when he came in "Blanco" was at the door (I had been out there petting him while he was under the portal out of the rain) and he spoke to him calling him by name and he made a lunge at Jim. I told Hattie good night after Mr Howard had gone away and she gave me an awful good kiss[.]

Jim is going to stay with me all night to night and all the time Howe is gone and he is now stripped off and in bed while I am writing as fast as possible with my sleeve rolled up.

Monday; 22.

Well to day has passed away very much pleasanter than I had expected[.] on account of the absence of Howe I expected I would be quite lonely. I studied and recited my Spanish to day and in the presence of a Laguna Indian who preached in Spanish yesterday and stays with Mr Gorman until he returns to Laguna—he is a licensed preacher and preaches among his own Indians in their pueblo.

This afternoon I employed myself by reading in Roger's Poetical Works some notes of which I took down in my Index Rerum. Willie has not been down here to day. Jim and Eddie were both over here this afternoon and also Harry Whiting with a pistol shooting.

I went up to the Fonda and played two games of billiards—with Boone or the new nick-name he goes by is "Critter." I beat him the first game and strung him the second—I made one thirty-two run on him at that—he got disgusted I believe with the game but he had just won seven or eight dollars. I then looked at Doctor Kavanaugh and Doctor Hale play two very amusing games in which Kavanaugh played his Salt Lake game—getting on the table to make licks—they came out even one and one. George Gardenhire has a little bank of monte but I came very near getting cleaned out to night. Dunn and I hunted to night for a baile but could find none. But it is late and I am tired—I will not get to kiss Hattie to night, Que cosa tan mala!!

Tuesday; 23.

Well I have passed through another of my happy days for such they are now and the happiest I perhaps will ever see but still I do not know. I recited two lessons in "Ollendorff" to day a little after the time. I played two games or three games of checkers with Ed Rose this afternoon and I rather beat him —two games of three. I have played no billiards to day. While I was in the Fonda two fortunate things happened—father came home and the Eastern Mail came in—McKinstry conductor—he said that high water had detained [them] at Cow Creek, Walnut Creek and Pawnee Fork—five days detention—I do not know whether they will fine them or not—I expect not. I did not get any letters, but a catalog from Sam Dodds and one or two papers. Howe received or I rather for him a great many papers which I and father have been reading—father received some letters in the mail. I went over to see the "folks" this evening or night rather and Beck played some for me on the piano and for the rest of the folks. I staid until about 9 1/2, O'clock when Jim came home with me. Hattie came out and told <u>Jimmie</u> and <u>I</u> good night in <u>her [poor?] way</u>!! Long will I remember Hattie and she is <u>wanting</u> to be remembered <u>long</u>. I read some in Rogers' Works to day—father has been lecturneering for Gallegos.[10] Jim is setting by reading.

Wednesday; 24.

Well to day has passed and has increased my billiard account two dollars and a half. I have played eight games with different personst most with Dick Simpson—seven games three of which I won and four I lost. I lost one with Willie Rencher—I cannot play with him without being disgusted at some thing. I recited in Spanish to the Parson as usual—I also read about a page in a Spanish book. I disgusted or rather wounded Jimmie's feelings this afternoon while in Mr Howards for which I was sorry and Mrs Edgar sent over to see me to know what it was about and I explained to her what I thought it was but he is still not in a very good humor with me. Eddie came over to stay all night with me to night and is now in bed and <u>perhaps</u> asleep. You may talk about this thing and that being nice but the most excellent— the choicest, sweetest—in fact the "<u>ne plus ultra</u>" of things at least to me is —an affectionate, warm and voluntary <u>kiss from one you love</u>—such as Hattie gave me to night when Eddie and I came home—it was a <u>treat decidedly</u>. When I came home I went in and let father pick open a little pimple or boil on my forehead. And now I am through the rotine of the day. I asked Jimmie's pardon—I am sorry about that but I intend to let him alone[.] I expect he will come around after while—his father scolded him a little Eddie told me[.]

Thursday; 25.

Well to day I have varied a little from my usual rotine—I did not recite in Spanish this morning[.] I was copying off a letter of father's to Col. C. St. Vrain[11] which took me all morning and in the afternoon although the parson told me I could come up and he would hear me but I forgot it entirely. Battaile, Editor, Kelly and Wheeler[12] came in to day Louie Dickens and Col Clemens yesterday.

Jimmie I believe has not got in a good humor with me yet—I expect though he will before long. I have been thinking of going to Taos tomorrow but I have found out that I am not going. Louie Staab is going to Albuquerque Monday and perhaps I may go down there with him. Howe will soon be back. I had a talk with Mc Kinstry to day who is trying to find employment.

Battaile said he would come over and stay all night with me to night but as yet he has not made his appearance. I do not know whether I will go over to see Hattie to night or not. Father is up town some where. I beat Ed Rose at checkers to day—I have played no billiards to day.

Friday; 26.

Well I have made quite a bad out at billiards to day[.] I lost three games— two with Dick Simpson and one with Juan Tapia. I was fifty ahead once in one of the games I played with Dick. I recited in Spanish this morning as usual and after I came home and had been sitting a short time who but Howe should walk in just returned from San Meguil. I heard him "hawk" at the gate and I thought it was like him but thought it was father. He went up to dinner when the time came where they all shook hands with him and seemed glad to see him. I had translated a letter from father in Spanish but very poorly done but he put it in good Spanish directly. I have been reading the papers tonight—I made my eyes a little sore last night reading. Battaile and he have gone over there to see them to night. I expect they will have a nice time[.] if they do not it is their own fault. I am getting so I can write a little better with this fountain [pen] every day.

From some cause which I am not able to explain I feel like writing to night and although I have nothing in particular to say yet I will give some items. Jimmie has not yet got in a good humor with me yet I believe— I spoke to him this evening but he did not feel inclined to make up. I will try to get him to make up with me three times and if he will not then he can go for all I care. Battaile I expect will have quite a nice time for he has not seen the parler since the piano and rest of the things since they have come. Howe

I expected would let Battaile into the secret of his going to get married but I suppose he is a little scrupulous but I do not blame him in the least.

Howe has not his gold pen he loaned General Pelham and from the appearances he will not get it until some time yet. Father is sitting in the other room reading the Washington Star, which with Waverly Magazine, Harper's Weekly, Louisville Journal, Richmond Despatch, and Dollar Newspaper I have been employing myself since candle light. I will have Howe to sleep in the room with me to night. I was looking at a very pretty hand to day written to father in a letter to him from Faut & Co—written by some of the clerks there and a good hand it is. The Eastern Mail came in this evening but I did not receive any letters nor papers.

Saturday; 27.

Well! Another week closes with to day. and now let us take "una mirada" at both and see what we have done. I am certain of one thing that I have spent too much time and money at billiards and checkers. I have played every afternoon this week almost with Ed Rose with whom I am pretty well matched, we play about the same game I believe but I cleaned him badly this afternoon—I beat him three out of four games. I have not played any billiards to day which is quite a fortunate occurence—but what am I thinking about I played two games with Howe one of which I beat and lost one. He played two games with Willie both of which he lost. I recited my usual lesson to the parson as usual—I am now to the fiftieth—that was my lesson to day.

The only thing interesting which has happened to day was Howard and I going down to Stephens to witness the christening of one of his children. Seth or Steph[13] I should write was tight—as fellows generally get—we staid but a short time and then came away—disgusted!

Howe, Battaile, Willie, and Mr and Mrs Wilkins were there at Mrs Edgar's for I heard them talking. I came over home and took this book—my good old friend which will accompany me many long days yet to come. Howe has given his as he always said he would up—when he got married which is now faster approaching. Father started below to day—for El Paso and will be gone about three weeks.[14] Demetrio was here this morning after a piece of music Howe is going to lend him.

Sunday; 28.

Another week begins with to day—will I live until the close and if I do will I spend my time better than in the week which has passed and gone? I hope so.

I rose about my usual time—soon enough to dress for supper or breakfast I should say. I dressed and went to Sunday School and taught Jimmie Gorman and Eddie Edgar.

I and Battaile both went over together to go to church with Beck and Mrs Edgar, I with [the] latter B. with the former—Howe staid at home with Hattie. We had quite a nice sermon or a good preached one—Beck said it was a little too long was the only objection. I went over and staid until after dinner with them and so did Howe as a matter of course. After dinner Beck, Eddie and I all went to see how large Santa Fe, River, was but all the water had run down before we got there and nothing but the dry bed was there. I and Howe went to Vespers in the Catholic Church [which] was a ceremony I never before witnessed—they played on an organ or melodian I expect it was and sung. Howe has gone over there again to night.

Willie was here this evening. I got a letter out of the post Office for Howe from ma this afternoon. I am improving I think in penmanship. Howe does not write in his journal any more—it seems wrong and sad.

Monday; 29.

Well I find myself without much trouble a day behind. Jim was over to night and first since our rumpus and staid all night with me—every thing went off very smoothly. I recited my Spanish as usual. I read in "Shakspeare" to day a play and a half. The first was "Romeo and Juliet" and part of "Macbeth." I did not play any billiards to day. This evening I, Beck and Eddie all took a ride—first in the direction of the States then South until we struck a road that led into town and then we road out the Taos road and then came home. The Band came out and played just as we were started off. Jim and I went to bed but it was some time before we could go to sleep. But I am run through and had better stop.

Tuesday; 30.

This morning we all rose early and took a walk out on the mountains. Howe started a little before Jim and I and overtook Hoxie and the Squire whom he joined. Jim and I went after them but they hid from us by Squire['s] suggestion and when we found them it tickled the Squire considerably. Jim and I did not speak to them but went on and took our walk and came back— we got caught in a little shower but Howe, Hattie and the Squire got wetter than we did. It rained this morning pretty hard and just about the time I wanted to go and recite so I postponed it until after dinner when the Parson heard me. Howe has been reciting in Spanish to Mr Elison—I think he begun yesterday. He has been pasting scraps in Hattie's Scrap-Book nearly all the morning—we had a fire this morning. I cut out pieces out of papers all day and pasted in my Scrap-book some. I read also some in "Shakspeare" finished "Macbeth." I played three games of billiards to night with Mantel—beat him playing off. Willie and Gardenhire had a big game to day and Willie lost playing off but George Waldo and Barry Simpson said they would pay if he lost before he begun—he beat Dick Simpson though three games to day even and Dick was tickeled to death almost when Gardenhire beat him. Jim and Howe are now both in bed and I will follow suit. "<u>Scissors</u>" deviled Mantel to night considerably.

Wednesday; 31.

Well this morning was the examination at the Convent which I attended in company with Howe and <u>all the folks</u>. The exercises were <u>very</u> good considering that this is Santa Fe and the Territory of New Mexico.

The exercises consisted of performances on the piano & essays after which presents were awarded to the pupils in this manner[.] the present was given to the child or the padre who took it to one of the parents of the child who presented it to the child—it was a long and tedious way for the parents had to be singled out of the crowd. Louie Staab and I have been talking of going to Alburquerque and we took a notion after dinner we would make a start. After dinner then we mounted our horses and set off at a brisk speed. After we had passed through Agua Fria—a little, "lugar"—six miles below Santa Fe two Mexicans overtook us and traveled with us until we came to the "Mojada"[15] as it is called which is at the foot of a mesa we pass over on our journey—this I believe is called twenty miles from Santa Fe—here one of our compañeros left us and three of us went on together. On the middle of the mesa we met a lot of Mexicans who said the Navajoes were close around stealing—which we afterwards found to be a lie.

On leaving the, Mojada we went in a lope stopping at intervals to let our horses "<u>blow</u>" until we came to an Indian pueblo called, San. Domingo— where Howe and Mr Howard went to see the Indian dance—which is thirty miles from S. Fe. Here we came in full view of the, Rio Grande of New Mexico—we first see five or six miles from the Mojada. And here our other partner left us and a bad impression in our minds as to his veracity for he said he was going to Algodones to which we were going. From here (to use a common expression) we, "made tracks" for Algodones—ten miles or fifteen miles distant. We met several Indians going to the pueblo San Domingo about sun down. We passed by San Felipe also and arrived at Algodones at ten min. after 5. O'clock—making forty-five miles in six hours which I think is good traveling. This is the first day.

NOTES: Chapter 6

1. Watts' terms "National Democrat Party" and "democrat party" are confusing.

Many politicians in New Mexico identified themselves as Whigs when that party held national office. In 1853, when Democrat Franklin Pierce won the Presidency by a landslide, Whigs and other politicians interested primarily in expediency began to identify themselves as members of the Democratic party, hence "National Democrats." New Mexico politicians who opposed these fellows identified themselves as "regular Democrats," although they were called by a variety of names, including "Douglas," "Buchanan," and "states rights" democrats. The *Gazette* called these men (whose main figures were Spruce M. Baird W.W.H Davis, and Padre Gallegos) "Baird bob-tail democrats." The *Gazette* also announced a convention of "the National Democracy of Santa Fe County" for August 14, 1858, to nominate "National Democratic Candidates for the Legislature."

Howard R. Lamar suggests that political "parties" in early territorial New Mexico were not groups with clearly defined political philosophies. Rather, "party" was a label under which this leader or that organized his followers. "Rather than parties," Lamar writes, "New Mexico had cliques, usually led by one man and generally organized for the specific purpose of winning an election or controlling patronage."

In retrospect, this seems a practical policy, considering that the Congressional Delegate was the Territory's spokesman. "He was," Lamar writes, "its lobbyist for patronage, troops, and appropriations as well as the consultant for Indian affairs and the advocate of annuities." As New Mexico's chief spokesman and most important politician, the Delegate needed a well organized, loyal "party" structure back home. Any particular political philosophy was secondary. See Lamar, *Far Southwest*, pp. 100-101; and *Gazette*, 24 July, and 28 Aug 58.

2. Jim Houston's stabbing of Chastine is an example of the kind of entertainment which plagued early Santa Fe. Of this bloody brawl, Kingsbury wrote Webb, September 10, 1859: "We got safely through Election day without any serious fights, only one man killed in Santa Fe over the election. Several weeks ago Jim Houston stabed [sic] Chasteure [sic] ... during a political argument, from which wound he died, Houston is now on trial for his murder. This probably kept the parties cool on election day ... . Santa Fe is getting worse and more unsafe every day, during the sitting of this Grand Jury they have brought in no other enditements [sic] except those for murder. There are now 6 or 8 cases before the court. These wild sporting characters are increasing every week, and it is really unsafe here for a quiet man. If I escape with my life I shall consider myself lucky." See Elder and Weber, "Trading in Santa Fe," Ch.11, p. 37.

3. Very likely "Mr and Mrs Houton" were Joab Houghton and his wife. In an entry for Sunday, December 7, 1856, James Ross Larkin mentioned visiting Mrs. Houghton and others. Within the next few days Larkin visited several other people often mentioned in Watt's Journal—Drew, Smith, Lt. O'Bannon, Mrs. Wilkins, and Dr. "Cavanaugh." Since the circle of friends is about the same in both the Larkin and Watts accounts, it seems likely that "Mr. and Mrs Houton" were in fact Mr. and Mrs. Houghton. See Barbour, ed., *Reluctant Frontiersman,* pp. 108-109.

4. Doctor Steck was Michael Steck, the Indian agent. Born in Pennsylvania in 1818, Steck graduated from Jefferson Medical College in 1844. After practicing in Pennsylvania for several years, Dr. Steck was appointed agent for the Mescalero Apaches by President Fillmore. Later, President Buchanan appointed him the Superintendent of Indian Affairs for New Mexico.

Dr. Steck was a harsh critic of General Carleton's policy of exiling the Navajo to the Bosque Redondo reservation at Fort Sumner. He eventually resigned from the Indian Service over this point. In 1868 the Navajos were released and permitted to return to their homeland.

Having resigned from government service, Dr. Steck joined Stephen B. Elkins in gold mining ventures in the territory, and became reasonably wealthy. After returning to Hughesville, Pennsylvania, however, he lost his money in various railroad ventures and promotional enterprises. He died on his farm near Winchester, Virginia, in 1883.

See Keleher, *Turmoil,* pp. 506-507, n. 137; Lamar, *Far Southwest,* pp. 125-28; Horn, *Troubled Years,* pp. 104-100; and appropriate pp. in Edwin

R. Sweeney, *Mangas Coloradas: Chief of the Chiricahua Apaches* (Norman, 1998).

5. "Doctor Fulkenson," (elsewhere in the journal spelled "Fulkison") has not been identified.

"Clem Howard" was Clement W. Howard, whom Governor Rencher appointed notary public for Taos County on August 3, 1858. See "Executive Record Book 1," p.196, NMRA.

6. Merrill Ashurst was one of several early day lawyers in New Mexico. Howard R. Lamar calls these men—Houghton, Watts, Wheaton, Baird, Clever, and others—"pioneer lawyers." They were generally shrewd, avaricious, and interested in political influence, in working the opportunities afforded by land grants, and in promoting the railroads. Most of them ran cattle and sheep on the public domain or on the vast land grants they succeeded in confirming. In writing of the Territory in the 1850s, Lamar describes the place as "a paradise for lawyers and politicians."

Born in Alabama, where he had been a state legislator, Merrill Ashurst came to New Mexico in 1851 and began practicing law. He was territorial attorney general from 1852 to 1854. Elected to the territorial assembly, he became speaker of the house of representatives in December 1857. He served a second term as attorney general from 1867 until his death in 1869.

While he was an assemblyman in 1859, Ashurst pushed through a charter for the Southern Pacific Railroad.

Ashhurst was the prosecutor in the famous case in which William L. Rynerson was tried and acquitted for the murder of Judge John P. Slough in 1867. Twitchell described Ashurst as "a man of unusual ability, a convincing orator and very successful as a prosecutor."

A moral and intellectual gymnast of supreme agility even amongst lawyers, Ashurst would take any side willing to pay. Franz Huning told an amusing story about him. In the fifties, a lawyer named Skinner was murdered at Juan C. Armijo's home in Ranchos de Albuquerque. "When the news reached Santa Fe," wrote Huning, "there was a great uproar, speeches were made in the Plaza, threatening all sorts of violence to the Mexicans. Among the most violent was Lawyer Ashurst. Only a day or two afterwards [however], Mr. Ashurst went to the Rio Abajo. After his return he made no more speeches against the Mexicans; he had been retained by J.C. Armijo to defend him in this murder case. He eventually cleared him in the courts."

Ashurst reportedly joined O.P. Hovey and others in stealing the pollbooks of Rio Arriba County while they were being brought to Santa Fe in September 1855. The *Gazette* reported that Ashurst, Hovey, and company held up attorney general Wheaton and probate clerk Elias T. Clark at gunpoint near Pojoaque Creek and took the pollbooks from Clark's saddlebags.

Interested in land grants as investments, Ashurst and Charles P. Clever purchased José Albino Montoya's interest in the vast Pablo Montoya Grant in March 1862 for $225. Two years later Ashurst sold his half of this share to Judge John S. Watts for $150. A younger, more voracious, and much more successful territorial lawyer, Thomas B. Catron, studied the intricacies of land grant law as a student in Merrill Ashurst's office.

Although territorial lawyers had a reputation for the amount of liquor they consumed—no one ever saw Kirby Benedict uninebriated, and Hugh N. Smith drank himself to dealth—Merrill Ashurst's style was to go out on an occasional blind bender (the exception was Judge Watts, who apparently never touched liquor). John M. Kingsbury mentioned Ashurst's condition to Webb, December 24, 1859. Writing of "attaching" a certain party so as to recover a debt, Kingsbury added: "I should do it today but Ashurst and the whole town is on a Christmas spree and I must wait for him to get sober ... Whiskey will get them all after a while ... When shall I get out of this hole of dissipation [sic]."

See Twitchell, *Leading Facts*, II, p. 411, n. 337; Lamar, *Far Southwest,* pp. 105, 138-39, 140; Keleher, *Turmoil*, p. 204, n. 43; Horn, *Troubled Years*, pp. 127-28; Remley, *Bell Ranch*, pp. 68-69; Elder and Weber, "Trading in Santa Fe," Ch. 12, pp. 38-39; Huning, *Trader on the Santa Fe Trail*, pp. 23-24; and *Gazette*, 22 Sept 55, and 12 Dec 57.

7. "Tasker" was Joseph Tasker, a twenty-nine-year-old man, born in New Hampshire. The 1860 Census lists him as a "messenger." See 1860 U.S. Census.

8. Judge William G. Blackwood was a member of the territorial supreme court during what Twitchell calls "the second judicial period." A native of South Carolina, Blackwood and Miguel Antonio Otero had met while the two were law students in St. Louis. Otero later married Mary Josephine, Blackwood's Sister. In 1858, Blackwood was appointed a justice of the New Mexico supreme court through the influence of Otero, then Delegate to Congress. Howard R. Lamar notes that, with Southerners holding key offices (Governor Rencher, Secretary Jackson, Judge Blackwood), Otero was "well on the way to establishing a machine in New Mexico" when political circumstances at the national level overturned his cart. With Lincoln and the Republicans elected, Otero's Washington influence was "severely limited" and "by 1861 he was out of office." See Twitchell, *Leading Facts*, II, pp. 393-95; Lamar, *Far Southwest*, p. 105; and Miguel Antonio Otero,

My Life on the Frontier, 1864-1882, repr. (Albuquerque, 1987), pp. 284-85.

9. This was the deputy surveyor, R.P. Kelley. It seems likely that "Mayhall" and "Hager" were members of Kelley's survey party. Governor Rencher appointed one J.W. Hager notary public for Socorro County on August 24, 1858. See "Executive Record Book 1," p. 197, NMRA; and *Gazette*, 3 Apr 1858.

10. Padre José Manuel Gallegos represented the native or "home rule" branch of the "Democrats" against Miguel Antonio Otero of the so-called "National Democrats." Gallegos and Otero were old political enemies, Gallegos always aligned with local interests, and Otero—St. Louis educated and married to a Southern woman, Judge Blackwood's sister—always aligned with "national" interests. The two ran against each other several times for Delegate, beginning at least as early as 1855 when Otero unseated Gallegos who had beaten William Carr Lane in the 1853 election.

The curious point here is the mention of Judge Watts—first a Whig, then a rock-ribbed Republican and Lincoln-man—"lectioneering" for Padre Gallegos in 1859. The explanation probably lies in the personal hatred—with somewhat mysterious roots—between Watts and Otero, which led Watts to make remarks personally offensive to Otero and Otero to challenge Watts to a duel with pistols. This duel they actually fought, though neither man got hurt. See Lamar, *Far Southwest*, pp. 102-104.

11. "Col. C. St. Vrain" was Cerán St. Vrain, of the famous Missouri trading family.

Arriving in America from France in 1770, Cerán's grandfather settled in Missouri. Soon two of his sons followed, Charles and Jacques. Charles would become Lt. Governor of Spanish Louisiana, while Jacques, Cerán's father, settled near St. Genevieve.

Jacques left ten children, one of whom—teenage Cerán—was placed in the home of merchant Bernard Pratte, a wealthy Indian trader. The giant young Cerán, a handsome, friendly, sensible boy of unusually good judgment and immense energy, soon headed for Taos in company with a partner, Francois Guerin. They took with them a load of trade goods on credit from Bernard Pratte and Company. Cerán spent the winter in Taos, supplied trappers in return for a percentage of the beaver, and made friends everywhere he went. Lewis H. Garrard, who knew him, described Cerán as "a gentleman in the true sense of the term, his French descent imparting an exquisite, indefinable degree of politeness, and, combined with the frankness of an ingenuous mountain man, made him an amiable fellow traveler."

In about 1830 Cerán and Charles Bent, another Missourian, launched one of the great trade houses of the Southwest. Adding their brothers, Marcellin St. Vrain and William Bent, the partners were known far and wide as "Bent, St. Vrain and Company." In 1832 or 1833 the company completed "Bent's Fort" on the left bank of the Arkansas about twelve miles upstream from its junction with the Purgatory or "Picketwire" Creek as mountain men called it. Bent's Fort became a central trading post for the Plains tribes and a resupply point for travelers on the Santa Fe Trail. Bent, St. Vrain and Company were to be, Lamar wrote, "the exploiters of a vast Southwestern empire."

The company was a uniquely successful operation because of the energy, vision, and timing of its founders, as well as its effective organization. Charles Bent, the senior partner, took charge of purchasing and transporting supplies. William Bent, who enjoyed the company of Indian people and who married Indian wives, remained at the Fort to run the daily operations. Cerán St. Vrain kept the Company's store in Taos, ran a branch in Santa Fe, and sent trade goods as far away as Chihuahua and Sonora.

Cerán became a Mexican citizen, eligible for the grants of land Governor Manuel Armijo so lavishly handed out. On January 2, 1844, he and Cornelio Vigil took possession of the vast "Las Animas" or "Vigil and St. Vrain" Grant, a big piece of what is now southeastern Colorado. Although something like 4,000,000 acres were requested in the application for confirmation, only a little over 96,000 acres were eventually patented. Still, this was a very handsome sweep of land.

After Charles Bent was murdered in the Taos Rebellion in 1847, Cerán parted company with William Bent and struck out on his own—an investor in land, in railroads, and in banking. From Taos, he moved, to Mora, where he operated a flour mill in a building which is still standing. He died at Mora in 1855.

In his day, Cerán St. Vrain was as well known and well liked as any man in the territory. Governor Calhoun once described him in a letter as "long a citizen here, every way reliable and intelligent."

See Twitchell, *Leading Facts*, II, p. 121, n. 87; Lamar *Far Southwest*, pp.43-47; Garrard, *Wah-to-Yah*, p. 58; Keleher, *Turmoil*, p. 54; Westphal, *Mercedes Reales*, pp. 28-31, 54-55, 152, 296, n. 24; Lamar, ed., *Reader's Encyclopedia of the American West*, pp. 1060-61; and David Lavender, *Bent's Fort* (New York, 1954).

12. "Wheeler" and "Editor" have not been identified. Since they appear to have been in the company of surveyors—Battaile, Kelly, and Clemens—it seems likely that they were members of the survey party, perhaps chainmen or camp tenders.

13. "Steph" Stephens may have been one R.M. Stephens, a thirty-five-year-old carpenter, born in Tennessee.   See 1860 U.S. Census.

14. I have not been able to discover what business Judge Watts had in El Paso although he often went downriver at least as far as Mesilla and probably on to El Paso. He had often gone to Doña Ana and Las Cruces to hold court after 1851 when he was appointed to the territorial court. Franz Huning gives a lively account of a band of Santa Fe lawyers, including Judge Watts, going to Doña Ana for court in about 1857.   See Huning, *Trader on the Santa Fe Trail*, pp. 59-61.

15. What Watts calls the "Mojada" was probably a village or a spring and resting place at the foot of the vast east-west escarpment which overlooks the Rio Grande valley roughly twenty miles south of Santa Fe. Marc Simmons explains that this escarpment became, about 1660, the division point for what were known as the "Rio Arriba" and the "Rio Abajo," upper and lower New Mexico along the Rio Grande. Today the interstate highway from Albuquerque climbs straight up the brow perhaps a mile or so east of the old road, which drops down by switchbacks to a very old village at the foot of the hill.

Known as "La Bajada Hill," this great brow lay within "La Majada Grant." Situated in Santa Fe and Bernalillo counties, La Majada Grant was confirmed by the Court of Private Land Claims for 54,404.10 acres. See White, Koch, Kelly, and McCarthy, Attorneys at Law, and the New Mexico State Planning Office, *Land Title Study* (Santa Fe, 1971), p. 230, # 89; and Marc Simmons, *Albuquerque, A Narrative History* (Albuquerque, 1982), P. 38.

Frances "Fannie" Ann Watts Bancroft,
John's sister and wife of Albert Little Bancroft.
Photo by George D. Morse, San Francisco.
Courtesy: California Historical Society, FN-29908.

BOOK III

FALL 1859

"It is raining outside ... . Such nights as these have a tendency to make me feel melancoly but one blest with the priveleges that I am and surrounded with so many comforts as I ought never to think of getting melancholy and never of grumbling." — *Sunday, 25 September 1859*

"I went up in town and got shaved. I went over to see the girls and kissed them all. — *Friday, 7 October 1859*

"Dick Simpson was caught sleeping with Mrs. Generet by Mrs. Green, Date and John Kingsbury and they told him he had to do one of two things—marry Mrs. Generet or leave the Territory and he chose the latter[.] at least he has left the town. Frank Green got in to night—they will not be so free in his house now[.] He will straighten them out." — *Friday, 7 October 1859*

"I went home with Willie and he and I and Sallie sat under the portal and sung, 'Gentle Annie,' and 'When Stars are in the Quiet Skies' and he played an accompaniment on the guitar—he sung air—Sallie ... alto ... and I bass—we made right good music together." —*Thursday, 13 October 1859*

September; 1859.

Thursday; 1.

Well to day we left two things two things and came to two-
which are the following; Algodones and August we left behind
and came to Albuquerque and September which I now have
as the month which I left home for Santa Fé, for the good
of my health—for the month in which college takes—the
month of the Election and last but least the month
in which I will see the dearest thing on earth to me
— my brother, Home, married. All hail, then September!!

My travel to and stay in Albuquerque will be confined
to the Jews whom I will some what describe. Louis is
the best Jew I ever saw. From Algodones we started in
company with Aaron Zeckendorf, Simon (Rosenstein) with
his little girl of about five years and a fellow driving them
— for they rode in a carriage. They started two hours earlier
from S. Fé there we and but and not get there until 12.
O.clock. We started after breakfast across the river which
has here and there trees scattered along its banks. Last night
we had a chat with Crenshaw who is going up to S. Fé
at the hotel in Algodones which is kept by a fellow called
Townsend — no relation suppose to the man that makes the Sarsaparilla. We traveled along until we met Clever coming up
from Albuquerque where he and Gallegos has made speeches the
day before — he was hoarse. We passed through an Indian pueblo after leaving Algodones and next came to Bernalio where Simon
and all of us stopped and eat grapes out of the vineyards —
there is where Simon's mother-in-law lives—we Louis and I also
stopped at Major Weldon's or Weldon's I do not which is the
proper way to spell it where we took three glasses of pure wine
a piece for the Major pressed it out himself and I knew it was
pure. We stopped a little while in Alameda at a Chihuahuan's
who stayed and kept store there—a strong Gallegos man and a clever
fellow. We staid there a while—for it was raining when Cotton
and a brother of his rode up—we waited a short time and then
all four put out in the rain—I borrowed a coat of Antonio
Lerma—for that was his name. We soon came in sight of the
flag staff and at last into the town. We stopped at Aaron Zeckendorf, a Jew that keeps store there.

Chapter 7

September 1859

Thursday; 1.

Well to day we left two things two things and came to two—which are the following; Algodones and August we left behind and came to Alburquerque and September which I now have as the mo[n]th which I left home for Santa Fe, for the good of my health—for the month in which college takes—the month of the Election and last but [not] least the month in which I will see the dearest thing on earth to me—my brother, Howe, married. All hail, then September!!

My travel to, and stay in Alburquerque will be confined to the Jews whom I will some what describe. Louie is the best Jew I ever saw. From Algodones we started in company with Aaron Zeckendorf, Simon (Rosenstein) with his little girl of about five years[1] and a fellow driving them—for they ride in a carriage. They started two hours earlier from S. Fe than we did but did not get there until 12. O'clock. We started after Breakfast down the river which has here and there trees scattered along its banks. Last night we had a chat with Crenshaw who is going up to S. Fe at the hotel in Algodones, which is kept by a fellow called Townsend[2] —no relation I suppose to the man that makes the Sarsaparilla, We traveled along until we met Clever coming up from Alburquerque where he and Gallegos has made speeches the day before—he was hoarse. We passed through an Indian pueblo after leaving Algodones and next came to Bernalio where Simon and all of us stopped and eat grapes out of the vineyards—there is where Simon's mother-in-law lives—we (Louie and I) also stopped at Major Wilden's or Weldon's I do not [know] which is the proper way to spell it where we took three glasses of pure wine a piece for the Major pressed it out himself and I knew it was pure. We stopped a little while in Alemada[3] at a Chihuahuian's who stayed and kept store there—a strong Gallegos man and a clever fellow. We staid there a while—for it was raining when Cotton and a brother[4] of his rode up—we waited a short time and then all four put out in the rain — I borrowed a coat of Antonio Lerma[5] —for that was his name. We soon came in sight of the flag staff[6] and at last into the town. We stopped at Aaron Zeckendorf, a Jew that keeps store there.

Friday; 2.

Well Louie and I as I said stopped and slept in Zeckendorf's store— after a good sleep I feel fresh and ready to go and take a look at the second town, or city if you choose, of New Mexico. They have three billiard tables here to commence with and exceedingly large balls—I mean large pockets for the balls are very small. Alburquerque has a flag staff which they say is higer than ours in the middle of the plaza.

The situation is in the valley of the Rio Grande and now on account of the rain the streets are full of water.[7] I had a letter from Mr Gorman to Mr Clark[8] which I left in his store—sutters store—which I found by inquiry and also I asked about Violand who was in his employ[.] I found [him] sick with the rheumatism in his knee—he said he had been sick more than a week — he has never been sick much most any one could tell from his impatience and restlessness—poor fellow I feel sorry for him. I have played billiards to day with the man that keeps the establishment, three games with Louie Staab on, a three bit table—I beat him playing off. Last night I and Simon took a game and he beat me. I had some grapes to eat to day. I took dinner with Simon and so did Louie. Cotton is going to Las Lunas to day to make a bet on a horse race—he still has Kavanaugh's horse which he bought of him for $500. 1 went over to see Violand again this afternoon and was introduced to Mr Young and Harrison. I met Fitzgerald in Bernalio and spoke to him—no more—he is the wildest fellow I ever saw. Again to night I slept at the same place I did last night. Louie was busy trying to make purchases all day— they talk a great deal about the election and claim the county for Otero by at least four hundred votes. I was over again to see Nick to night and staid a while and then went over to the billiard room where I found Louie playing billiards with Simon. I here saw and had a short conversation with Mr Clark.

Saturday; 3.

Well I staid again with Zeckendorf's and after breakfast having had our horses brought out—after I had been over and told Nick good by we started for Algodones, which we expect to reach some time to day. Simon went along with us. Louie stopped along at the ranches to make some purchases and I having become tired came on to Alemeda—eight miles from Alburquerque—by myself and talked with Antonio Lerma until Louie came up when we had our horses put up and got us quite a fine dinner among which was chicken and grape jelly of which Louie and I pitched into like hungry folks. While we were eating it rained terribly and a good while but in a bout a half an hour we started off for Algodones. When we came in about two miles of Bernalio we saw a terrible black cloud coming up so we put out in a gallop and got to Major Wilden's just as it was sprinkling and blowing very hard—we found the Major "tight" and we had to take a couple of glasses of wine with him before we could get off and then he had us lay down on the bed and he and Louie went to sleep but I kept awake. When we came away I played a good trick off on the Major and Louie too—I acted as though I was tight to their great sport and laughter and Louie thought he had a good tale on [me]—that I was tight—I laughed at him considerably. Louie also said he was sun burnt but I said his face was read from the bitters he took. About dark we came to Algodones where we found Crenshaw and Lieut. O'Bannon who were just from Santa Fe and were going to Alburquerque to the election. We had a short conversation and then Louie and I went to bed early—for we intend to start out at 2, O'clock in the morning—we tried to start a baile that night but spoke of it too late. We were both tired when we went to bed but I did not go to sleep for a long while afterwards.

Sunday; 4.

Well to day is the last day of my journey. I woke up at 12, O'clock in the night last night and asked Louie what time it was and finding it so soon we went to sleep and were awakened by Townsend at 2, O'clock according as agreed and then we got ready and when our horses were saddled we put out. At day light we were twenty miles on our way and at 9, O'clock we were at Delgado's Ranche—twelve miles from Santa Fe. Here we unsaddled our horses and let them take a feed on green oats—after they had rested and eaten we saddled and came on to Santa Fe where we arrived at about 12, O'clock. Thus ended my trip to Alburquerque and in all I had a pleasant and profitable trip. I did not keep any written journal while gone but trusted to my memory for all I have written. I played eight or ten games while in Alburquerque and made also besides [various?] friends.

We had tolerable good weather while going and coming and pretty good while there. They have miserable water there I think—the river water although they brag on it a great deal. I would think though that it would be quite unhealthy—it is so low and there is so much water standing which in a short time stagnates and I should think bring on disease.[9] On[e] thing commend[ed] Alburquerque, which is the trees which grow along down the bottoms or valley of the Rio Grande—to see which river was the principle thing that I went to Alburquerque [for]and I would not have missed seeing that alone for a great deal—I would hate to go home saying I had never seen the Great river of New Mexico but I have and after I have seen the Taos valley I will be willing to go home and [be] fully satisfied with my stay in New Mexico.

Monday; 5.

Election Day.

Well I am rested now from my trip and hard ride of yesterday and am all right for the election which comes off to day and which will decide who is to go to Congress to represent New Mexico. Father is now in Doña Ana and will be for two weeks more I expect. Well the day passed off I believe very quietly—Howe[,] Doctor Kavanaugh, Fulkison and Willie Rencher all went up to Tecuque to see that the Otero men who had been sent up there did not bully and run off the Gallegos men—Howe said they like to have had two or three fights and Kavanaugh told a little bullying dutchman if he did not shut his mouth he would break it for him, which dried the Dutchman up and [he] was seen and heard no more.

Hovey had his Ambulance going with Otero printed on a piece of some kind of cloth and Bowler's hack was going with Gallegos on it—both were running all the time and full of voters. As usual on such occasions, there were enough of drunken men—Charly Thayer and Dick Simpson in the crowd. As one fellow said there was a waste of horse flesh. Col. Grayson[10] had some fire works to night which looked very pretty and are the first I have seen since I have been in the Territory. I and Jim went up there and staid until they were over and then we went around to the poles of the lower precinct where they were counting out the votes but they were not near done and we came away[.] Jimmies ma let him come over and stay all night with me and we had a very nice time.

Tuesday; 6.

Well here I am sitting by myself at home by the fire and in a half a notion to have the blues but still I will drive them off. Well this morning we heard from the lower precinct—Howe was over there though last night when they finished counting them. Gallegos got a majority of one hundred and seven in the lower and eighty-five I believe in the upper—Howe says eighty-nine—in Tecuque Otero got two majority—in Galestio ninty—Placer 33 majority for Gallegos[,] Agua Fria for Otero fifty I believe. The mail came in to day— the new contracters bring it in fifteen days. I am glad that it does not come in on Sunday. I did not recite in Spanish to day. I called on Mrs Rencher who is getting almost well—she is going out to the Las Vegas springs[11] soon.

Howard has some watch chains which he has been wanting to sell me but I have no money to buy which is the worst part. I played three games with Howe to day at the discount and beat him two out of three.

I have [also?] Ed and I are great checker players lately, been playing checkers to day and got beat badly. Howe and Hattie went to see Mrs Jackson to night and he has just come home. Jim and Eddie were here to night but soon left. I do not feel like writing to night much.

Wednesday; 7.

I have not finished posting up for the time I was gone to Alburquerque although I wrote some to day. I studied and recited in Spanish as usual. I played three games of billiards this morning with George Waldo and he beat me playing off. I have read some in Spanish in the Reader and also in "Shakspeare" in, "Taming the Shrew." I read all the afternoon and did not get through one play. Jim and Eddie were both over here to night. Howe and I went up town and I took another game with George Waldo and beat him. Howe and Smith played on the upper table with new balls. I saw an old man who knows Howe, pa and myself to night—lives in Algodones—I had a little talk with him. Nothing of much interest happened to day that I know of or recollect.

Thursday; 8.

Well here I am at the close of another day, the most of which I am sorry to say has been literally <u>idled away</u>—and especialy this afternoon in which I did nothing but look at those who played billiards and played checkers with Ed Rose. I however recited in Spanish at my hour and after which I read in the, Spanish Reader until dinner time. My money is nearly all gone and I see but very few of my bills paid. Howe collected the rent and had about half of it stolen, he thinks by Uncle Tom.

I played three games of billiards—with Barry Simpson two— he gave me twenty-five and I strung him both games, and strung Louie Staab one game in which I made forty—the most I ever run—Howe has made as many as seventy-four when playing with me.

I took a walk this morning with Howe up to Fort Marcy after breakfast just while Uncle Tom cleaned up. To night I told Howe I would come by for him but when I went I thought they had company and the Squire coming along I walked on over home and since I came have finished up posting while I was gone—played on the guitar a little. We do not know for certain whether Otero or Gallegos is elected.

Friday; 9.

Well the election is or rather has strongly changed—the Otero party are blowing since they have heard from some of the counties where Otero got a majority. I recited as usual in Spanish. I went up town after dinner and played three games of checkers with him and beat him two of three. To night I beat Manuel playing off—gave him fifteen at that after which I went down to Mrs Edgar's where I found Sallie, Willie, Miss Knelly and her sister Lizzie whom Mrs E-r thinks the best looking. I had quite a nice time but but got no kiss from any of them when I came away. I was at court a little while to day. I did not read any to day in Shakspeare or any where but newspapers. I will leave for the States in about two weeks now I guess which seems very near.

Saturday; 10.

And here ends another week and very little has been accomplished by me. I recited in Spanish although it is Saturday and contrary to the custom of all schools.

I have played three games of billiards to day—two with Col. Menes and one with Willie R. who as usual beat me—I beat one and coronel one. The stage came in this evening and Battaile and Clemens came up and they say that Otero will be elected. Father will be up about next Saturday or Sunday. I played checkers with Ed Rose to day and as usual he beat me. He is going to the Springs Monday which I am glad of for I will not be beat with him any more and bothered—I am glad he is going. Battaile was over here to night and talked a while. Howe is over at the folks I suppose. It rained like the mischief to night. I will not get off to the States before October I fear.

Sunday; 11.

To night I have been looking at some good writing and I am now trying to imitate it as near as possible—it is writing of a clerk in Fant & Co's Banking House and he is an excellent writer as can be told from his writing.

I rose about my usual hour this morning and went to breakfast after which I came home and dressed myself for church whither I went after the bell rung. We had a pretty fair sermon and about the right length for me. I went to church or rather to Sunday School the first thing this morning.

I did not go to church this afternoon but staid at home with Howe. I wrote one letter this afternoon and to Mary Miner although I did not receive one in the mail. Battaile was over here to night but went over to see the ladies immediately—Howe went and borrowed some good black ink of Hovey. It is reported that father and Otero are going to have a duel—Battaile and Col Clemens both said they had challenged each other. Mr Jackson was over to see us this afternoon. We have had a fire all day—it is a little cold. I read a great deal in the, "Sunday Times" to day and cut several pieces out for my scrap-book. I took dinner at Mrs Edgar's to day as usual.To night's Journal is the best I have written and from looking at H.E. Offley's writing.

Monday; 12.

Well I am through another day. I did not recite in Spanish to day for at the time I had not studied the lesson well and therefore I did not go over to recite but thought I would wait until dinner time which I did and then went off and forgot it. The reason I did not have my lesson at the proper time was because there was an old man in here from Algodones talking to Howe and I was listening.

Hugh Smith was taken suddenly sick this morning and it was thought he would not live until dinner but he has through the whole day—the sickness is of a kind I cannot classify but it certainly is from the "site" or quantity of liquor he has drunk—they say (the doctors) that he cannot possibly get well. I expect prehaps that I will go out home with Battaile to morrow again. To night I played three games of billiards—two with "Scissors" one of which I won and on[e] with Doctor Hale [Hall?] which I also beat. It rained quite hard to night

     Remember, remember, the 22nd of September
     The wedding knot, should ne'er be forgot.

Tuesday; 13.

Nine more days and it will all be over and Howe will be a married man, and then I will have finished my nights of sleeping with him. Battaile did not go home to day—Hugh Smith died about 6. O'clock this morning—his corpse is very natural—poor fellow! there is a young man who had drunk himself to death as many have and are still doing every year. The funeral will come off tomorrow. I neither studied nor recited my Spanish to day until after dinner.

This morning before Howe and I were up that old Mexican that lives in Algodones came in to see him with a "fiador" [Watts may mean a "viador," or "traveler"] with [him]—Howe got up and talked with them for some time and then I rose and when washed and dressed we went up to breakfast. The mail came in a short time before dinner and I received a letter from Seth Tuley which I immediately answered. I have been reading in the papers this afternoon also to night. I played two games of billiards to day with Col Means both of which I beat—I have played checkers to day with Ed Rose four games—two and two I believe we came out. I read some in [Ballard's?] Pictorial to night. Howe went over to see his intended to night. Howe got his first <u>fee</u>[12] to day and made his second speech yesterday which I heard and which [was] in Spanish.

Wednesday; 14.

Well to day as was appointed at 9. O'clock—the burial of Hugh Smith came off, but on account of some delay they did not leave his residence until 10. O'clock. He was a Mason and and was buried by that order in the grave yard of that and the Odd Fellow order. The new band was employed and the most splendid was played I ever heard I believe—there was and excelent crowd if the expression is allowable quite long—the most I have ever seen in this country at one funeral more than three hundred in the line I should think. Howe showed me cousin John Wilber's grave which I did not know before. I did not recite to day—lost three games of billiards with George Gardenhire and beat George Waldo one; but my light is giving out and I will have to stop. Major Baker came from Alburquerque and said that father and Otero had had a duel—that they had three shots a piece and neither hit and they concluded to quit.[13]

Thursday; 15.

Well another day has passed and as usual I went through my daily duties—I studied and recited in Spanish at my usual hour. This morning about 9. O'clock Willie came running in and said that they were just starting for the Hot Springs at Las Vegas where they will be gone the governor said until next week. I have not played any billiards to day but checkers with Ed Rose and chess with John Kingsbury whom I beat—it is a pretty even game between us. I have been in court a great deal and to day—Howe made another speech in a criminal case which has taken up the whole day and until 10. O'clock at night and then they were not done—they have left the jury to decide and [adjourned?] the court. Hattie sent for me to come over to see her at 10. O'clock this morning but I had to study my Spanish then and did not go. I have read some in Shakspeare to day "Anthony and Cleopatria". We look for father in the next mail.

Friday; 16.

Well the week is drawing to a close and every day shortens my stay in New Mexico—I expect that we will start prehaps next Monday week—that will be three days after the marriage. I recited as usual to day in Spanish at the proper hour 11. O'clock. I played a game with a fellow to day and gave him thirty and the discount and beat him. I have not been in the court-house to day—tomorrow is the last day of court but they will not be half done. We look for father tomorrow in the mail. Squire came home early this morning for breakfast having started at 1 or 2. O'clock and come about twenty miles I believe—he has been distributing presents to the Indians (Utahs and Apaches) at Abicuiu. The new band played in the plaza this afternoon. To night Howe and I went over to see the folks—they all gave me "jissy" for not coming over oftener. I have read some in Shakspeare to day and now I believe I am about done for I can think of nothing more at present. I am uncertain whether I will keep a journal across the plains or not—I expect I will have notes at least[.]

Saturday; 17.

Well another week has passed and gone and very little have I accomplished when it is all sumed up. As to day was Saturday I did not recite any in Spanish. I played two games of billiards one with George Gardenhire who only made made twenty-nine on the first string—on the lower table—and one with Col Means giving him twenty-five and he beat me four points. I bought some grapes of an old man or boy rather and gave an old beggar a picaune. I have played eleven games of checkers with Ed Rose to day six of which I beat—five this morning and six this afternoon. I read some in Shakspeare to day. I have very little to say nowadays. I received a letter from Fannie to day in which she gave me a scoring—Aunt Lou has another baby—Fannie Bell is its name. I answered Fannie's letter to night. Otero I expect came in to night—I hear the band playing—Howe received a letter from father to day in which he said he had fought the duel reported with Otero and resulted as reported but was forced into it by Otero and his friends.

Sunday; 18.

Well this is the last week that Howe will be a single man—four more days and he will be a married man—next Thursday is the day—I expect pa will not be here. I dressed and went to Sunday School after I came from breakfast. I also went to church at 11. O'clock and with Beck at that where we found the house full. The Parson preached the funeral sermon of Hugh N. Smith—the house was full and the sermon was a good one. I took dinner as usual at Mrs Edgar's. I staid over there until three O'clock and then came home and laid on the bed about an hour and then went up town and staid until supper time. I saw Otero to day at a distance with Squire Collins and saw his wife at church. The Parson was to preach a sermon (funeral—of Smith) also in Spanish this afternoon in the court house but he could not get in at the appointed hour and so he had to preach in his own church. I have been reading in a Sunday School book—I returned two this morning and took out two[,] one rather this afternoon. I received my wedding ticket this evening. I have three letters for the mail.

Monday; 19.

<u>The Concert.</u>

I went through my Spanish as usual—played one game of billiards with George Waldo and he beat me—a game of backgammon with Spanish Juan[.] he beat me—five or six games of checkers most of which beat, but the crowning thing to day or rather to night was a Concert given by this new band which has just come out and which was splended. Admittance was fifty cents—there were but few programmes and those were written by Mr Howard who has been actively engaged all day in assisting them.

There were fourteen pieces and in two parts and the best of the performance I think was "<u>a solo</u>" on the violin—I think the man thay played is named <u>Athlick</u>—at least he is certainly the best violin player I ever heard. He imitated on the violin, a flute, an organ, a fife, a drum, a Scottish bagpipe, and played the devil's dream with a perfect rush and in two or three ways different from each other. There were most of the ladies that are in town. Howe has sent out his wedding tickets to day. I feel like all <u>my</u> music is no music at all since I have heard such good—but I will go to bed—it is time—the house was pretty full.

Tuesday; 20.

Well day after day passes away—two more days will not close without my seeing the union of, <u>the happy couple.</u> I was going all morning hunting wedding clothes and did not recite in Spanish. I played no billiards to day nor checkers. I got pants at the tailors for $10. boots at [Loui's?] for $8. and vest I think at $5.50. 1 have just been running around to day. Tomorrow night is another concert. Howe and I went over and played some on the guitars for the girls—while we were playing Miss Knellie Shoemaker and Doctor Beck Jr[14] [came in]—the mail came in on horse back to day having broken down in Apache Cañon—the tounge of the coach was broken somehow. I did not get any letters or papers but read some in Howe's.

Wednesday; 21.

<u>To Howe.</u>

This is the <u>last</u> night of Howe's being a batchelor and as he has no journal I will devote to nights Journal to him. I did not recite any Spanish to day. I played six or eight games of checkers with Ed Jones to day and once for the peaches—a treat—and I beat him and we went out and found some fine ones which Ed paid for and I helped eat. I have been helping them over at Mrs Edgar's all afternoon with Howe—we have been making festoons of cedar to hang along the wall. I went to the Concert to night but I thought that it was not as good as the first although the house was full. I expect I will smoke a cigiar before I go to bed as I did two or three nights ago and just to keep <u>Howe</u> company who is smoking.

It will be a year the 19th of Oct. that is coming which would make me here a year but I will not be here when that comes during which time I have slept, eat and roomed with Howe but after to night I will, "<u>hang up the fiddle and the bow</u>."

I am glad though not only that he is going to get married but in whom I think an excellent choice—I hope he will live <u>happy</u> and contented and may he still be <u>true</u> as he ever has been.

Good By.

John Watts.

J. Howe Watts.
Santa Fe.
N. M.

~   ~   ~

[Note: Pages 145 and 146 with entries for September 22 through 24 have been torn out of the journal. "Thursday 22nd" is double underlined in the upper left corner of what was page 145, but the rest of the page is gone. These missing entries probably described the wedding. One conjectures that the subject was so painful for the boy John that he destroyed the entries.]

~   ~   ~

Sunday; 25.

To day is the day that college always takes up on but I suppose it will not commence until tomorrow—college will be advanced almost a month when I enter and I will have to tug away though.

Father says he is going to contest Otero's election on account of illegal votes. I expect to spend one more Sabbath in New Mexico before I start for home—I hope we will get off. Jimmie E-r has a carbuncle on his neck and I am afraid that he will not be right well by that time. It is now ten minutes of 7. O'clock—It is raining out side—Howe has just come over to look at some papers of Howe. Well it is now twenty-two minutes of 8. O'clock.

Howe has just gone although it is raining quite hard and thundering—he says he has to write three letters—one to "Pug," on[e] to Bettie and one to ma. I fear I am not improving in writing as fast as I ought neither am I keeping in the same style of writing that I thought to improve on. Father is out some-where I cannot tell where—I suppose he will be in in a few minutes or at farthest by bed time. It still is coming down heavy. Such nights as these have a tendency to make me feel melancholy but one blest with the priveleges that I am and surrounded with so many comforts as I ought never to think of getting melancholy and never of grumbling—such a thing I never will do but will rest as well satisfied as I can.

The bells are mournfully tolling which makes me think of home and the dear ones that are there. I have just been reading a Sunday School book called "Ancient Philosophy"—it treats of the different philosophies and various doctrines of the Ancients.

Monday; 26.

Well I have rather bad news to relate to night which is—pa will not g[o] before two weeks from to day which is news I do not like at all—he says the stage will be full is the reason why he does not go—I will lose at college at least a month, but still I suppose it is all for the best so I will wait with patience and not bother myself about the future. I got the parson a lesson to day in Spanish and we read two chapters in the New Testament—in Ephesians. I took my watch to Howard to day to have him fix it and he gave me another to carry while he fixed mine—he gave me a double cased silver watch which is big and heavy enough. I commenced hunting up and arranging things to day but I guess I need be in no hurry now father is not going as early as he expected[.] But here is pa with the Eastern mail so I'll stop and read a while after I finish writing before I go to bed. Four Republicans came and father is now reading them. I was over at Mrs E-r's for supper with Howe and pa—we had quite a nice supper and then I went in Howe's room and sat and talked with all the folks until a few minutes ago when I came home.

Tuesday; 27.

My Journal from now until I go home will be very monotonous and uninteresting unless some thing out of the ordinary round of things takes place. I recited two lessons to the Parson to day in Spanish. I went up in town after dinner and Mr Howard and I went out walking upon the hills North but it was too warm—I felt extremely lazy. To night I went over to Mrs E-'s and took my guitar and Howe and I played for them—Beck played on the piano while Howe and I were in the little room or Howe and Hattie's room—we had quite a nice time. We sat and laughed and talked and [they] said they would miss me so much when I went to the States. Hattie sat by me and we eat candy. I had lots of kisses from Hattie—two just as I came home and plenty before—she calls me her sweetheart. Us four sat in there together by ourselves—Mrs E-[,] I, Howe and Hattie. Father has just asked me if I did not want to go to Taos tomorrow with him and I of course said yes [...?] but right now I think I will go to bed.

September 1859.

But here is pa with the Eastern mail so I will stop and read a while after I finish before I go to bed. [etc ?]

~ ~ ~

[Note: Pages 149 and 150 were left blank in the Journal and filled with other items. These include financial figurings, practice penmanship, and a brief biographical statement about Charles Sumner.]

~ ~ ~

Wednesday; 28.

Taos Visit.

Well! today as I expected and spoke of in yesterday's journal I and father started for Taos. I could not get a horse until almost dinner time. I first went to get Stephens mule but it had gone out in the herd so I came home and while talking to pa in came Hovey and said he could [pay?] or rather let me have a horse that he was getting shoed then at the shop which he said I could have by 12. O'clock—so I concluded that that was the best I could do and father the same so I waited. We did not get started though until after dinner—about 2. O'clock. Father took a pair of saddle bags in which I had a clean shirt, socks and dancing shoes. I had my shall to ride on and put on me when cold—father had one also—father road his horse and I a little pony of a white and brown spots—father also had a shall—thus equipped we left to go as far as we could—father said he expected to the Cañada—twenty-five miles from Santa Fe in Rio Aariba County. We went along rather slowly—we passed through Tezuque six miles from Santa Fe and two miles below it the Pueblo of Tezuque in our left. Along here runs quite a nice little stream which serves the rancheros for water to drink and water their fields—it is good cool water from the mountains. We trotted on over mountains country until we came to, Pejuate, an Indian Pueblo and name—eighteen miles from Santa Fe—in the right hand of this place is another called Namba which is situated at the foot of the mountains—in this place (pa says) a few years ago they killed some of their people who were accused of being witches. We rode on conversing together until about 7. O'clock in the night—when we came to Cañada—just before entering which we crossed a little mountain stream called Las Truces (The Grant).[15] We staid at the house of a Mexican friend of father's—who was formerly the prefect—he gave us some supper—he was sick in bed on the floor—father had a long talk with him to which I listened after which we were shown our room where we tired and sleepy were glad to enter and compromise with the fleas and Morpheus.

Thursday; 29.

This morning we rose quite early and rode along up the Rio Grande ten miles for breakfast at a friend's of fathers—Mr Clark[16] —he has quite a pretty place on the Rio Grande—the place he lives in is called Los Luceros (The Evening Stars)[.] Here we stopped about an hour and a half until we got our breakfast and about 9 1/2 O'clock we started to go from there to Taos a bad road of forty-five miles.

~ ~ ~

[Note: Pages 153 through 156 in the journal are blank, except for practice penmanship, and pages 157 through 160 are missing. Watts may have intended to fill the blank pages from a small, pocket-sized notebook, as he sometimes did. Unfortunately, these were never filled in.]

NOTES: Chapter 7

1. Aaron Zeckendorf, born in Hanover, Germany, was a twenty-five-year-old merchant who listed real property valued at $500 in Santa Fe in 1860. That year he attended, at the home of Levi Spiegelberg, the "first Yom Kippur held at Santa Fe."

The Zeckendorfs, who had come to New Mexico in the 1850's, were based in Albuquerque. Their widespread business operation included Santa Fe, Mora, and Grant Counties. After the Civil War, they moved to Tucson where they engaged in various enterprises in southern Arizona, including supplying forts. See 1860 U.S. Census; and Tobias, *Jews in New Mexico*, pp. 29-30, 42, and 73-75.

Simon Rosenstein's "little girl of about five years" was, in 1860, six-year-old Antonia Rosenstein. Born in New Mexico, Antonia was a student at the Santa Fe Female Academy in 1860.

Her father was an Albuquerque merchant who had married a Mexican woman. In 1860 he had a personal estate valued at $22,000. Young Franz Huning took a job clerking in Rosenstein's store on the south side of the plaza in Albuquerque in the mid 1850s. From there, Rosenstein moved to a corner location, then within about a year to a "building on the west side of the plaza." Huning suggests that Simon was a drinker who permitted drinking and card playing. On one occasion he was drunk while a cheating incident involving Judge Kirby Benedict occurred in his store.

Simon could also be slow to pay his debts. John M. Kingsbury wrote his partner Webb on May 19, 1860, that he had been trying to collect. "I am constantly stirring up all our old nest eggs, but with very little success. Rosenstein has not returned yet, his clerk sent me last week $300.+ on account. If I succeed in collecting anything this week I shall send you some checks by next mail." Four months later—on September 8—Kingsbury wrote again: "I have some little doubt now about the balance due from Rosenstein. He may pay it but it will be slow. He bought goods in the states & I know that he is paying his debts there to the pr[ejudice] of those he owes here. He is a grand scamp & is capable of doing almost anything. Still I believe he can pay us if he will."

Perhaps a violent man, Simon was on one occasion arrested by soldiers, held in the guardhouse of the military post in Albuquerque, then blindfolded, "stripped, and bound, and scourged." On another occasion he was assaulted. His marriage ended in divorce in 1866.

In 1867 Rosenstein was involved in a business venture in Las Vegas. See 1860 U. S. Census; Tobias, *Jews in New Mexico*, pp. 37-40, 45, 75; Huning, *Trader on the Santa Fe Trail*, pp. 55-58; and Elder and Weber, "Trading in Santa Fe., Ch. 13, p. 58, and Ch. 14, p. 30.

2. The "fellow called Townsend" may have been one Edward C. Townsend, a twenty-nine-year-old farmer, born in New York. In 1860 Townsend owned real property valued at $3,500 and personal property valued at $800. His wife, Aria, was a twenty-eight-year-old woman, born in Ireland. See 1860 U.S. Census.

3. "Alemada" is the village of "Alameda,"presently a residential community in Albuquerque's North Valley.

4. "Cotton and a brother" may have been M.L. Cotton, a thirty-two-year-old trader, and Thomas L. Cotton, a twenty-year-old clerk. Both were born in Mississippi. See 1860 U.S. Census.

5. Antonio Lerma lived along the road in or near Alameda. On a trip from Santa Fe to Albuquerque with Attorney Clever, Judge Kirby Benedict was once thrown out of a buggy and injured. He was taken to the home of Antonio Lerma for medical attention. See Hunt, *Kirby Benedict*, p. 84.

6. The old flagstaff in Albuquerque's plaza was something of a landmark. Franz Huning recalled its being placed by Major Carleton about 1856, not long after Huning first arrived from Santa Fe. Carleton, at the time commanding the local Army post, had also added a sundial and begun a dug well in the plaza.

Huning wrote that the plaza was much larger then than now, that "it extended south and east" and that "before the flagstaff was built, the soldiers, cavalry as well as infantry, had their drills on it." Stationed there were "two companies of dragoons and generally two companies of infantry, with the regimental band." See Huning, *Trader on the Santa Fe Trail*, pp. 55-57.

7. Franz Huning remarked on the water standing in the streets of Albuquerque. The plaza, he wrote, "was also much lower than it now is, and after every heavy rain a large pond would form and many times when I opened the store early in the morning, I could have shot wild ducks from the store door." See Huning, *Trader on the Santa Fe Trail*, p. 56.

8. "Mr Clark" ran a store with the Spiegelberg brothers in Albuquerque, the "contents" of which, according to the *Santa Fe Weekly Gazette*, were "appropriated by the Texans" in 1862. The *Gazette* noted that "Mssrs. Clark and Spiegelberg Bros." were "sutlers for the regulars and volunteers." After the War, Clark apparently sold the remainder of his interest to the Hunings. See Simmons, *Albuquerque*, p. 183, and p. 402, n. 30, 31.

9. Franz Huning commented on the bad drinking water in Albuquerque in the mid 1850s: "One discomfort we had to contend with," he wrote, "viz., the water for domestic use had to be hauled from the river (or from [the] acequia) and was always more or less oily and in winter hard to get at." See Huning, *Trader on the Santa Fe Trail*, p. 57.

10. In 1860, Col. John B. Grayson was a fifty-three-year-old Army officer, born in Kentucky. He was elected president of the Historical Society of New Mexico at the first meeting of that society in Santa Fe in December 1859. In 1860, Col. Grayson owned real property in Santa Fe valued at $56,000.

He was in Santa Fe in January 1858, when the *Gazette* carried a notice of his "for the supply of government stores." The following April, the *Gazette* noted that a fire which burned the "fodder" and "the fodder house attached to the corral of Judge Houghton" had come near destroying, not only "the residence of Judge H., owned by H.N. Smith, Esq.," but also "the buildings occupied by Col. J.B. Grayson."

In September 1860, Col. Grayson was still buying supplies for the Army, for John M. Kingsbury noted: "Marsh has got 400 head of cattle on the road if these get here safe and can effect a sale to Col. Grayson he will be out of the woods at once. The cattle are from Arkansas and coming on Tom's [Tom Green's] Neiotio [Neosho] route. They look for them to arrive every day."

Col. Grayson was apparently something of a gay blade for all his fifty some years, for James Ross Larkin attended a colorful "Bayle or Mexican Party" at the colonel's quarters in December 1856. "1 went & found it a grand Fandango," Larkin wrote. "Every one was there almost (except the decent American ladies)—officers, gents, gamblers & all with their mistresses. Champagne &c. flowed in abundance & the party was a lively one. I was soon satiated & tired of it—came away and retired."

According to Marian Russell, a "Captain" Grayson and his child wife had a sad story. As Russell tells it, Grayson was ordered to the front during the Civil War. He left his sixteen-year-old bride of one month in the convent at Santa Fe for protection. Soon word came that Grayson had been killed in action. His wife then stayed on at the convent "as that seemed to be the only home that she had."

Eventually a young rancher named George Hebert fell in love with her, and, with the help of Bishop Lamy, the two met and were married. They spent the rest of their lives at the Hebert ranch near Glorieta. "They were always happy and always in love with each other," says Russell.

Col. Grayson had a son, also named John B. Grayson, Jr., who was an attorney in New Orleans in 1858.

See 1860 U.S. Census; Hunt, *Kirby Benedict*, p. 173; *Gazette*, 16 Jan, and 17 Apr 58; Barbour, ed., *Reluctant Frontiersman*, p. 108; Russell, *Land of Enchantment*, pp. 95-96; Elder and Weber, "Trading in Santa Fe," Ch. 14, p. 31; and *Gazette*, 22 May 1858.

11. The hot springs near Las Vegas, later the site of the Montezuma Hotel, were for years a favorite place of rest and recuperation. Franz Huning bathed at the springs for about a month in May or June 1852, for rheumatism. While there he visited with the local people, who took baths and washed their clothes in the springs, and he survived an Indian attack, in which an arrow grazed his face. At that time the local people had built a two-story log cabin at the springs for the use of the bathers. See Huning, *Trader on the Santa Fe Trail*, pp. 53-55.

12. J. Howe Watts, who had been reading law with Mr. Jackson, had been preparing for the bar.

13. Little is known of this duel other than what is reported in Watts' journal. Twitchell remarks that Watts "in a speech at Mesilla, made some remarks relative to the Otero family which resulted in a bloodless duel between the two." See Twitchell, *Leading Facts*, II, p. 310. Seemingly, the two later became political friends for Otero's son wrote that Lincoln, upon Watts' "urgent request ... appointed [Otero] Secretary of the Territory and Acting Governor in 1861 ... ." See Otero, *My Life on the Frontier, 1864-1882*, p. 283.

14. "Doctor Beck Jr" must not be confused with Preston Beck Jr. The latter, born in Indiana, had acquired the huge "Preston Beck Grant" of 318,699.72 acres on the Pecos River east of Anton Chico. He operated a ranch on the grant and a well-known store in Santa Fe.

The legal history of the Preston Beck Grant is as complicated as any in the Territory. Originally granted to Juan Estevan Pino in 1823, this handsome grant later passed into the hands of Preston Beck Jr., who applied for its confirmation to Surveyor-General Pelham. Pelham adjudicated the property on September 20, 1856, and recommended for confirmation. After confirmation by Congress, the trouble began, for surveys showed that roughly 120,000 acres of the Beck and the Anton Chico grants had overlapping boundaries. Legal procedures over these boundary issues went on until the 1930s and were carried all the way to the U.S. Supreme Court.

Preston Beck Jr. also operated "Beck and Johnson's" store on the plaza in Santa Fe in the 1850s. James Ross Larkin mentioned visiting "Mr Becks of Beck, Johnson & Co" on November 17, 1856. The *Gazette*, calling Beck a "public spirited citizen," complimented him for "planting shade trees in front of his store" on the plaza in February 1858.

Preston Beck Jr. died as a result of knife wounds received in a fight with a clerk, who died at the scene. Knifed in the abdomen, Beck lived until the evening of April 7. The *Gazette* spoke of "his extensive mercantile engagements, ramified throughout the entire Territory" and recalled his "correct business habits, courteous and hightoned bearing, and manly and generous qualities of head and heart" which it said had "won for him an esteem and confidence rarely enjoyed by any man."

Like everyone else in Santa Fe in those days, however, Preston Beck Jr. had his enemies. The merchant William S. Messervy hated him. Messervy wrote John M. Kingsbury on September 16, 1855, that he would rather have his store building stand empty than rent it to Beck.

"Doctor Beck" was another man although there are similarities between the two other than the last name. Doctor J.J. Beck was the executor of Preston Beck's estate. He too died as a result of wounds in a knife fight. On March 3, 1860, John M. Kingsbury wrote his partner Webb: "I have a horrid & fatal affair to tell you of. It happend [sic] between Henry Oneil and Dr. Beck in which the Dr. was killed. The Dr. was a quick, passionate man." Kingsbury gives the detail: Beck alledgedly attacked O'Neil for refusing to sign "some sort of a paper which H. thought unnecessary and objected." O'Neil shot Dr. Beck in the left eye alledgedly in self defense because the doctor "was coming to him with the knife." Beck "immediately fell and expired in about 10 minutes, never spoke." O'Neil "gave himself up immediately," and was set free by the court who believed his story of self defense.

Kingsbury added that Doctor Beck had been engaged to Nelly Shoemaker. "They were to be married some time in April." Nellie Shoemaker, mentioned by both Kingsbury and Watts, must have been an attractive girl. In a letter to Webb, Kingsbury noted that "Capt. Shoemaker" had recently gone to "the States" and had "left 3 of the daughters here with Houghton's family." See *Gazette*, 27 Feb, and 27 Mar 58; Oliva, *Fort Union*, p. 66, n. 89; *Land Title Study*, p. 222; Westphall, *Mercedes Reales*, pp. 81, 220-24; Barbour, ed., *Reluctant Frontiersman*, p. 103; and Elder and Weber, "Trading in Santa Fe," Ch 1, p. 4,n. 10, Ch 13, pp. 12, 26-27; and Keleher, *Turmoil*, p. 128, n. 54.

15. Las Truchas Grant, northeast of Santa Fe, was a Spanish grant of 1754.

16. The "Mr Clark" mentioned here was Elias T. Clark of Los Luceros. Clark had been the Secretary of the territorial legislative council, in December 1853. John M. Kingsbury noted Clark's death in a letter of May 28, 1860: "Elias T. Clark of Rio Ariba [sic] died last week of dropsy, his

remains were brought here and intered [sic] by the Odd Fellows. Report says that his estate will not pay his debts in full."

Los Luceros, where Clark lived, was an old community, capital of the departmento of Rio Arriba under the Mexican government, and county seat of Rio Arriba County from 1855 to 1860. Now a private residence, the old court house is still standing. Los Luceros is five miles south of the present community of Velarde.

See Twitchell, *Leading Facts*, II, p. 208, n. 145; Elder and Weber, "Trading in Santa Fe," Ch. 13, p. 57; and Fugate, *Roadside History of New Mexico*, p. 227.

Chaper 8

October 1859

Friday; 7.

Well I feel some what rested and fresh and active after my long and tiresome ride of yesterday and also the day previous. I rose pretty early this morning and after washing and putting on clean clothes I went up to the parsons and had a fine breakfast which I most assuredly appreciated. After breakfast I came down to my room when Howe came over who was also here before breakfast. I went up in town and got shaved. I went over to see the girls and kissed them all—they are all as usual in excellent health. I sat and chatted with them until most dinner time and then I came over home and from here went up in town to wait until dinner time which fortunately for me soon came and I filled my chair and eat twice as much I suppose as any of the rest of the folks. I have a little memorandom of my little bills here which I want to settle up before I leave for the States to which country I hope to leave for in a few days—next Monday. I paid Some of my debts to day—the Parson for one—I paid my board bill. Howe paid me $45. to day—the rent of the houses—he had already paid Uncle Tom $5. for September which I had not paid when I left. I find I will have to write a back or round hand— I cannot write a good running hand and then I write it quite slowly in the bargain. I feel some what better than ridding all day. I went over to see the ladies again to night—father, Doctor Kavanaugh, Sallie and Willie all came in while I was there—had quite a pleasant time. The Governor and family have returned from the Springs—when I have not learned. Dick Simpson was caught sleeping with Mrs Generet by Mrs Green, Date and John Kingsbury and they told him he had to do one of two things—marry Mrs Generet or leave the Territory and he chose the latter at least he has left the Town. Frank Green got in to night—they will not be so free in his house now[.] He will straighten them out. I played a game of billiards with Howe to day <u>even</u>, as a matter of course he beat me.

Saturday; 8.

Well here it is again—I have been talking all about going and not going to the States next Monday all day—Whiting says he will not let the Stage go out Monday and when he says any thing of course it is law. Mr Edgar says if he was mail contracter he would let the mail go it but would send out a Stage. I rose about my usual hour and father took breakfast with me at Mr Gormans. I have paid all but two of my bills—one to Louie Staab and my billiard bill, the former $41. and the latter $22. and some [cents?]. I have been over at Mrs Edgar's nearly the whole day talking to them—I have also been packing my trunk which will be awful heavy—about a hundred pounds. Jimmie is going to take a small trunk only. I got a letter from Sam Dodds to day and Howe one from ma and Gus Lynch who I think is fishing for Fannie whom he will never get, if I can help it sure. Neither will pa or Howe consent to it so Mr Lynch cannot come in there. I have been doing nothing in the world all day but run around town. Hoxie, Howe, and Jimmie were all over here to night, father was here. I went with Beck to the Convent this afternoon and she bought some peaches and grapes and then came over here to my room and eat them. I had a most excellent dinner to day and have an invitation to eat dinner with Mrs Edgar tomorrow. I am doing some very poor writing here I think so I will try the other hand. Mary Miner has married that excuse for a man called Ben Wolfe[1] —but when I get ready to get married I have no doubt but that there will be some lady that will have me. Mrs Miner told that I had asked for Mary once which from my age any one would know I did not want to get married. I say emphatically with the Mexicans, "que quelan." Sam Dodd's letter was a good long one. They had better wait until I ask for their daughter for I never have yet.

Sunday; 9.

Well I rather guess that I will not go to the States on next Monday—the Squire thinks it is best that I should go with pa and Jimmie too. I dressed as usual and went to breakfast. Father took breakfast with me[.] he has concluded I believe to board there until he leaves for the States. I went to church and Sunday School as usual—eat dinner at Mrs Edgar's with pa. I also went over to night and I found Eddie with a very bad tooth-ache and while I was there Doctor Kavanaugh came and commenced to pull Eddie's tooth but it hurt him a little and he would not let the Doctor pull it. Jimmie has come over to stay all night with me and is now in bed and father tambien while I am writing. Hattie is a little sick—got a bad cold. I[t] has been quite a pretty day and one which Mrs Pelham cannot find fault with.

Howe has lately been doing a good deal or more properly a great deal of writing for pa but I am not fond of writing for I write such a poor hand[.] I wish I could write [a]good hand for I like good writing.

Monday; 10

Here I find.myself a day behind by some bad management and my journal is short enough without putting off what little I do write a day—well I have let a day run by but now I will tell why. Howe and Cotton were playing billiards [most?] late last night and so I was tired when I came home and did not want to write and so went to bed. Cotton owed pa forty dollars of gambling money and father told him if he would give Howe thirty-five he would have a chance to win it all back and Cotton took the game and they played in the afternoon eleven games I think and Howe beat him eight of them—half of the time pa bet ten and the other twenty dollars—Tom Bowler bet with him three times and and won every time first a fifty dollar—then one hundred then fifty again.

To night again they played and Cotton won seven out of nine or ten games at $25 a game so that father and he in the end came out about even. Tom Bowler did not bet any at night. I did not get any Spanish to day. Eddie has the tooth ache still but will certainly get it pulled.

Tuesday; 11.

Well to day we have been waiting all day for the mail but none came—there are two mails now behind and it is surmised from hostility from the Indians. Howe and Cotton took it again this morning and Howe beat Cotton seven out of ten games I think—at least he beat Cotton badly—he did not play any to night. We all went to the concert. George Waldo and Tom Cater have been playing all day at twenty and the discount[.] I do not know who is ahead. I was over to see Hattie and Howe a little this afternoon. The concert was good—Miss Snowflake was one of the participaters to night—she came out on the stage and danced very nicely. I have read a little in Shakspeare to day and that is about all I have done.

Wednesday; 12.

And still there is no news of the mail and many and different are the surmises of its fate. I rose about my usual hour and father and I both went to breakfast together. I have made this a billiard day—a day of billiards or a day in which I played at billiards considerably. This afternoon or forenoon rather I will take first[.] I played one game with Bob Riddlesbaugher—he giving me fifteen and again this afternoon I played again with him[.] I beat him both—I played three with Cotton's brother and beat all three and to

night four with Cotton at thirty and the discount—all of which I beat him—
father was betting on the game—$10. on the first two and $20. on the last
two—after which we came home and I sat down and wrote the above. I read
"Hamlet" to day in "Shakspeare" which is all the reading I have done and
not a bit of work. I still have to write with a steel pen for I have no other
kind. I was over to see folks this afternoon but she was not at home. Howe
was over to see us and took a sleep this afternoon.

Thursday; 13.

Well to day has passed and it now remains for me to post up as the
saying is among Howe and I. I rose about my usual hour this morning and
went to breakfast with father. After breakfast when I came home I found
Howe sitting here by the table writing. I played two games of billiards to day
with "Scissors" winning one game and losing one. My billiard account for
this month at present is $1.50 which is very little compared to what I have
had and to others bills. I read some to day in Shakspeare but did not finish
even one play. I have a steel pen I got of Vigil which I like very well although
it writes pretty thick. It is amalgamation pen I think—it looks like those kind
at least. To day a party went out to Tzuque after peaches but came back
without having procured a single one (so they say) but got a few apples. The
party consisted of Misses Knelly Shoemaker and Lizzy[2] —Beck and Hoxie—
Howe, Battaile, Doctor Kavanaugh and Fulkison and Wilbar. I went up to
see the Governor and Lady to night—Mrs Rencher is not at all well she is
taking the neuralgy again I am afraid—she has here face tied up with a
handkerchief. "Comadre Lus"—as they call her washed four shirts and one
handkerchief for me to day, at least I got them to day—she charged me—
"cuatro reals"—which I quickly paid. I went up in town to night but nothing
of interest was going on and I went home with Willie and he and I and Sallie
sat under the portal and sung, "Gentle Annie," and, "When Stars are in the
quiet skies" and he played an accompaniment on the guitar—he sung air—
Sallie tener or alto rather and I bass—we made right good music together.
The mail from Fort Union arrived to night but I have heard no news yet.
I am afraid I will not get off to the States soon—at least it looks so at
present. But I feel tired and sleepy enough to go to bed.

Friday; 14.

To day has passed without my playing any billiards—so there is that
much saved but I went to the concert and there again I lost fifty cents—
I paid the Parson $5. this morning—he came in with his market basket and
he said strapped. I have been reading Shakspeare to day—I read, "Measure

for Measure" and commenced, "Merchant of Venice" which is a fine thing. I went by for Sallie to go to the concert but she did not want to go and so I went alone—we had quite a fine concert in which Miss Snowflake appeared again. Jimmie had a piece of his composing which he was delighted with and which was a very good piece—entitled the, "Artful Dodger"—one verse of which brought in Joe Hurch's flour of peas and beans.[3] After the Concert father and I went up to the Fonda where we saw Lon Hickland and Judge Blackwood both of whom are from Taos. There is quite a large bank of monte and quite a number betting—Commings and Charly Thayer have the bank. It has been quite a pretty day but I have done very little[.] I cannot tell when I will go to the States now—Mrs Kelly is back[.] I saw her at the Concert—no more is said about Dick Simpson. "Bob" took Miss Jinnie to the Concert to night. Father has gone to bed while I write—it is late—11. O'clock.

Saturday; 15.

Well I hope it will not be many more days before I will leave for home!! I hope so at least—father thinks of starting Monday in the Southern mail —Jimmie will go with me and I hope and expect to have a fine time. I rose about my usual hour and went to breakfast after which I came home and employed myself in packing up my trunk which is all fixed and as we will go the Southern route I think I can take my guitar. We have been moving all day our things over to Mrs Edgar's. Howe is going to leave for below tomorrow and I and pa and Jimmie Monday I hope. I cannot tell yet where I will sleep—all the beds are out[.] Howe had them off.

Sunday; 16.   10. O'clock less 7 minutes.
Adios Nuevo Mexico.

This day's journal as is indicated above is a, Farewell to New Mexico. As this is the last journal I expect to write in Santa Fe and in New Mexico I thought I would devote it to thoughts on the subject above mentioned. I and Jimmie Edgar expect to start for El Paso tomorrow morning in the stage and wait in El Paso for pa a week unless the stage is empty and then we will go on. I have had some delightful times in Santa Fe and New Mexico and when I think I am going to leave it my wishes and heart fain would still remain here but it is my interest and good which will be increased by going and therefore I must go and ought to without complaint. The Squire, or Col. Collins gave me an order on John Kingsbury for $150 and a draft on New York for $100. which is for Jimmie's expenses and support. It is the hour above marked—I have just finished packing my trunk and am sitting in my drawers writing, while father is sleeping. I am going to take my guitar—a present from Howe. I have given father a list of my debts which he says he will settle. I went to Sunday School, church and eat dinner and supper at Mrs Edgar's who is sick with a cold. Father is going to give me $20 dollars and [an] order on Vincente St. Vrain[4] for more if I go on to St. Louis. Howe went towards Alburquerque to day in an extra stage—he is now going to all the courts below and will be gone he says six weeks—Hattie will be all by herself—I was over there, all the afternoon[.] I got a purse at Louie Staab's for 75 cts. I cannot write much to night. As I have to get up early I will now say to Santa Fe and New Mexico, <u>Good By</u>—<u>Farewell</u>—at least for two years and perhaps <u>forever</u> —   Adios! Adios! Adios!!!

~   ~   ~

[Note: Pages 168 and 169 are blank in the Journal. Page 170, dated Monday, November 21, 1859, was written in Bloomington, and gives, among other things, a brief account of the trip. The following is a selection from that entry:]

"Monday; 21. Well here <u>I</u> am again not only keeping my journal but under peculiar circumstances—the last day that I pened was in my room in Santa Fe N. Me. and at the present time I am between fifteen hundred miles to two thousand from that dear place—there I daily saw father, <u>Brother Howe</u> and sister Hattie, Beck and many more acquaintances which I see no more ... and perhaps <u>never</u>!!! I leave them in the hand of Him who doth '<u>all things well</u>'. But I cannot indulge my thoughts in this direction further although <u>very</u> pleasant—'Journal' we must away and trace our speedy trip to El Paso and after a weeks stay there, on the overland mail in twelve days to St. Louis without one night's sleep for eleven days. Jimmie and pa came with Journal and we had quite a nice trip on the whole. I kept a Journal across in my note book with a pencil which I fear will be rubbed out before I have time to copy it off—a sad catastrophe is it not Journal? I went to my first theater in St. Louis[.] Murdock performed in one of the plays—if not all.

I arrived in Bloomington—<u>My Old Home</u>!—on last Tuesday—tomorrow a week but was so busy that I could not attend to <u>Poor Journal</u>! Thus you have lain neglected in the drawer without any notice and even have not been let out once to say, '<u>How do you do</u>!' ... . We brought in two bottles of wine from El Paso Texas or rather Mexio and father who is going to Washington has gone by Cincinnati to present them to Mr. Longworth for he wrote a letter to father asking him about the grapes and wine of El Paso. To day I entered and went to my first recitation ... . I entered the Junior Class without the languages—Jimmie the Preparatory. I wrote a long letter to Squire Collins giving an account of Jimmie's expenses with an account of our crossing the plains ... . I had a sty coming across the plains and now have another one ... ."

NOTES: Chapter 8

1. Ben Wolfe was seemingly one of Watts' many acquaintances back in Indiana.

2. "Lizzy" was one of Nellie Shoemaker's sisters. Captain Shoemaker had several daughters.

3. Possibly the phrase "Joe Hurch's flour of peas and beans" was an "in" joke about the poor quality of the flour produced by the miller Joseph Hersch and sold to the Army in Santa Fe in 1859.

A Santa Fe merchant and miller who was thirty years old in 1850, Hersch owned a gristmill on the Rio Chiquito (now Water Street) in Santa Fe by 1852. That year he had an Army contract to deliver 50,000 pounds of flour. He soon became one of four millers who supplied nearly all of the Army's flour in the territory before 1860. The other three large suppliers with their own mills were Cerán St. Vrain of Mora, Simeon Hart of "Hart's Mill" at El Paso, and Antonio José Otero who operated a mill at Peralta.

By 1858, Hersch built a mill on the Rio Chiquito using a steam engine for power. Hauled into the terrritory for use in placer mining in the Ortiz Mountains, the engine could turn out "some hundred fanegas" of flour per day according to the *Gazette*. In 1858, the Army contracted with Hersch for 266,500 pounds of flour, and in 1859 for 320,000 pounds. Thus, Hersh was the largest supplier in New Mexico that year.

However, the departmental inspection in 1859 concluded that Hersch's flour was "indifferent—or bad." And in 1860 the Secretary of War ordered that flour of this quality no longer be accepted. Hersch received no further flour contracts. Nonetheless, he apparently had done well for himself, for the value of his real property had grown from $300 in 1850, to $40,000 in 1860. See Tobias, *Jews in New Mexico*, pp. 34, 37, 39; and Frazer, *Forts and Supplies*, pp. 80-81, and 105-107.

4. Vincent St. Vrain, a member of the famous family of traders originally from Missouri, lived in Mora. See Keleher, *Turmoil*, p, 484, n. 10.

The Brady photo of John Watts *(left)*, taken during his stay in
Washington, D.C. c. 1862-64. This is about as he looked when
he kept his journal in Santa Fe.
Courtesy Hallack Watts Hoag.

Epilogue

John Watts attended Indiana University as a junior from the fall of 1859 through the spring of 1860. He studied chemistry, calculus, and "Moral Philosophy" during the fall semester; Latin, Greek, Calculus, Logic, and "Mechanics" during the spring; and read, among other books, Washington Irving's <u>Astoria</u>. He rose regularly at four or five a.m., built a fire in the stove, and got his lessons by candlelight (later by coal oil lantern). Before attending "prayers," with which the university began each day, he opened the library, where, as "Deputy Librarian," he "let books out" to students.

After recitations with the professors, which took up most of the morning, he studied again in the afternoon, then did chores, which included hoeing potatoes, pruning grapevines, stopping at "Aunt's" for a bucket of milk on the way home from the post office, splitting and stacking firewood in the woodshed, bringing in next morning's fuel, and, occasionally, "planting" fence posts for his grandpa. He often took meals at his grandma's, where for Thanksgiving, 1859, "most of the relations ... assembled" to devour three turkeys. "We had feasting, decidedly and emphatically feasting," he wrote. "There were an awful sight of children there more than I have seen in a long time."

In the evenings John visited friends, took lessons on the violin, attended various church functions, wrote letters (including a regular exchange with brother Howe in New Mexico), and "posted" in his journal. He was apparently popular, for he was elected junior class speaker for the senior graduation in 1860, and chose "Washington Irving" as his topic. He took part in a debate in January, 1860, in which the question was, "Should Mexico be annexed to the United States?"

"The affirmative (which I was on)," he noted on January 27, 1860, "gained it two to one." He was also a Protestant in a southern Indiana community of decidedly Protestant attitude. "Cousin Matildy asked me all about Howe and his wife," he wrote, December 24, 1859, "and thought it strange that he should marry a Catholic."

John spent the summer of 1860 in Washington, boarding at Mrs. Carter's house with his mother and two of his sisters, Lou and Mollie, touring with them, and copying legal depositions for his father in the Clerk's Office of the U. S. Court of Claims. He filled the pages of his journal with details of daily life, of tours of the Patent Office, the Interior Department, the Corcoran Gallery and the Smithsonian, and of trips to Baltimore and Mount Vernon, where, he noted, in spite of "a placard telling visitors not [to] pull any flowers or injure the shrubbery ... I noticed the ladies made things fly."

He was especially impressed with the Capitol and its grounds, which he described in great detail in the journal, as well as with the usual tourist attractions—the "original manuscript" of the Declaration of Independence, and General Washington's "portfolio, Camp Trunk, Part of his tent when in Battle, His Table, chairs, and cane." He took regular walks. "This morning I went into the Rotunda and upon the dome," he noted July 31, 1860, "where I could get a splendid view of the city." On August 2, 1860, John, Lou, and Molly went with a grand picnic of fifty people by steam-powered canal boat on the "Ohio and Chesapeake Canal" to the "Great Falls" of the Potomac.

Graduating from Indiana in 1861, John went back to Washington with his father, who was New Mexico's Delegate to Congress from 1861 to 1863. Again the family boarded at "Mrs. Carter's," at 4 A Street, North, a house located where the Supreme Court building stands today. Life at Mrs. Carter's was all pleasure. "Breakfast at 9, Dinner at 4, Tea at 7," John had described it on July 25, 1860. "At breakfast I was introduced to Mrs. Carter and her famous daughter Phoebe and also the much talked of and abused Senitor King, who is a very fat ... jolly old man—a perfect Falstaff for laughing at and telling jokes."

From Mrs. Carter's, Judge Watts could walk across the street to the Capitol in the morning while John could hike over to the Pension Office of the Interior Department at 7th West and F North to work as a clerk. During his two or three years in Washington, he joined a group for a photograph by Matthew Brady, or, more likely, by Brady's assistants. His father took him to meet the President. Both Judge Watts and Lincoln had stumped for William Henry Harrison for President in 1840, Watts in Indiana, Lincoln in Indiana and Illinois. According to the *Bloomington Post* of February 7, 1840, Judge Watts had given "a bold, masterly and eloquent discourse" at a Whig rally in Bloomington.

Years later, John recalled a humorous story the President told when he and his father visited the White House. Lincoln, Judge Watts, and Judge [David] Davis had been speakers at a Whig gathering in 1840. "Do you remember, Judge, my opening address, near the Illinois and Indiana line in the campaign for Harrison for President?" Lincoln asked of Judge Watts.

"Well, Judge Davis spoke first and you second, and I the last. I opened like this: 'Fellow citizens I have had something happen to me today that never happened before, and I am sure will never happen to me again. I have spoken after two men uglier than myself.'"

Telling light stories probably diverted Lincoln from the horrors of the War and also from his grief at the death of his eleven-year-old son, Willie. Young John Watts met Lincoln's boys and remembered becoming acquainted [with Willie]: "we saw many of the sights of Wash. together," he wrote. John remembered being a pall bearer at Willie's funeral at Rock Creek Cemetery in February 1862.

John also recalled in sharpest detail an important scene of Stephen A. Douglas speaking during the presidential campaign of 1860. The Democratic party had split that year, northern Democrats nominating Douglas, southern Democrats nominating Vice President John C. Breckinridge, states-rights champion from Kentucky. Grappling for his political life, Douglas chose to campaign actively, speaking wherever crowds assembled. Lincoln, following tradition and the advice of friends, chose to make no statements, to remain silent and let the Democrats fight it out.

A keen account of a tired Douglas speaking in the very early hours of the morning at a Bloomington whistle stop, Watts' journal captures the nub of the Senator's difference with Lincoln. Douglas believed that citizens of the territories, as well as the states, had the right, by majority vote, to choose their own social institutions, including that of slavery. "The true doctrine was Non-Intervention by Congress," as he put it. In contrast, Lincoln held that "life, liberty and the pursuit of happiness" were rights guaranteed all men, that no man had the "right" to own another.

In Watts' account, the train pulled into Bloomington after midnight, September 30, 1860. At 2:20 A.M., Douglas stepped out of his car. A large crowd had already waited more than an hour. "The band was on the platform of the Depot and a crowd inside with three torches (turpentine balls on iron)[.] when the train came up three cheers were given for D-s and the Band playing," John wrote. The Senator looked "something like his photographs ... but worn out - tired - sleepy - and hoarse."

Douglas "said one sectional party appealed to northern passion against the South and the secessionists vice versa—said when Congress touched slavery it caused disturbance—the true doctrine was Non Intervention by Congress—someone cheered for L-n—said took part of that to himself for his Republican friends would never [have] heard of L-n if it had not been for him—said cars (locomotive having whistled) were the greatest tyrants on earth[.] Mrs Daily said 'Not in this country.' D-s [said] 'You are not married?' Mrs D. 'Yes I am'—, said he did not believe even the Wide Awakes would be up this early—said L-n would not be elected no difference about cheering—thanked them and retired in a jam—train whistled and left."

In late 1863 or 1864 John returned to Santa Fe where he clerked briefly for his brother Howe, who had become Army Paymaster for New Mexico during the Civil War. About 1865 or 1866 John moved to Fort Bascom on the Canadian River in San Miguel County, where his father owned a ranch acquired largely as legal fee for his work in confirming two vast grants—the Pablo Montoya Grant and the Baca Location Number Two. Watts registered a "Double W" brand in San Miguel County on June 25, 1868—possibly for "Watts and Watts," or for "Watts and Wardwell" (William V.B. Wardwell, who had come to New Mexico with the California Column, was a trader in New Mexico, and a son-in-law of Judge John S. Watts).

Young John intended to run the Canadian River ranch. He had a lively time. He recalled selling milk, butter, and melons to what few soldiers there were at Fort Bascom, and contracting to put up hay and furnish beef to the fort "at good figures." But the Indians more than once stole his livestock. At one time "about a mile from the Fort" a band of Comanche and Kiowa drove off $6,000 worth of stock. They shot and killed John's superintendent, Dick Maguire, wounded a laborer named Montoya, "and shot at me," John wrote, "but my horse was so restive and scared they missed me."

Another time, roving Navajo pulled up corral posts at night and drove off $4,000 worth of mules and horses. "My men followed them to Fort Sumner (eighty-one miles from my ranch) and we found my stock, but the Indian Agent would not let us take [it] as it would 'make the Indians mad,'" John wrote. Since "we could not help ourselves we had to submit." But "such outrages were so <u>common</u>," he added, "that little attention was paid to them and the only consolation you received was congratulations that all of us were not <u>killed</u> and <u>scalped</u>." The agent told Watts to "make out a list of animals lost and their value and I will send it to Wash. for payment!"

Clearly the hard breaks of the ranching life were not for John Watts. "I stayed there about two years," he wrote, "when the Indians stole me out and I left." He moved back to Santa Fe, and in 1872, four years before his father's death in Indiana in 1876, he took a job as a "collection clerk" at the Second National Bank of Santa Fe at a salary of $25 a month. He remained until about 1884, becoming a "cashier" at $150 a month, and performing nearly every job, including sweeping the floor, dusting the furniture, and building a fire in the stove on chilly mornings. During these years in Santa Fe, Watts was three times president of the Literary Club. He was elected a member of the Historical Society of New Mexico in January 1881.

He was also married in 1880, to Susan Jane Barnes. Born at Estill Springs plantation, Estill County, Kentucky, December 30, 1851, Susan had moved to Santa Fe from Kentucky, when her father, Colonel Sidney M. Barnes, was appointed United States District Attorney for New Mexico. A former Colonel of the 8th Kentucky Volunteers of the Union Army, Col. Barnes, who owned Estill Springs plantation, had freed his slaves as the Civil War began, and enlisted in the Northern cause. John and Susan Jane Watts would have one child, a daughter named Loraine (later Loraine Watts Hoag).

Meantime, John's brother, Howe, mentioned almost daily in the journal, also lived eventfully. The boys' three sisters were Frances ("Fannie"), Mary ("Molly"), and Louisa, ("Lou"). Howe was named for the family of their mother, Elizabeth Ann Howe, whose father, Joshua 0. Howe, was a successful Bloomington merchant and a trustee of Indiana Seminary, later Indiana University. Howe graduated from Indiana in 1857 (four years before John) and moved to Santa Fe. By 1860, at twenty-two years of age, he was an attorney with real property in Santa Fe valued at $2,000 and with a seventeen-year-old wife, Hattie Edgar Watts. Howe worked at various jobs over the years, describing himself in 1890 as a "mining engineer and United States Mineral Surveyor; Lieutenant-Colonel during the War, [and] Adjutant General of the Territory under Governor Lew Wallace." An 1883 issue of *The Indiana Student* noted that he was "Vice President of the Bonito and White Oaks Mining Company" of White Oaks, New Mexico.

At some point, Howe moved his wife and several children to the Republic of Honduras, where he took up farming. He wrote John in January 1897: "We are poor folks here now, but happy and [in] good spirits ... . I have a fine banana patch and almost live on bananas and milk." He wrote again on March 28, 1898, of planting oranges and lemons and of putting out 67,000 coffee trees, "but expect to finish the full 100,000 by next Christmas." He told John: "I don't think I ever enjoyed better health and I am sixty years old today ... . the climate is perfect and I am well and content." Howe eventually moved on to San Pedro, California, where he died on April 21, 1921.

*   *   *

While Howe and his family moved on, John resigned from the Second National Bank of Santa Fe and settled in Wichita, Kansas, in 1886, where he organized the West Side National Bank. He worked as its cashier for four years. In February 1890, he was appointed a federal bank receiver. Thereafter he settled his family in Newton, Kansas, in a fine Victorian style home at 228 West Eighth Street (still standing in 1996, in beautiful condition). Remaining in government service as a bank receiver and examiner until his retirement, he died at home on January 10, 1925, having lived in Newton for about thirty years.

His wife Susan, known as a sociable woman of "gracious and lovable character," lived at home at 228 West Eighth until her death sixteen years after her husband's, on May 31, 1941. Both she and John Watts lie buried in a Newton cemetery.

Information for Preface, Introduction, and Epilogue

Address to the Santa Fe Literary Club as retiring president, 5 Sept 1880, handwritten document, in Hallack Watts Hoag Collection, Newport Beach, California.

Bancroft, Frances Watts, biographical statement, 1886, about John S. Watts, in Wm. H. English Ms. Collection, W. H. Smith Memorial Library, Indiana Historical Society, Indianapolis, Indiana.

Bloomington Post, 7 Feb 1840.

Huning, Franz, *Trader on the Santa Fe Trail: Memoirs of Franz Huning* (Albuquerque, 1973).

"In Memoriam, John Watts" (obit.), *Newton Evening Kansan-Republican*, 16 Jan 1925.

"J. Howe Watts," in *The Indiana Student*, IX, 4 (Feb 1883), p. 96.

"John Watts" (obit.), *Newton Evening Kansan-Republican*, 10 Jan 1925.

"Joshua Howe Watts," *Indiana University, Its History from 1820 ... to 1890* (Indianapolis, 1890), p. 219.

"Mrs. John Watts" (obit.), *Newton Evening Kansan-Republican*, 4 June1941.

Myers, Burton D., "Joshua Owen Howe," *Trustees and Officers of Indiana University, 1820 to 1950* (Indiana Univerity, 1951), p. 24.

Official document from the Historical Society of New Mexico notifying Watts that he has been elected a member, 11 Jan 1881, Hoag Collection.

"San Miguel County Brand Book, Number 1" [1867-1873], NMRA.

Smith, Leonidas, "An Address Delivered February 10th, 1857 on the Occasion of the Anniversary of the Santa Fe Literary Club" (Santa Fe, 1857), in Huntington Library. Copy by Dr. Robert R. White.

Watts, John, "Biography of John Watts," autobiographical statement, typed, unpbl. ms., Hoag Collection.

_____, *Journal*, in Monroe County Historical Museum, Bloomington, Indiana.

_____, pencilled biographical statement, entitled, "Jno. W. Newton Kans., Nov 4, 1921," Hoag Collection.

Watts, Joshua Howe, letters to John Watts, Jan 1897, and 28 Mar 1898, Hoag Collection.

John and Susan Watts' burial site, Newton, Kansas.
Courtesy David Remley.

Susan Barnes Watts, John's wife, with their daughter Loraine
Courtesy Hallack Watts Hoag.

INDEX

236